Data Analytics Applications in Education

Data Analytics Applications in Education

Edited By
Jan Vanthienen and Kristof De Witte

CRC Press
Taylor & Francis Group
Boca Raton London New York

CRC Press is an imprint of the
Taylor & Francis Group, an **informa** business

AN AUERBACH BOOK

CRC Press
Taylor & Francis Group
6000 Broken Sound Parkway NW, Suite 300
Boca Raton, FL 33487-2742

First issued in paperback 2021

© 2018 by Taylor & Francis Group, LLC
CRC Press is an imprint of Taylor & Francis Group, an Informa business

No claim to original U.S. Government works

Printed on acid-free paper

ISBN-13: 978-1-4987-6927-3 (hbk)
ISBN-13: 978-1-03-209629-2 (pbk)

Visit the Taylor & Francis Web site at
http://www.taylorandfrancis.com

and the CRC Press Web site at
http://www.crcpress.com

Contents

PART III POLICY RELEVANCE AND THE CHALLENGES AHEAD

Editors

Kristof De Witte is a tenured associate professor at the Faculty of Economics and Business at KU Leuven, Belgium, and he holds the chair in "Effectiveness and Efficiency of Educational Innovations" at Top Institute for Evidence-Based Education Research at Maastricht University, the Netherlands. Kristof De Witte is further an affiliated member of the CESifo Network (Ludwig-Maximilians University and Ifo Institute). At KU Leuven, Kristof De Witte is director of the research center "Leuven Economics of Education Research." His research interests include education economics, performance evaluation, and early school leaving. He has published his work in many international academic journals, including *The Economic Journal*, *Journal of Urban Economics*, *European Journal of Operational Research*, *Economics of Education Research*, *European Journal of Political Economy*, and *Scientometrics*.

Jan Vanthienen is full professor of information systems at KU Leuven, Belgium, Department of Decision Sciences and Information Management, Information Systems Group, where he is teaching and researching on business intelligence, analytics, business rules, processes and decisions, business information systems, and information management. He has published more than 200 full papers in reviewed top international journals (such as *MIS Quarterly*, *Machine Learning*, *Management Science*, *Journal of Machine Learning Research*, *IEEE Transactions on Neural Networks*, *Expert Systems with Applications*, *IEEE Transactions on Knowledge and Data Engineering*, *Information Systems*, and *Health Information Management Journal*) and conference proceedings. He is a founding member and currently coordinator of the Leuven Institute for Research in Information Systems (LIRIS) and co-chairholder of the bpost bank research chair on Actionable Analytics, and the Colruyt-Symeta Research Chair on Smart Marketing Analytics. He received an IBM Faculty Award in 2011 on smart decisions and the Belgian Francqui Chair 2009 at FUNDP on smart systems. He is co-founder and president-elect of the Benelux Association for Information Systems (BENAIS).

Contributors

Tommaso Agasisti
Department of Management,
  Economics, and Industrial
  Engineering
Politecnico di Milano School
  of Management
Milan, Italy

Cristian Barra
Department of Economics and
  Statistics
University of Salerno
Salerno, Italy

Bruno Broucker
Public Governance Institute
KU Leuven
Leuven, Belgium

Ana S. Camanho
Faculdade de Engenharia
Universidade do Porto
Porto, Portugal

Johannes De Smedt
Management Science and Business
  Economics Group
University of Edinburgh Business
  School
Edinburgh, United Kingdom

Sergio Destefanis
Department of Economics and
  Statistics
University of Salerno
Salerno, Italy

Kurt De Wit
Data Management Unit of the
  Education Policy Department
KU Leuven
Leuven, Belgium

Silvester Draaijer
Faculty of Behavioral and Movement
  Sciences, LEARN! Academy
Vrije Universiteit
Amsterdam, the Netherlands

Grazia Graziosi
Department of Economics, Business,
  Mathematics and Statistics
University of Trieste
Trieste, Italy

Wim Groot
Top Institute for Evidence Based
  Education Research (TIER)
Maastricht University
Maastricht, the Netherlands

Joris Hindryckx
VIVES University College
Kortrijk, Belgium

and

Top Institute for Evidence Based
  Education Research
Maastricht University
Maastricht, the Netherlands

Francesca Ieva
Department of Mathematics
Politecnico di Milano
Milan, Italy

Chiara Masci
Department of Mathematics
Politecnico di Milano
Milan, Italy

Anna Maria Paganoni
Department of Mathematics
Politecnico di Milano
Milan, Italy

Maria C. Andrade e Silva
Research Centre in Management and
  Economics
Católica Porto Business School
Porto, Portugal

Wouter Schelfhout
Antwerp School of Education
University of Antwerp
Antwerp, Belgium

Vania Sena
Business and Local Government Data
  Research Centre
University of Essex
Essex, United Kingdom

Mara Soncin
Department of Management,
  Economics, and Industrial
  Engineering
Politecnico di Milano School
  of Management
Milan, Italy

Henriette Maassen van den Brink
Top Institute for Evidence Based
  Education Research (TIER)
University of Amsterdam
Amsterdam, the Netherlands

Seppe K.L.M. vanden Broucke
Department of Decision Sciences and
  Information Management
KU Leuven
Leuven, Belgium

Chris van Klaveren
Faculty of Behavioral and Movement
  Sciences
Amsterdam Center for Learning
  Analytics
Vrije Universiteit
Amsterdam, the Netherlands

Roberto Zotti
Department of Economics and
  Statistics
University of Salerno
Salerno, Italy

Chapter 1

Introduction: Big Data Analytics in a Learning Environment

Kristof De Witte and Jan Vanthienen

Contents

The abundance of data and the rise of new quantitative and statistical techniques have created a promising area: data analytics. This combination of a culture of data-driven decision making and techniques to include domain knowledge allows organizations to exploit big data analytics in their evaluation and decision processes. Also, in education and learning, big data analytics is being used to enhance the learning process, to evaluate efficiency, to improve feedback, and to enrich the learning experience. Before discussing some possibilities and issues in the use of learning analytics in education, we define its concept.

1.1 Data Analytics

With data available in large quantities, data analytics refers to a set of techniques and applications to explore, analyze, and visualize data from both internal and external sources. Applications can range from business intelligence (BI), enterprise reporting, and online analytical processing (OLAP) to more advanced forms of analytics, such as descriptive, predictive, and prescriptive analytics. Descriptive analytics identifies relationships in data, often with the intent to categorize data into groups. Predictive analytics exploits patterns found in historical data to make predictions about future behavior. Prescriptive analytics suggests decision options and shows the implications of alternative decisions.

Data can be of many types, and may originate from many sources: internal transaction data, web data, location data, browsing behavior, driving behavior, government data, and so on. With the increased digitization of society, a wealth of data is ready to be explored. The data explosion, however, has created a gap between the volume of data generated and stored, on the one hand, and the understanding and decision making based on these data, on the other hand. Traditional analysis techniques such as query and reporting or spreadsheet analysis are unable to cope with the complexity and size of current data sources.

This is where advanced analytics comes in, generating automatic *descriptions* of the data in terms of (human-interpretable) patterns, and *predictions* of unknown or future values of selected variables using, for example, clustering, classification, or regression techniques. In data analytics projects, however, a lot of effort is still devoted to collecting and integrating the available data; data preparation and cleaning; building, testing, and refining models; and finally, communicating results or triggering actions.

Data analytics has huge potential and is changing the world. The technical and managerial issues resulting from the adoption and application of data science in multiple areas are worth exploring (Baesens et al., 2016).

1.2 Data Analytics in Education

Rogge et al. (2017) argue that data analytics applications and functionalities provide a broad range of opportunities in the public sector. Their review reveals that governments worldwide have announced plans and road maps to support the development of big data in both the public and private sector. Education economists, in particular, are increasingly using the availability of large datasets (Rogge et al., 2017). As every step a student takes in the online world can be traced, analyzed, and used, there are plenty of opportunities to improve the learning process of students.

First, data analytics techniques can be used to enhance the student's learning process by providing real-time feedback, or by enriching the learning experience. The latter might take place in adaptive learning paths that provide a tailored learning environment for students. Thanks to the use of data analytics, the learning environment can better correspond to students' characteristics in terms of cognitive abilities, earlier acquired knowledge and skills, interests, learning style, motivation or meta cognitive abilities. While similar adaptive and differentiated learning is difficult to realize in a physical classroom, it is relatively easy to realize in the online classroom. We discuss this more extensively in Chapters 2, 4, and 9.

Second, data analytics can be used to support the instructor or teacher. Using data analytics, the instructor can better trace, and take targeted actions to improve, the learning process of the student. By combining comprehensive student data with learning outcomes—in terms of student success, dropout, or cognitive skills—of earlier cohorts of students, the learning outcomes of the evaluated student can be predicted. Forewarned by similar indicators, instructors can pay additional attention to those students who are at risk of lagging behind. Moreover, the instructor can obtain descriptive analytics from the progress that students are making in online courses, or their use of tools in the electronic learning environment (see Chapter 2). In addition, the instructor can use data analytics to detect fraud by students (see Chapter 4) in a cost-effective way. Creating quality indicators (Chapters 7 and 9) for courses is also facilitated by data analytics.

Third, we see possibilities in using data analytics to measure the performance of instructors. Today, it is relatively difficult to compare and assess the performance of instructors. If the performance of instructors is measured by students' evaluations of teaching (SET), instructors with poor SET scores may argue that they face a more challenging student group, a more demanding topic, or that the students do not take the course seriously. Thanks to the abundance of data, these and similar arguments can be examined, and SET scores can be adjusted accordingly. De Witte and Rogge (2011) provide a model to do so. We will return to this issue in Chapter 5, where we discuss performance at the faculty level.

Finally, for policy makers, it is often unclear how schools use their available resources to "produce" outcomes. By combining structured and unstructured data from various sources, data analytics might provide a solution for governments that aim to monitor the performance of schools more closely. In Chapter 6, we discuss some techniques to relate resources to outputs (e.g., test scores, graduation scores). While similar techniques have existed for some time, school performance scores can now better capture the observed heterogeneity in school, student, and neighborhood characteristics, thanks to the increasing availability of data. This will facilitate the use of these performance scores for policy purposes.

1.3 How Has This Become Possible?

The upsurge in data analytics is a result of the automatic recording and ready availability of data in electronic form. The main enablers of this evolution are the availability of cheap data gathering, data storage, and computing technology. Information systems store and manage data about student background, registration, program, and performance, and all these data can easily be exchanged, combined, and processed.

Moreover, the introduction of learning management systems and online learning applications allows huge amounts of data about the learning process to be collected in real time and at the source. Analogous to clickstream analysis or customer journey mapping in marketing domains, the availability of data about the learning process allows student behavior throughout the learning experience to be analyzed and described. This amount of education data, combined with student, course, and instructor information, makes it possible to use either traditional reporting techniques or more advanced forms of analytics, such as descriptive and predictive analytics.

1.4 Why Data Analytics Has Become Important

With the possibility of collecting and analyzing educational data comes the potential for enormous benefits through the proper use of data analytics. Policy makers (acting as principals in a classical principal–agent setting) are increasingly aware that, thanks to quantitative and qualitative data, they can better monitor the activities of the organizations they are funding (the agents). In fact, data analytics facilitates data-driven decision making such that, for instance, schools or universities can be better-compensated for their efforts in teaching students from disadvantaged backgrounds.

In addition, the availability of data allows stakeholders to assess the effectiveness (i.e., doing the right things) and efficiency (i.e., doing the thing right) of their interventions (see Chapter 10). While there is constant innovation in education (e.g., teachers who experiment with a different didactical instruction method), most of these interventions are not examined on their efficiency or effectiveness due to the absence of reliable data from before and after the implementation of the intervention. Data analytics can provide a solution.

At the same time, we need to be careful with the abundance of data. While combining data from various sources might create privacy issues, dealing with the overwhelming amount of data can also be an intricate issue (Chapter 9). It also forces us to think about such normative questions as whether we should store the data that are gathered during the student learning process. If we answer this question in the affirmative, to evaluate the effectiveness and efficiency of educational innovations, the question of how long we should store the data automatically arises.

Similar questions show that data analytics in education should not be the domain of a single discipline. Economists should discuss the possibilities, issues, and normative questions with a multidisciplinary team of pedagogists, philosophers, computer scientists, and sociologists. By bringing together various disciplines, a more comprehensive answer can be formulated to the challenges ahead.

This book provides a start to this discussion by highlighting some economic perspectives on the use of data analytics in education. We hope that the book marks the start of an interesting and multidisciplinary discussion such that, in the medium term, data analytics in education will seem as natural as a teacher in front of a classroom.

1.5 List of Contributions

This book on data analytics in education is structured in three distinct parts. The first section, consisting of three chapters, discusses the use of data analytics in to improve the student learning process. The second section, with four chapters, details the use of data analytics to measure the performance of faculty, schools, and students. In the third section, two chapters are devoted to the policy relevance of data analytics and the challenges ahead.

1.5.1 Data Analytics to Improve the Learning Process

Part I of the book begins with a chapter by Johannes De Smedt, Seppe vanden Broucke, Jan Vanthienen, and Kristof De Witte. The chapter focuses on supporting the automated feedback learning environment through process mining. It discusses some new ways to process student data, for example, by social network analysis. As similar data are shown to predict student performance, these can be used by instructors to obtain insights into student's behavior and to act accordingly in real time.

Chapter 3, by Wouter Schelfhout, provides a model, based on learning communities, as a platform for growing data use. Research indicates that data use by schools and teachers is not widespread, and where it does occur, is often superficial. In this chapter, we argue that schools and teachers are not open to data use because the essential conditions for integrating it in daily practice are not met in many schools. There is a profound lack of an effective professional development policy, which should start with the core processes and concerns of schools and teachers. Equally important is the frequently observed absence of shared instructional leadership as a basis for shaping this policy. Developing different forms of learning communities—in focused interactions—will provide a platform for addressing these challenges and needs, while at the same time promoting a gradual increase in the integrated use of data. Learning how to gather specific process data on teaching practices must form part of educators' professional development cycles to reach these goals. This will form a basis to give meaning to school internal output data and to school external data sources. Cooperation between schools and with external stakeholders such as education networks, governmental education departments, and school inspectors will be needed to support this endeavor. As part of this contribution, a holistic model of "data for development" will be defined.

Chapter 4, by Silvester Draaijer and Chris van Klaveren, discusses the impact of fraudulent behavior and the use of learning analytics applications. Online quizzes are frequently used to prepare students for summative achievement tests. To encourage student participation, extra credits can be awarded to students who pass these quizzes. While anecdotal evidence indicates that offering quizzes carrying extra credit can result in fraudulent behavior in which students cheat to inflate their scores, there is as yet no empirical evidence investigating the extent of score inflation among, and its impact upon, cohorts of students. In this chapter, the impact of fraudulent behavior of first-year Dutch law students on weekly online quiz scores is studied. Exogenous variation in feedback to students was used to identify the impact. This exogenous variation was generated by abruptly, and without prior notice, ceasing to provide direct feedback to students on online quizzes. The main finding of the study was that the average quiz scores dropped by 1.5 points (on a scale of 0–10) immediately after the unanticipated feedback change. This result, first, supports the anecdotal evidence that online quizzes may not be a valid representation of student knowledge due to fraudulent student behavior. Second, and more importantly for this volume, fraudulent behavior may cause online quiz data to undermine the effectiveness of learning analytics applications.

1.5.2 Data Analytics to Measure Performance

Part II of the book focuses on the use of data analytics to measure performance.

Chapter 5, by Cristian Barra, Sergio Destefanis, Vania Sena, and Roberto Zotti, shows how data analytics can be used to disentangle faculty efficiency from student effort. In particular, this chapter provides an empirical methodology that allows monitoring of the performance of university students through data that are routinely produced and stored by universities. This approach disentangles the portion of the students' academic achievement controlled by the institutions' activities from the portion directly influenced by the students' own efforts, offering novel insights into the performance of universities and potentially supplementing the information from the standard league tables. The procedure is applied to a sample of 37,459 first-year students from a large university based in the South of Italy from the 2004–2005 to the 2010–2011 academic years. The evidence suggests that the efficiency with which faculties deliver their materials matters to female students and to students from low-income households. Pre-enrolment information such as the high school grade and type are good proxies of the student's own effort.

Chapter 6, by Maria C. Andrade e Silva and Ana Camanho, focuses on the measurement of performance at school level. In the majority of European countries, evaluation of schools is at the heart of the educational system as a means to guarantee the quality of education. Every year, in most countries around the world, students perform national exams. Their results are analyzed by several stakeholders, including governmental agencies, the media, and researchers on educational issues. Current advances in information and communication technology (ICT) and data analysis techniques allow schools to make use of massive amounts of data in their daily management. This chapter focuses in particular on the use of students' data to benchmark schools. It illustrates the potential contribution of the information gathered and analyzed through data analytics to promote continuous improvement in schools' educational processes.

Chapter 7, by Kristof De Witte, Grazia Graziosi, and Joris Hindryckx, provides a methodology to handle the abundant data in the learning process. Using a unique and rich dataset of a large European higher vocational institute, this chapter examines which student, teacher, learning, and didactic characteristics can explain differences in students' performance. It proposes a two-step procedure, rooted in the data analytics literature, to select, in a data-driven way, the relevant variables from a large number of potential covariates. First, an importance measure of the variables is computed by repeatedly performing the Lasso variable selection technique on bootstrap subsamples of the original dataset. Second, the results of the bootstrap Lasso selection model are included as *a priori* information for a Bayesian factor approach. This allows the computation of the posterior probability distribution of different models, that is, the inclusion probabilities of potential variables. From this perspective, the chapter suggests an innovative approach to variable selection; by incorporating prior information into Bayesian analysis that is different from the standard choices (e.g., uniform distribution assumption).

Chapter 8, by Tommaso Agasisti, Francesca Ieva, Chiara Masci, Anna Maria Paganoni, and Mara Soncin, provides insights into using data from administrative sources. While public administrations collect data from various sources (e.g., test scores, income, taxes, juvenile offences, school history, medical records, and traffic violations), similar data are not combined in most countries (notable exceptions are the Netherlands and Hungary). Chapter 8 starts with a discussion on how administrative datasets are structured. It then provides some examples of well-known educational datasets: the PISA data, collected by the Organization for Economic Cooperation and Development, and the Italian Invalsi data. Chapter 8 concludes with some empirical applications of similar data to measure the performance of schools.

1.5.3 Policy Relevance and the Challenges Ahead

The third and final part of the book focuses on policy relevance. In Chapter 9, Kurt De Wit and Bruno Broucker define what is typically understood as "Big Data." They apply the concept to higher education, and focus on the data-related issues that need to be addressed. The authors specify what a governance structure for Big Data in higher education would entail. In particular, they focus on IT governance, internal governance, and external governance. Next, they illustrate what this can actually mean in practice by examining recent developments in Belgium (Flanders), at both the Flemish higher education system and higher education institution levels. This case is interesting because data-driven decision making, supported by interconnected databases and purpose-built analytical tools, has expanded at both levels in recent years.

The final chapter of the book, written by Wim Groot and Henriëtte Maassen van den Brink, makes the case for evidence-based education. Evidence-based education is the philosophy that education should be based on the best evidence about what works. This means that specific educational interventions, strategies, and policy science should be evaluated before being recommended or introduced on a wide scale. Without evidence, these interventions should be introduced on an experimental basis, such that their effects can be evaluated scientifically. The availability of large datasets may facilitate the paradigm of "evidence-based education."

References

Baesens B., Bapna R., Marsden J., Vanthienen J. and Zhao J. (2016). Transformational issues of big data and analytics in networked business. *MIS Quarterly*, 40(4), 1–12.

De Witte, K. and Rogge, N. (2011). Accounting for exogenous influences in performance evaluations of teachers. *Economics of Education Review*, 30(4), 641–653.

Rogge, N., Agasisti, T. and De Witte, K. (in press). Big data and the measurement of public organizations' performance and efficiency: The state-of-the-art. *Public Policy and Administration*.

DATA ANALYTICS TO IMPROVE THE LEARNING PROCESS

I

Chapter 2

Improved Student Feedback with Process and Data Analytics

Johannes De Smedt, Seppe K.L.M. vanden Broucke, Jan Vanthienen, and Kristof De Witte

Contents

2.1 Introduction

The growing number of students attending higher education institutions requires tutors to come up with solutions tailored toward these big groups, while maintaining the same quality of student support. A smart way for achieving such feedback is the introduction of automated feedback techniques, enabled by the vast number of electronic support systems that help teachers in their activities. Online fora, assessment environments, and other educational support systems do not only provide an environment to manage course content, but also the means to and the data of interacting with students in a fast and personal way.

This chapter focuses on supporting the automated feedback learning environment through process mining, a novel research area on the verge of data mining and business process management. Traditionally, a "process" is viewed as a series of business activities that need to be executed to achieve a particular goal, although here, the process reflects the steps of the learning flow of the student throughout the time span of a course, both in what they do (the learning activities) and in the data that is generated. The information coming from keeping track of the student's learning trajectory can then be utilized to: provide immediate feedback and suggest next best courses of action, provide monitoring systems to tutors to know which parts are troublesome for students, and even to help construct predictive models that can assess the probability of students passing exams, for instance. The application of process mining is studied from the practical case of supporting a programming course with information systems in the form of an online compilation and feedback mechanism, which helps students grasp the different concepts in the form of exercises and mirrors it to the performance of other students over different years.

2.2 Related Work

The field of learning analytics has been gaining traction in recent years. The prevalence of (big) data, and especially techniques to tackle large datasets, has vastly extended the possibilities to support large groups of students. In this section, the basic concepts and existing work on the field of learning analytics will be discussed in the context of process mining and programming. While it is in no way intended to recapitulate the related work sections of previous chapters, some major works that introduced data analysis in the educational environment are discussed in Section 2.2.1. Next, the more detailed and applied works are discussed in Sections 2.2.2 and 2.2.3.

2.2.1 Learning Analytics

Learning analytics surfaced as a separate research area only recently, enabled by the vast amounts of datasets generated by new supporting information systems, such as online platforms, Massive Open Online Courses (MOOCs), and so on. Seminal works includes the work of Siemens (Siemens and Long, 2011; Siemens and Baker, 2012), and Baker (Baker and Inventado, 2014), focusing on the basic concepts and applications that can be established in learning environments. The advancement of automated systems, which has seen a large increase in computational power, allows for analyses that were previously unthinkable. Key applications include variants of the classic data mining tasks, that is, classification, clustering, regression, social network analysis, and pattern mining. An overview of applications and their required dataset types is shown in Table 2.1. Also, visualization of learner data (Duval, 2011) plays a big role in descriptive analytics.

A key part of the analytics exercise should be to entail an automated feedback cycle, which not only provides insights from a tutor's perspective, but also informs the student (Clow, 2012). This can be done not only by, for example, automated assignments and online dashboards, but also by providing actionable work points that were obtained from the analysis.

Table 2.1   An Overview of Data Mining Techniques and Their Corresponding Applications and Data in Learning

Technique	Application	Data
Classification	Determining a student's profile	Grades, forum activity, prior education, demographic information
Clustering	Retrieving student profiles, strategies	Grades, assignment content, time of submission
Regression	Predicting student exam scores, pass rates	
Social network analysis	Find collaborators of student groups	Forum discussions, social media data
Pattern mining	Find successful resolution strategies	Multi-staged exercise solutions

2.2.2 Automated Feedback Systems

The automated grading and analysis of (coding) assignments already has a long and rich history. Many research papers have focused on the topic, including the efforts of Kay et al. (1994), Cheang et al. (2003), and Singh et al. (2013). The former studies a system that automatically scores programming exercises at the University of Singapore, while the latter provides a recent approach for automated feedback generation with a very extensive methodology. Singh et al. (2013) start with a reference model to which they can compare student efforts with an error model to find common mistakes. Automated feedback in this context enables tutors to effectively score larger student bodies by making use of scaling systems, baseline solutions, and individualized feedback. It reduces the time educational staff have to spend on repetitive tasks inherent to grading, allowing teachers to focus on finding truly representative cases that reinforce students' understanding of the subject matter. Furthermore, it enables the tutor to automatically match the submissions to detect duplicate solutions, hinting at plagiarism (Clough, 2000). Finding such works is typically done by using natural language processing and incorporates techniques that go beyond just one-on-one code or text matching, analyzing the similarity in the line of reasoning. Also, online repositories can be used to find students copying solutions from other locations.

The downsides that are tied to automated feedback include the fact that students now have potentially unlimited attempts to tailor their solution toward the baseline, making them lazy and unobservant. As they receive immediate feedback, they can keep uploading new versions of their solution in order to obtain a perfect score. However, by also using new examples during the correction phase, this effect can be mitigated.

2.2.3 Process Mining

The body of analysis techniques for historic or real-time, event-based data is called process mining (van der Aalst, 2016). The field encompasses retrieving the process models that are present in the data, by building workflow-type models and their various aspects, for example, the contributors, data, timing information, and so on. An event is considered to be an execution of an activity or event type. The research area is situated on the verge of machine learning and data mining techniques, business process management, and information systems. Process mining has already been applied in numerous other learning analytics settings, including the efforts of Pechenizkiy et al. (2009) and Mukala et al. (2015), among others. They cover the basic applications that process mining offers, such as retrieving the paths that students followed toward constructing their solutions, as well as the timing information and different behavioral clusters (Bogarín et al., 2014). Furthermore, process mining has an extensive background in finding deviating behavior by making use of simulation and conformance checking (van der Aalst et al., 2012).

2.3 Automated Feedback Environments

The challenge of teaching large bodies of students requires new ways of setting up interaction that is still tailored toward the individual. By using automated feedback environments, technology has provided an adequate solution that combines the typical method of supporting students through assignments and tests with large-scale computing for processing them. In this section, such a set of solutions is discussed in detail. The approach has been used by the authors to support a programming course, and it provides the data that will be used in the next sections to illustrate the power of analytics in an educational context.

2.3.1 The Online Corrector

In the context of educating students on the subject of programming, an extensive amount of educators' time is devoted to constructing and correcting exercises. Moreover, it is key that educators provide useful and detailed feedback on these exercises. However, manually correcting assignments on a weekly basis is intractable for a small team of tutors. Hence, a fitting solution was found in the automated correction of students' submissions. The system allows students to download the assignment and upload a personal solution as many times as possible. The most far-reaching change that the tutor has to cope with is the streamlining of the nature of the exercises in order to comply with the way the corrector processes the output generated from student solutions. To do so, students are provided with a template solution "skeleton." This way, they can focus on the programming problem, rather than on the convoluted set-up of programming environments. In addition, the compatibility with the Online Corrector is guaranteed, for example, in terms of inputs and outputs.

Second, the uploaded solution will be executed under several testing conditions and inputs, generating text and file output that can be matched with the given "to-be" solutions of the tutor. This overcomes the imprecisions that were reported in Kay et al. (1994), where slight differences in text output created oversensitive solutions. In Figure 2.1, a screenshot can be found of a result generated for an assignment. Notice that the student received the maximum score for all five scenarios that were offered. Since the environment is offered in a web-based package, it is platform independent and offers compatibility with all the different operating systems. This overcomes many impracticalities that are often witnessed with standard programming environments.

2.3.2 Immediate Feedback

The greatest potential benefit for the student is in the way her/his solution gets evaluated. Immediate feedback is provided over multiple cases that test the code for inconsistencies and common mistakes. If grave errors are present, the student's

Figure 2.1   An example solution provided by the Online Corrector system. The student scores one out of six; that is, only one scenario was handled correctly by this solution.

is directed to the section of the code that is inhibiting the online mechanism from running the code. If the code is executable, several tests are performed to check the full range of the output that is generated. The approach is granular enough to point the student in the correct direction for later attempts.

2.3.3 Student Performance Tracking and Dashboards

The other benefit of using an (online) evaluation system, is the possibility to record each student's progress throughout the website. Indeed, incorporating such a tracking mechanism is paramount to set up a learning analytics environment; the (quality of the) data is of utmost importance for models to be built. The following data is stored during web sessions:

- Student ID (anonymous): used for identifying students in a privacy-sensitive manner. This is used to connect to other course data, such as grades, and so on.
- Platform: technical information regarding the device used to submit a solution
- Attempt:
  - Assignment: assignment chosen
  - Score: score obtained for the specific assignment
  - Compilation file: uploaded solution

This information is stored and an aggregate overview can be presented to the tutor at any given time. It enables the educational team to get a quick overview of the activity and performance of students. The system informs them about whether students are actively trying to solve the exercise, how many attempts are made on average, and what the evolution of the scores is over time. Afterwards, a direct connection with the final solution uploaded through the university portals can be made to assess the exercise's life cycle.

2.4 Process Mining to Improve Student Feedback

The basic principles and the efforts made toward learning analytics regarding process mining were discussed in Section 2.3.3. In this section, a detailed overview of the basic principles is discussed, along with important techniques and applications in a learning analytics context. However, the programming context is still used as a backdrop for illustration.

2.4.1 Preliminaries

As indicated earlier, process mining uses techniques both from process modeling and its corresponding languages as well as data mining. Therefore, it is important to get a grasp on the way process models are represented, as well as how they are derived from process data.

2.4.2 Business Process Models

A business process model is typically built up as a flowchart-like graph, containing activities (represented by rectangular shapes) and arcs directing the order of execution. Next to that, gateways introduce concurrency by splitting the flow in either exclusive or inclusive parts. They can be annotated with extra information, such as certain data variables, to steer the routing of work even further. The organizational aspect of a process is typically represented by different lanes and pools in the process. Each pool indicates a certain division in the overall system, while the lanes represent separate actor types. An overview of the online correction approach and the corresponding actions is given in Figure 2.2 in standard Business Process Model and Notation (BPMN) (Silver and Richard, 2009). Other commonly used process languages are Petri nets, Yet Another Workflow Language, and Event-Drive Process Chains (van der Aalst, 2016).

2.4.3 Business Process Mining

Process mining encompasses many different activities. The term "mining" is a somewhat misleading term, as the research domain is founded on three pillars: discovery, conformance checking, and re-engineering. Each pillar will be covered in the following sections.

2.4.3.1 Discovery

In order to extract business process models from event logs, there is the minimum requirement of having ordered recordings of activities. In Table 2.2, an example of a standard event log is given. The main task when starting a process mining exercise is to find a representation of a single "case" to which activities can be associated. Oftentimes, a case identifier is included by default in order to do so. In the table, however, there is no straightforward identifier to be found. Depending on the analysis that is pursued, it could be interesting to follow one exercise, one student, or one tutor per case. One way to achieve the right granularity exists in incorporating the exercise into the activities, hence obtaining information regarding the length and occurrence of submissions to the platform on an exercise-level granularity. Furthermore, Upload exercises are disregarded as an activity, as they only occur once at the beginning of the process. In Figures 2.3 and 2.4, the process mining tool Disco (http://www.fluxicon.com/disco) was used to obtain a basic overview of the process on two levels for three exercises. On the one hand, in Figure 2.3 the time perspective is highlighted. Activities are connected with arcs that display how much time on average has elapsed before the next activity starts. It shows when exercises are made available and whether students actively made multiple submissions through the online platform. This indicates students going through a learning phase. Only for Exercises 2 and 3 is this behavior clearly present, indicating that either the level of this assignment or the engagement from students was higher. In Figure 2.4, the same model is shown from the case perspective, that is, how many times an activity is executed. Here it can be seen how many repetitions are typically performed. Also, it shows that students tend to check their solutions after uploading as a safety check.

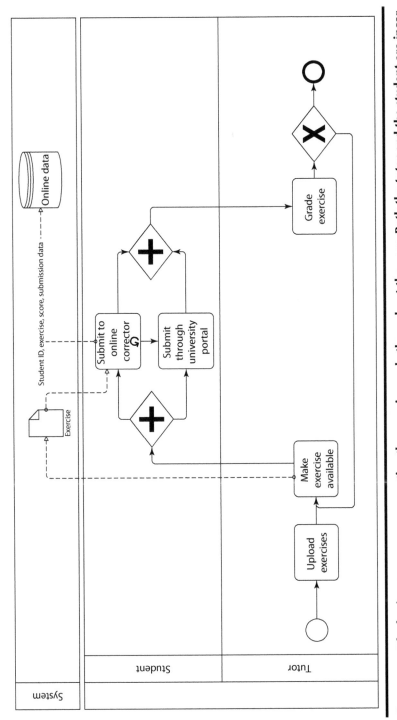

Figure 2.2 The business process representing the exercise cycle throughout the year. Both the tutor and the student are incorporated. The tutor makes an exercise available, after which the student has to submit through the online platform to practice (optional) and then submit a final solution.

Table 2.2 A Small Example of an Event Log Containing Events Generated by Students Using the Online Correction System

Event	Resource	Timestamp	Data
Upload exercises	Tutor_1	5/03/2016 15:07	Exercise = 1
Make exercise available	Tutor_1	6/03/2016 18:12	Exercise = 1
Submit to Online Corrector	Student_1	10/03/2016 9:41	Exercise = 1; Score = 2
Submit to Online Corrector	Student_1	10/03/2016 9:43	Exercise = 1; Score = 2
Submit to Online Corrector	Student_1	11/03/2016 23:42	Exercise = 1; Score = 5
Submit through university portal	Student_1	11/03/2016 23:49	Exercise = 1
Submit to Online Corrector	Student_2	10/03/2016 9:41	Exercise = 1; Score = 7
Submit through university portal	Student_2	11/03/2016 23:49	Exercise = 1
Grade exercises	Tutor_1	11/03/2016 10:05	Exercise = 1; Score = [8,9,...]

2.4.3.2 Conformance Checking

Once a process model is discovered, or in case there is a reference process model available, it can be checked to what extent its behavior aligns with (historic) event data. This is called conformance checking and can be performed in numerous ways. The basic principle boils down to replaying the behavior that was found in the event log over the process model that is at hand. This way, deviations in terms of steps that were taken that do not match the base model become apparent and can be used for further analysis. Consider the model in Figure 2.2 again and the event log from Table 2.3. In this example, student one submits her/his exercise without first submitting them to the Online Corrector. Clearly, this is not allowed in the process model in Figure 2.2.

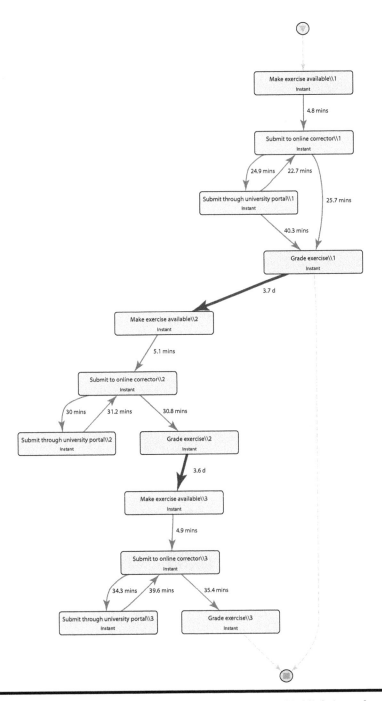

Figure 2.3 Process model discovered with Disco highlighting the time perspective.

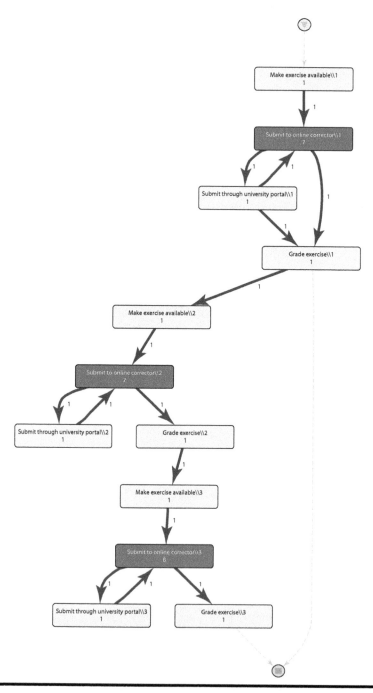

Figure 2.4 Process model discovered with Disco highlighting the case perspective.

Table 2.3   An Event Log That Does Not Match the Process in Figure 2.2

Event	Resource	Timestamp	Data
Upload exercises	Tutor_1	5/03/2016 15:07	Exercise = 1
Make exercise available	Tutor_1	6/03/2016 18:12	Exercise = 1
Make exercise available	Tutor_1	6/03/2016 19:31	Exercise = 2
Submit through university portal	Student_1	11/03/2016 23:49	Exercise = 1
Submit to Online Corrector	Student_2	10/03/2016 9:41	Exercise = 1; Score = 7
Submit through university portal	Student_2	11/03/2016 23:49	Exercise = 1
Grade exercises	Tutor_1	11/03/2016 10:05	Exercise = 1; Score = [8,9,...]

There are many reconciliation strategies for tackling such inconsistencies (van der Aalst et al., 2012). The missing event can be considered an error in the event log; it was not recorded by the system by mistake or removed during data processing. In this instance, the model can act as if the event has happened in order to be able to continue replaying the rest of the trace. Another peculiarity in the event log is the making available of Exercise 2 right after Exercise 1. This is also not allowed by the model. In this case, the event can be skipped in the model, as there is no way to execute the model like that. This means that later, when Exercise 2 is needed, the model has to either insert it or postpone the execution to comply with the log.

In the end, the goal is to find a set of executions that yields the smallest cost between log and model. There are different ways to process these reconciliation procedures. For example, it might be very important that the student does not skip the online step. In order to reflect this, a higher cost can be assigned to that activity.

2.4.3.3 Re-Engineering

The final pillar of process mining entails the improving of a process according to the insights that were gathered from mining and conformance checking.

Again, this encompasses all the different aspects that are tied to a process. When performance analysis uncovers that a certain part of the model takes a long time to progress, it might be due to the way the activities are ordered, or it might be because one particular resource handles it while being overwhelmed by others, hence constituting a bottleneck. Many of these analyses are performed by doing a simulation.

In the end, it is also important to close the loop with the process model that was actually expected to come out of the information system. That is, deviations that are due to a gap between implementation and design can be resolved or fixed in the information system. Likewise, both the process model design and implementation can be modified to be more in line with what users expect in terms of activity flow.

2.4.4 Social Network Analysis

An important part of process mining is the analysis of its so-called resources, that is, the entities involved in the execution of a particular activity. This task is usually part of the discovery phase and can be done in different ways (Song and van der Aalst, 2008). Typically, techniques that retrieve resource information make use of the handover-of-work, that is, the interconnections between (human) actors in a process, to build a social network. Note that, in contrast with techniques that retrieve control flow information, the social network is built over cases, not from cases. Hence, it gives an overview of who delegates and receives works throughout the full event log. Social networks are built up of graphs that connect all the different nodes, that is, people in the network when there is evidence of cooperation. This is measured by, for example, the number of times they interacted, or the value of their transactions, and so on. This information is stored in adjacency matrices, which are symmetric matrices that assign values between the actors. In Table 2.4, an example of a small adjacency matrix is given. One of the main goals of constructing social networks is to find communities of interacting actors. These can be used to find, for example, the spread of media campaigns over time, fraud, or research collaborations. The communities can be indicated in the graph to get a grasp of their size and their spread.

Table 2.4 An Adjacency Matrix

-	a	b	c
a	1	1	0
b	1	0	1
c	0	1	0

2.4.4.1 Case Study

One of the key applications of social network analysis for learning analytics is to find communities of students that cooperate to solve exercises and assignments. This can be used to detect plagiarism, but also to identify whether cooperation actually stimulates them, or whether it leaves them with an insufficiently clear view of the course matter. This analysis was also used for the programming course. By making use of the information of the assignments, the online platform, and the final submission, it is possible to retrieve the similarity of solutions and hence bundle the similar solutions. This was done on a weekly basis to obtain a view of how the cliques were formed throughout the teaching period. In Figure 2.5, an overview is given of 6 weeks of assignments. In Week 2, the first small groups are formed, as shown in Figure 2.5a. Next, throughout Weeks 6–9, the cooperation intensifies, with larger groups being formed. In Week 10, a very big community is created. Presumably, the smaller groups merged into the bigger to solve the exercise. In Week 11, this effect is less noticeable. These insights provide extra background information for the tutor. First of all, while there is cooperation, it is only present to a certain extent. Furthermore, the formation of smaller groups (i.e., between two and four students) is not discouraged in general, as students can learn from each other. The bigger groups, however, reflect a different situation; members of big groups are typically students that copy the solution of a strong student to obtain good grades and demonstrate participation in the course. They have little notion of how and why their solution is correct, and as such do not study the course material in an adequate manner. The fact that Week 10 shows a big discrepancy in terms of participation is mainly due to the assignment's subject: recursion. Recursion is a hard topic, especially for novice programmers, as it requires a very good understanding of coding as well as many trial-and-error runs during development. The results gave the tutors the insight that, indeed, this exercise was hard, and students who could not easily obtain a correct answer themselves consequently turned to other sources for help. Finally, in Figure 2.6, all the information of all the weeks is condensed into one graph, based on the amount of times students appear in the same group.

2.5 Predictive Analytics to Forecast Student Performance

Given the process analyses and data that was gathered from students' actions, an overview is now given of other different data mining approaches that can be used toward obtaining insights into student data. As explained earlier, data mining focuses on different tasks, such as prediction, description, regression, and so on. Remember that, from a tutor's view, it is not just the aim to predict student

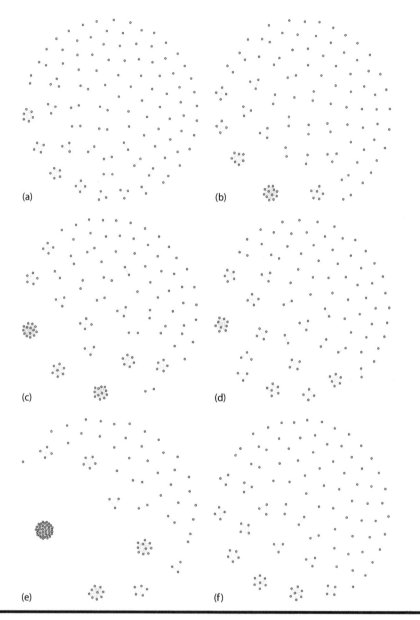

Figure 2.5 Overview of the social networks present in 6 weeks' data.

performance by any means, but rather to obtain an insight into the important features influencing the result that reflect parameters that can be adjusted in newer iterations of the course. In this section, different features extracted from the portal, the university system, grades, and Online Corrector are condensed into descriptive and predictive models.

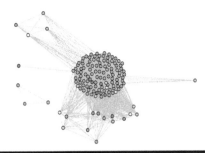

Figure 2.6   Full social network of students' assignments over 12 weeks, with communities indicated in different colors.

2.5.1 *Student Attributes and Basic Analysis*

The following attributes (also sometimes referred to as variables or features) are used for analysis:

- Score: The final score that students received for the exam
- Exercise cluster (ex_i): The cluster/part of the social network in which the student is present for Exercise i
- Difference (diff_ex_i): The amount of minutes the student submitted her/his assignment before the deadline
- Community (clust): The community in which the student resides, obtained from the social network analysis in Section 2.4.4.1

Naturally, some of these attributes are correlated. Hence, an overview of the correlation is given in Table 2.5. First, the amount of minutes submitted before the deadline is strongly correlated with the cluster that the student ends up in. This gives reasonable evidence that the groups are organized and have similar submission strategies. Also, between different assignments this effect is sometimes present, for example, in the number of minutes to the deadline of Assignment 11 and the cluster of Assignment 12. Besides these results, all correlation is relatively low. The correlations will be taken into account when constructing analytical models.

Next, a chi-squared weighing is performed to obtain a notion of the goodness of fit, that is, to what extent a certain variable is able to capture the attribute chosen for prediction. In the following table, the values are shown in terms of predicting the score by means of the other variables. Clearly, the community has the biggest explanatory power among all the variables, with roughly the same value as the network the student resides in, for Exercises 3 and 4. A student's place in a certain part of a social network has strong explanatory power regarding the student's scores, except for in Assignment 1. This corresponds with the fact that the first exercise was very easy, hence confirming that achieving a higher or lower grade has little value when predicting a student's final performance. Compared to the clusters,

Table 2.5   Correlation Matrix of All Variables

	Ex1	Ex2	Ex3	Ex4	Ex5	Ex6	Ex7	Ex8	Ex9	Ex10	Ex11	Ex12	diff ex1	diff ex2	diff ex3	diff ex4	diff ex5	diff ex6	diff ex7	diff ex8	diff ex9	diff ex10	diff ex11	diff ex12	Clust
Ex1	1.00	0.02	0.15	0.15	0.24	0.00	0.20	-0.09	0.03	0.07	0.09	0.21	-0.92	-0.21	-0.11	-0.13	-0.37	-0.04	-0.18	-0.04	-0.28	-0.13	-0.22	-0.22	-0.22
Ex2	0.02	1.00	0.02	0.02	-0.12	-0.22	-0.05	0.07	-0.07	-0.16	0.09	-0.13	0.03	-0.40	-0.02	-0.13	-0.03	0.00	0.05	-0.05	0.02	0.04	-0.01	0.06	0.04
Ex3	0.15	0.02	1.00	1.00	0.07	-0.01	0.11	-0.07	0.05	0.00	0.10	-0.06	-0.14	-0.04	-0.15	-0.49	-0.36	-0.24	-0.28	-0.11	-0.08	-0.17	-0.23	0.00	-0.10
Ex4	0.15	0.02	1.00	1.00	0.07	-0.01	0.11	-0.07	0.05	0.00	0.10	-0.06	-0.14	-0.04	-0.15	-0.49	-0.36	-0.24	-0.28	-0.11	-0.08	-0.17	-0.23	0.00	-0.10
Ex5	0.24	-0.12	0.07	0.07	1.00	0.06	0.15	-0.16	-0.14	0.21	0.03	0.16	-0.32	-0.10	0.06	-0.18	-0.54	-0.21	-0.14	0.03	-0.18	-0.10	-0.12	-0.18	-0.23
Ex6	0.00	-0.22	-0.01	-0.01	0.06	1.00	0.15	-0.05	0.07	0.23	-0.11	0.07	0.02	-0.05	-0.07	-0.15	-0.52	-0.09	0.02	0.04	-0.13	-0.06	-0.04	-0.04	0.09
Ex7	0.20	-0.05	0.11	0.11	0.15	0.15	1.00	-0.05	0.07	0.23	0.07	-0.04	-0.17	0.08	-0.11	-0.14	-0.05	-0.13	-0.43	0.08	-0.14	-0.13	-0.09	0.00	-0.14
Ex8	-0.09	0.07	-0.07	-0.07	-0.16	-0.05	-0.05	1.00	-0.12	-0.17	0.14	0.04	0.06	-0.11	0.09	-0.09	0.02	0.13	0.01	-0.38	0.07	0.22	0.13	-0.01	0.18
Ex9	0.03	-0.07	0.05	0.05	-0.14	0.07	0.07	-0.12	1.00	0.09	0.12	-0.03	0.00	0.00	-0.08	-0.04	-0.15	0.03	-0.19	-0.03	-0.49	-0.16	-0.24	-0.02	-0.06
Ex10	0.07	-0.16	0.00	0.00	0.21	0.23	0.23	-0.17	0.09	1.00	0.01	0.04	-0.10	0.08	0.07	-0.11	-0.10	-0.22	-0.21	0.01	-0.12	-0.72	-0.10	-0.11	-0.24
Ex11	0.09	0.09	0.10	0.10	0.03	-0.11	0.07	0.14	0.12	0.01	1.00	-0.07	-0.09	-0.04	-0.14	-0.09	-0.16	-0.12	-0.19	-0.25	-0.12	-0.12	-0.56	-0.02	0.08
Ex12	0.21	-0.13	-0.06	-0.06	0.16	0.07	-0.04	0.04	-0.03	0.04	-0.07	1.00	-0.26	-0.05	-0.06	0.12	-0.16	-0.15	-0.08	0.00	-0.19	-0.06	-0.03	-0.71	-0.06
diff ex1	-0.92	0.03	-0.14	-0.14	-0.32	0.02	-0.17	0.06	0.00	-0.10	-0.09	-0.26	1.00	0.24	0.12	0.15	0.42	0.03	0.23	0.01	0.28	0.14	0.19	0.26	0.23
diff ex2	-0.21	-0.40	-0.04	-0.04	-0.10	-0.05	0.08	-0.11	0.00	0.08	-0.04	-0.05	0.24	1.00	0.31	0.26	0.28	0.13	0.02	0.13	0.04	0.00	0.00	0.16	-0.06
diff ex3	-0.11	-0.02	-0.15	-0.15	0.06	-0.07	-0.11	0.09	-0.08	0.07	-0.14	-0.06	0.12	0.31	1.00	0.22	0.16	0.26	0.21	0.00	0.10	0.05	0.04	0.06	-0.11
diff ex4	-0.13	-0.13	-0.49	-0.49	-0.18	-0.15	-0.14	-0.09	-0.04	-0.11	-0.09	0.12	0.15	0.26	0.22	1.00	0.44	0.29	0.46	0.23	0.04	0.22	0.14	-0.04	0.08
diff ex5	-0.37	-0.03	-0.36	-0.36	-0.54	-0.52	-0.05	0.02	-0.15	-0.10	-0.16	-0.16	0.42	0.28	0.16	0.44	1.00	0.37	0.38	0.18	0.37	0.15	0.34	0.20	0.25
diff ex6	-0.04	0.00	-0.24	-0.24	-0.21	-0.09	-0.13	0.13	0.03	-0.22	-0.12	-0.15	0.03	0.13	0.26	0.29	0.37	1.00	0.40	-0.01	0.16	0.30	0.23	0.15	0.03
diff ex7	-0.18	0.05	-0.28	-0.28	-0.14	0.02	-0.43	0.01	-0.19	-0.21	-0.19	-0.08	0.23	0.02	0.21	0.46	0.38	0.40	1.00	0.05	0.30	0.32	0.31	0.09	0.17
diff ex8	-0.04	-0.05	-0.11	-0.11	0.03	0.04	0.08	-0.38	-0.03	0.01	-0.25	0.00	0.01	0.13	0.00	0.23	0.18	-0.01	0.05	1.00	0.20	0.05	0.23	0.09	-0.04
diff ex9	-0.28	0.02	-0.08	-0.08	-0.18	-0.13	-0.14	0.07	-0.49	-0.12	-0.12	-0.19	0.28	0.04	0.10	0.04	0.37	0.16	0.30	0.20	1.00	0.23	0.29	0.27	0.52
diff ex10	-0.13	0.04	-0.17	-0.17	-0.10	-0.06	-0.13	0.22	-0.16	-0.72	-0.12	-0.06	0.14	0.00	0.05	0.22	0.15	0.30	0.32	0.05	0.23	1.00	0.26	0.17	0.30
diff ex11	-0.22	-0.01	-0.23	-0.23	-0.12	-0.04	-0.09	0.13	-0.24	-0.10	-0.56	-0.03	0.19	0.00	0.04	0.14	0.34	0.23	0.31	0.23	0.29	0.26	1.00	0.22	0.17
diff ex12	-0.22	0.06	0.00	0.00	-0.18	-0.04	0.00	-0.01	-0.02	-0.11	-0.02	-0.71	0.26	0.16	0.06	-0.04	0.20	0.15	0.09	0.09	0.27	0.17	0.22	1.00	0.25
Clust	-0.22	0.04	-0.10	-0.10	-0.23	0.09	-0.14	0.18	-0.06	-0.24	0.08	-0.06	0.23	-0.06	-0.11	0.08	0.25	0.03	0.17	-0.04	0.52	0.30	0.17	0.25	1.00

the number of minutes until the deadline have less predictive power. They can be removed in case correlation with other variables is too high.

2.5.2 Student Profiling

In order to get a grasp on the different profiles that took part in the course, clustering is applied to the data. A technique called X-means is used, which tries to minimize the distance between the data points in the same clusters, while maximizing distances between data points in different clusters. It is derived from k-means, in which k stands for the number of clusters sought. X-means will stop searching for new clusters when it does not find any evidence for achieving clusters that differ from the ones already retrieved. The different values were normalized first, that is, they were transformed in order to obtain comparable scales. Note that the variables representing the different clusters are categorical and hence should not be interpreted based on the value of the score, but rather on the difference compared to other scores. The algorithm retrieved only two types of clusters: one cluster of average-performing students and one cluster of students who obtained lower grades. The results are plotted in Figure 2.7. Students that perform worse on average are typically also in different clusters throughout the year, and they submit their exercises later. In the end they score lower, as can be seen at the right-hand side of the graph. Still, the majority of students' performances are relatively consistent. The group dynamics probably level out their performing, hence straightening the way they solve exercises. It is probable that worse-performing students worked on their own and took the course lightly, thus missing the overall approach that was applied by the group. The algorithm was unable to indicate any information regarding better-than-average students.

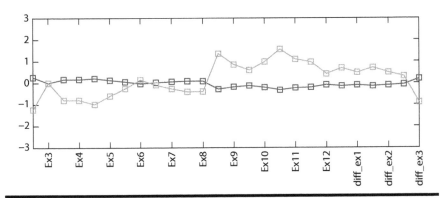

Figure 2.7   Average values of the variables in the clusters. Average students are indicated in black, worse-performing students in gray.

2.5.3 Predicting Student Performance

After getting a first grasp of the different student profiles that exist, predictive models are constructed in order to retrieve more in-depth information regarding the different variables and how they can be used toward modeling student performance. There exists a multitude of different techniques that can be used toward constructing prediction models. Some of the most widely used are (logistic) regression, support vector machines, neural networks, Bayesian networks, decision trees, and random forests. As explained earlier, it is paramount to use the right variables in order to obtain the best models. There are plenty of feature-selection techniques that can optimize the final goal, that is, finding a strong model that accurately represents the data. One such technique was already discussed in Section 2.5.1: chi-squared weighting. The weighing of the variables in the dataset can be found in Table 2.6. Alternatives exist, including principal component analysis, which combines variables in a way that reduces correlation among them. The downside, however, is that it is hard to relate the different constructed variables to the output. Next, the fitting technique used also depends on the types of variables and target variable that are at hand. Support vector machines, for example, are typically used for numeric data with high dimensionality. Logistic regression is used for binary target variables, that is, when only two possible outcomes are at hand, although extensions for multiple target variables exist as well. In order to avoid data being fit only around existing data, a set-up with training and test sets is typically produced. On the one hand, the training data is used to construct the model. On the other hand, the test set data is used over the constructed model to check performance and the generalizability of the model. A commonly used ratio to split the data is 70% training and 30% test data. In case the dataset is not large, or in case overfitting the data needs to be avoided at all cost, cross validation is often applied. It entails to iteratively use other data in the training and test set, for example, by leaving out 10% of the data 10 times. The end result is then a composition of the different outcomes. The results of binary classification are typically evaluated by making use of a confusion matrix. An example is given in Table 2.7, which displays the results of fitting a logistic regression on all variables for predicting whether a student passes (true), or fails (false). The table explains how well the algorithm is able to classify the data. The students that were predicted to fail the course that indeed failed the course, also known as true negatives (TN), can be found in the upper left-hand corner; students predicted to fail that did not fail are called false negatives (FN).

Positive observations can be categorized correspondingly. These metrics allow for constructing different evaluation criteria:

- Accuracy $\left(\dfrac{TP + TN}{TP + TN + FP + FN} \right)$: Expresses the extent to which the algorithm classifies all instances correctly

Table 2.6   Chi-Squared Weighting of All the Attributes

Attribute	Value
diff_ex3	15.55186
diff_ex8	15.64137
diff_ex2	18.66861
diff_ex10	18.89003
diff_ex11	20.86746
diff_ex4	21.65099
diff_ex12	22.67624
diff_ex7	25.80862
diff_ex1	28.02473
diff_ex5	32.48962
diff_ex6	34.09273
diff_ex9	40.55198
Ex1	56.56115
Ex11	135.091
Ex5	138.4916
Ex12	142.5164
Ex9	152.9203
Ex10	155.9722
Ex7	156.5083
Ex2	157.7327
Ex8	161.2573
Ex6	164.4453
Ex3	171.0156
Ex4	171.0156
Clust.	171.7689

Table 2.7 Confusion Matrix for a Logistic Regression Model Predicting Whether a Student Will Pass or Fail the Course

	True Negative	*True Positive*	*Class Precision*
pred. false	6	3	66.66%
pred. true	11	47	81.03%
class recall	35.29%	94%	

- Sensitivity $\left(\dfrac{TP}{TP+FN}\right)$: (recall) The amount of positive instances classified correctly

- Specificity $\left(\dfrac{TN}{FP+TN}\right)$: The amount of negative instances classified correctly

- Precision $\left(\dfrac{TP}{FP+TP}\right)$: The amount of true positive instances in all instances being predicted as true

The results show that the accuracy is relatively high, reaching 79.10%. Given the small amount of variables, especially in terms of different types of values, there is high predictive power in the dataset. The confusion matrix of another model that fits the same data without the different cluster variables (ex_i) is given in Table 2.8. The results are relatively comparable. Another metric that can be used to assess classification performance is the area-under-curve (AUC). It is used to express how much better the result is able to predict the outcome compared to a random classifier. The AUC is derived from the Receiver Operating Characteristic (ROC) curve, which plots the true positive rate (sensitivity) against the false positive rate (1-specificity) for various thresholds. The AUC is then the area under the ROC curve, scored on a scale of 0–1. The closer the curve approaches the upper left-hand corner, the better the classification, as this point represents the classification which contains no false positives and negatives. The ROC curves with their corresponding AUC scores are displayed in Figures 2.8a,b. Again, the high AUC values suggest

Table 2.8 Confusion Matrix for a Logistic Regression Model Predicting Whether a Student Will Pass or Fail the Course without the Cluster Variables

	Is Negative	*Is Positive*	*Class Precision*
Pred. false	3 (true negative)	0 (false negative)	100%
Pred. true	14 (false positive)	50 (true positive)	78.13%
Class recall	17.65%	100%	

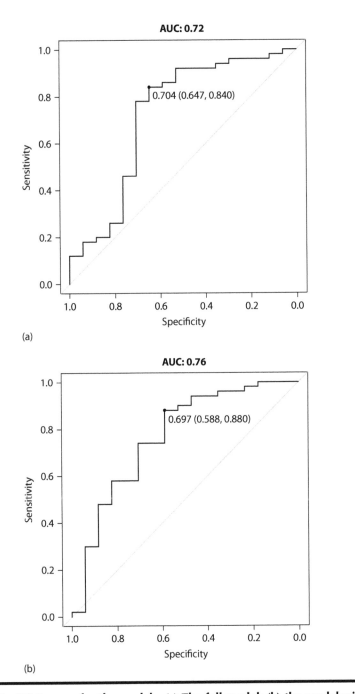

Figure 2.8 ROC curve for the models. (a) The full model; (b) the model without the cluster variables. The best-performing value is marked with its scores.

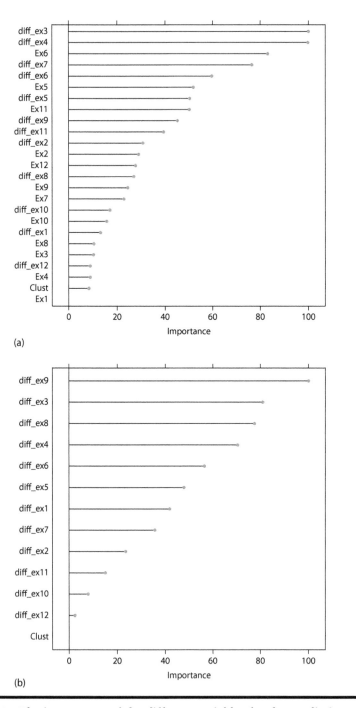

(a)

(b)

Figure 2.9 The importance of the different variables for the predictive models for the full model (a), and the model without the cluster variables (b).

that the models are well capable of predicting whether a student will pass or fail the course.

Finally, in order to gain insights into the models, the importance of the different variables is plotted in Figures 2.9a,b. One of the main determining factors appears to be the time of handing in certain exercises, as well as students being present in certain groups for the exercises. Notice that, despite the intuition established from the chi-squared weighting earlier, the community has very little impact. This can be due to the fact that the other variables explain largely what that variable can add to the prediction, but on a more fine-granular level.

Despite the fact that interesting results were achieved, there is a caveat to be added to the discussion. Although cross validation was used and the data mining techniques utilized were robust, the size of the data was still relatively small. Also, not every student actively participated in the course, introducing numerous missing values. Hence, it would require a second iteration of the course to confirm the findings.

2.6 Conclusion

This chapter shows new ways of processing student data by using both process and data mining techniques, such as deriving student flows, social network analysis, and predicting students' performance. The chapter shows how tutors can be supported by automated systems that eventually produce data that give insights into students' behavior. Real-life data was used to add a very hands-on aspect that can inspire tutors to produce their own analyses in future teaching endeavors.

2.6.1 Useful Tools and Links

Throughout this chapter, many software packages are used. A small overview is given here:

- Disco: A proprietary process mining tool that is tailored toward novice users. It offers guidance toward important and analyzing data, and it is compatible with the ProM framework. https://fluxicon.com/disco/
- ProM: An open-source process-mining suite that contains state-of-the-art algorithms, visualization, and so on based on the latest research in process mining. http://www.promtools.org/
- igraph: An open-source R plugin that can be used for social network analysis. http://igraph.org/
- RapidMiner: An open-source data-mining suite that covers a plethora of techniques and data-processing modules. http://rapidminer.com/

References

Baker, R. S. and Inventado, P. S. (2014). Educational data mining and learning analytics. In Larusson, J. A. and White, B., *Learning Analytics*, pp. 61–75. Berlin, Germany: Springer.

Bogarín, A., Romero C., Cerezo R., and Sanchez-Santillán M. (2014). Clustering for improving educational process mining. In *Proceedings of the Fourth International Conference on Learning Analytics and Knowledge*, pp. 11–15, New York: ACM.

Cheang, B., Kurnia, A., Lim, A., and Oon, W.-C. (2003). On automated grading of programming assignments in an academic institution. *Computers & Education*, 41(2), 121–131.

Clough, P. (2000). Plagiarism in natural and programming languages: An overview of current tools and technologies. Research Memoranda: CS-00-05. Department of Computer Science, University of Sheffield, United Kingdom.

Clow, D. (2012). The learning analytics cycle: Closing the loop effectively. In *Proceedings of the 2nd International Conference on Learning Analytics and Knowledge*, pp. 134–138. ACM.

Duval, E. (2011). Attention please!: Learning analytics for visualization and recommendation. In *Proceedings of the 1st International Conference on Learning Analytics and Knowledge*, pp. 9–17. ACM.

Kay, D. G., Scott, T., Isaacson, P., and Reek, K. A. (1994). Automated grading assistance for student programs. *ACM SIGCSE Bulletin*, 26(1), 381–382.

Mukala, P., Buijs, J., Leemans, M., and van der Aalst, W. (2015). Learning analytics on coursera event data: A process mining approach.

Pechenizkiy, M., Trcka, N., Vasilyeva, E., van Aalst, W., and De Bra, P. (2009). Process mining online assessment data. In *Educational Data Mining. Proceedings of the 2nd International Conference on Educational Data Mining (EDM)*, Cordoba, Spain, July 1–3.

Siemens, G. and Baker, R. S. (2012). Learning analytics and educational data mining: Toward communication and collaboration. In *Proceedings of the 2nd International Conference on Learning Analytics and Knowledge*, pp. 252–254. ACM.

Siemens, G. and P. Long. (2011). Penetrating the fog: Analytics in learning and education. *EDUCAUSE Review*, 46(5), 30.

Silver, B. and Richard, B. (2009). *BPMN Method and Style, Volume 2*. Aptos, CA: Cody-Cassidy Press.

Singh, R., Gulwani, S., and Solar-Lezama, A. (2013). Automated feedback generation for introductory programming assignments. *ACM SIGPLAN Notices*, 48(6), 15–26.

Song, M. and Van der Aalst, W. M. (2008). Toward comprehensive support for organizational mining. *Decision Support Systems*, 46(1), 300–317.

van der Aalst, W. (2016). Process Mining—Data Science in Action, Second Edition. Berlin, Germany: Springer.

van der Aalst, W., Adriansyah, A., and van Dongen, B. (2012). Replaying history on process models for conformance checking and performance analysis. *Wiley Interdisciplinary Reviews: Data Mining and Knowledge Discovery*, 2(2), 182–192.

Chapter 3

Toward Data for Development: A Model on Learning Communities as a Platform for Growing Data Use

Wouter Schelfhout

Contents

3.1 Introduction

Research indicates that data use by schools and teachers is not widespread and often happens in a superficial way (Schildkamp et al., 2014; Schildkamp et al., 2013; Young, 2006). In fact, this general observation makes good sense, because if one expect schools to (start to) use data, it is clear that there needs to be motivation and a good reason for the school leaders and teachers to do so (Firestone and Gonzalez, 2007; Ikemoto and Marsh, 2007). Integrating data use will be innovative for many schools and therefore demands effort (Schildkamp and Kuiper, 2010). Fundamental questions—the starting point for this contribution—must be posed: Why is data use not widespread and is often superficial? Do schools have good reasons to integrate data use in their school policy and daily operation? What is the added value? How can it be organized in such a way that there is an appropriate balance between efforts, yielding sufficient gains? This contribution will deliberately start from the core processes and concerns of schools, the challenges and needs that are consequences of this, the way in which schools could answer these challenges in general, and the role that the integrated use of data could play in this. At first sight, it will look like data use will not play the most prominent role in this story. However, starting "bottom-up" from the real needs and challenges of schools, we will give data use the balanced and nuanced place it deserves. We will do this by creating a school development model, to which data use will be linked (and not the other way around). As part of this endeavor, we assume that schools will gradually have to grow their data use and that this should happen in line with changing school policy and supportive organizational structures (Schildkamp et al., 2016). We also assume that schools had better start with "small data use" in order to be able to evolve toward use of "Big Data" that will really be integrated in school culture. Big Data use won't make a large and enduring entry into education if it doesn't start by supporting the core policy of schools: facilitating and fostering good education and, from the essential consequences of this goal, advancing school leadership and professional development policies (Supovitz, 2010).

Therefore, we start explaining our data model by stressing the core processes of learning, teaching, and coaching, and by indicating the most important players in delivering quality related to these processes: teachers and school leaders. Together, and in interaction with "normal teaching," schools nowadays are overwhelmed by societal challenges related to diversity, early school leavers, changing demands from the labor market, and inclusion of pupils with (learning) disabilities. From these challenges, expectations related to the role of schools are growing (Van de Werfhorst, 2014). Furthermore, school systems take a very big bite out of the national budget (as they should); therefore, it is clear that schools have to be able to account for the quality they deliver and to demonstrate in a clear way that they are busy ensuring and improving this quality (Ehren and Shackleton, 2015; Lewis and Young, 2013). As a consequence, school leaders—not forgetting their directing boards (private or public)—have a huge responsibility and are very dependent on the people who have to deliver the quality on the work floor: the teachers. Findings from over four decades of school effectiveness research have shown that the quality of teachers outperforms school features and classroom features (such as social composition) in explaining variation in students' learning results. A meta-analysis by Marzano (2012) reveals that approximately 13% of the variation in school performance can be attributed to the performance of teachers. The study results of students of ineffective teachers increase less than those of effective teachers and cumulative effects are alarming and traceable for at least four years (Haycock, 1998; Rivers and Sanders, 2002). The importance of what our teachers do for society and their impact on learning processes cannot be overestimated (Musgrove and Taylor, 2012). Therefore, one would expect teachers to be the key figures in a human resources and professional development policy, but this is very often not the case (Seddon and Levin, 2013), which is highly surprising when compared to companies (aiming for financial profit) in which personnel creating the most added value in the chain often get a very supportive human resources approach (Kehoe and Wright, 2013).

Research indicates that principals are working very hard, but mostly have to focus on, for instance, organizational and logistical tasks, as well as communication with students, parents, and stakeholders in the nearby and broader environment. In comparison, they are less busy with trying to get a better grip on the educational core processes (Grissom et al., 2013; Hoogendijk, 2013; Matena, 2013; Schleicher, 2012). There are different reasons for this, such as lack of time, teachers who don't want interference in their (pedagogical) freedom, and principals who respect this, but also a lack of knowledge and experience on the part of the school leaders related to instructional leadership and to professional development strategies that could foster quality improvement of teaching and learning processes in a bottom-up way (Leithwood and Riehl, 2003; Schleicher, 2012). In the following sections, we will discuss

- ■ The challenges related to the professional development of teachers that characterize (secondary) education
- ■ The general features of a professional development approach that can answer these challenges

- More specifically, the need for different forms of learning communities (and/ or teacher teams) to help concretize the general features of a professional development approach
- The need for shared instructional leadership to support this professional development approach and to embed it in a broader school policy aiming for continuing school development

The interaction between professional development policy, learning communities, and shared instructional leadership will be clarified within a growing theoretical model. As part of each of these sections, the need for a gradual integration of the use of data for supporting this innovative school policy will be discussed. From there, it will become clear that individual schools are not able to take on these challenges alone: cooperative structures between teachers and schools will have to be built and also supported in a focused way by macro educational players such as school groups, education networks, governmental education departments, and school inspection services.

3.2 Challenges Related to Professional Development of Teachers

Supporting and encouraging students' learning processes is the core responsibility of teachers. Expecting, supporting, improving, and developing these processes are the core responsibility of school leaders. However, a number of burdens and challenges related to the professional development of teachers impact—to a greater or lesser degree—all education systems in the world, and as a consequence, teacher development remains an individual and individually different endeavor (OECD, 2009, 2013). We represent this starting position—the importance of the core processes and the problem of insufficient professional development to support these core processes—in a schematic way in Figure 3.1.

3.2.1 Professional Development of Teachers: Meeting the Needs?

Research, for instance by Ballet et al. (2010) within the Flemish context or by van Veen et al. (2010) in the Dutch context, indicates that teacher professional development is still largely aimed at participating in rather traditional activities with the transfer of knowledge:

> Professional development is often reduced to the notion of "refresher courses" in which the external, short and transfer character of professional development occupies center stage .... The analysis also indicates

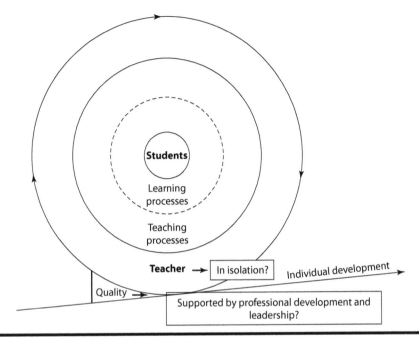

Figure 3.1   Learning and teaching processes at the core of a model of data use.

that professional development is mainly aimed at attending activities and that only to a limited degree there is attention for a particular translation of the content of these activities toward classroom practice or to multiplication of new insights towards colleagues.

(Ballet et al., 2010, p. 4)

Research on the British and NorthAmerican contexts indicates a similar lack of in-depth professional development (e.g., Evans, 2011; Wei et al., 2010). Also, the TALIS project (OECD, 2009) researching teacher professional development in 15 European countries and 8 countries in the rest of the world has proved quite revealing:

Analysis of the TALIS data reveals that despite high levels of participation in development activities, the professional development needs of a significant proportion of teachers are not being met. More than half of the teachers surveyed reported that they wanted more professional development than they received during the 18-month survey period. The extent of unsatisfied demand is sizeable in every country, ranging from 31% in Belgium (Fl.) to 76% in Portugal and over 80% in Brazil, Malaysia and Mexico.

(OECD, 2009, p. 82)

The TALIS project on teacher professional development indicates that "the degree of unsatisfied demand reported by teachers is troubling and may suggest a misalignment between the support provided and teachers' development needs in terms of content and modes of delivery" (OECD, 2009, p. 83). Teachers further report problems related to bridging the gap between abstract pedagogical theory (e.g., related to evaluation or differentiation) and the translation of this theory into daily teaching practice, applied to the specific curriculum they teach. Especially in secondary education, the subject-specific character of professional development remains limited, while the profound importance of content in professional development has been indicated by research, for instance, by Birman et al. (2000, p. 30), who argued that "The degree to which professional development focuses on content knowledge is directly related to teachers' reported increases in knowledge and skills."

This context has clear implications for teachers' possible focus on integrating data use into their teaching practice: if the basic needs aren't being met, why invest time in data use? Studies also reveal that more teachers than school leaders are negative toward data use. These beliefs are related to accountability or compliance matters or to a feeling of extended workload (Jimerson, 2014; Wayman and Stringfield, 2006). As Jimerson argues,

> This is significant in light of emerging research which suggests that educators respond more constructively to data use when they associate it with classroom-based improvement efforts rather than accountability or compliance efforts (Daly, 2009; Jimerson and McGhee, 2013; Tucker, 2010). Other research suggests that teachers are more embracing of data which they find relevant to their needs at the classroom level (Datnow et al., 2007; Marsh et al., 2006; Schildkamp and Kuiper, 2010).
>
> (Jimerson, 2014, p. 12)

However, several studies (Hubbard et al., 2014; Katz and Dack, 2014; Schildkamp et al., 2014; Staman et al., 2014; Wayman and Jimerson, 2014) demonstrate that some teachers and even school leaders lack the knowledge and skills to use data effectively. This doesn't mean that teachers and principals would not acknowledge the importance of data use, but they point to the problems they face with data use in their working context. One of the problems often mentioned is a lack of knowledge and skills related to the use of data on the part of the teachers, and directly related to this, a lack of professional development and training in the use of data (Vanhoof and Schildkamp, 2014).

3.2.2 Professional Development of Teachers: Part of School Policy?

Different factors foster or limit the degree to which teachers take steps to discover new educational insights and integrate them into their practice, including the individual characteristics and background of the teacher, the quality of courses that could be taken, school structures, school policy, school culture, and macro structures (Avalos, 2011; Borko, 2004). The research by Ballet et al. (2010) further indicates that "professional development clearly is a point of attention of school policy, but that this happens rather isolated, separate from the other school policy domains .... To illustrate: mentoring is rarely if ever integrated in a policy on professional development. A consequence is that a lot of energy is put into different initiatives without alignment" (Honig and Hatch, 2004). As part of this, professional development most often happens on an individual basis, isolated from other teachers (OECD, TALIS, 2013). Many secondary education teachers don't have direct colleagues teaching the same curriculum. On the one hand, this has the consequence that teachers can end up in an isolated position that they didn't choose (Elchardus et al., 2010; Goldberg and Proctor, 2000; Houtveen et al., 2006). On the other hand, there is less pressure in education, deriving from colleagues, to reflect on teaching quality. One "can close the class door" in a deliberate way (Cornbleth, 2002; Flinders, 1988). Further, the involvement of teachers with schools' professional development policies remains limited, and it is striking that most teachers are quite satisfied with this. They show almost no interest in being involved in policy making (Ballet et al., 2010; van Veen et al., 2010).

School leaders can make an important difference by creating a focused professional development approach. The mere provision of more training initiatives and obliging or expecting teachers to attend these initiatives will not suffice. It seems essential to integrate a professional development policy into a broader school policy, creating involvement from the teachers (Marshall, 2013; Timperley, 2011) and changing their beliefs related to professional development (de Vries et al., 2013). A similar logic holds for introducing data use in schools. Whereas encouraging professional development by means of providing training might appear to be a self-evident policy measure for introducing and developing data use in schools, empirical evidence clearly shows that other steps in this regard are still needed on different levels (Vanhoof and Schildkamp, 2014). For instance, as a consequence of the often-isolated position of the teacher in secondary education, there is no urge to reflect on possible differences in teaching practice between colleagues (Marshall, 2013). In the context where there are no direct colleagues teaching the same curriculum, one can argue that there are no real comparable data, but most of all there can be no culture of comparing data (e.g., comparing teaching method used to students' results) (Firestone and Gonzalez, 2007; Means et al., 2011).

In Section 3.3, we first discuss how data use should be part of an overarching professional development policy that complies with certain conditions, and not the other way around, that is, professional development for data use (Vanhoof and Schildkamp, 2014). To meet the challenge of encouraging in-depth professional development that will gradually be based on data, one has to look for different strategies of change and development, which are paired with commitment from the teachers (e.g., Guskey, 2000; Fullan, 2004; Wenger, 1998). Teacher teams (Vangrieken et al., 2015) or learning communities (Admiraal et al., 2012; van Keulen et al., 2015), in which teachers start to collaborate in a structural way, seem to offer opportunities toward more sustainable professional development solutions. We will discuss the use of different forms of learning communities in interaction with data use in Section 3.4.2. We further discuss the need for school leaders (also coordinating groups of schools) to structurally support and embed these learning communities in school policy (Schelfhout et al., 2015). In Section 3.5, we discuss an overarching condition for this: professional development strategies will have to interact with shared instructional leadership in order to embed data use in school structures in a sustainable and enduring way.

3.3 Effective Professional Development of Teachers and Data Use

A number of conditions will have to be met in shaping a school's professional development policy. The synthesis from Timperley et al. (2007) of the international evidence on approaches to professional learning and development can be used as a sound theoretical basis. The empirical studies used in this review comprised 84 different characteristics of professional development environments to determine which had the greatest impact on teaching effectiveness in terms of improving outcomes for students' engagement, learning, and well-being. The conclusions of the review identified that those approaches with the greatest impact were focused on meeting particular challenges or solving specific problems with respect to student engagement, learning, and well-being (Muijs et al., 2014). While gaining new professional knowledge and skills was embedded within this context, teachers were able to go beyond it by developing deep understanding in ways consistent with the principles of how people learn (Bransford et al., 2000; Schelfhout et al., 2006). These conclusions were brought together in a cyclical process of inquiry and building new knowledge, which is illustrated in Figure 3.2. In each of the phases in this process, data use could support reaching the goals. However, because most teachers are not used to connecting data with their daily practice in a profound way, we argue that bringing in these data should be done in a gradual way and with caution. We will discuss each of these phases in more depth in the following sections.

3.3.1 Setting Goals

The cycle begins with an analysis of student engagement, learning (results), or well-being in relation to the goals held for them (Timperley, 2011). It is clear that data plays an important role here. In an ideal world, one could suppose that the developmental process begins when schools and teachers gather data. However, many obstacles exist between the dream and reality. Schools often don't succeed in gathering relevant data (Wayman et al., 2012). The data that teachers and schools produce (e.g., student results on tests and exams, progress through secondary education, results in further education and on the labor market) often aren't experienced by

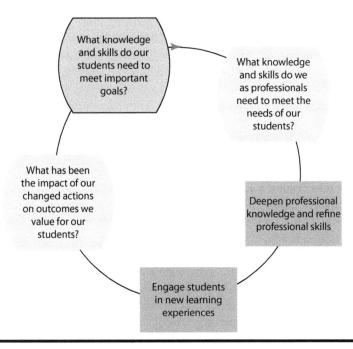

Figure 3.2 Teacher enquiry and knowledge-building cycle. (From Muijs, D., et al., *School Effectiveness and School Improvement,* **25(2), 231–256, 2014.)**

the teachers as a trigger for professional development (Means et al., 2011). Teachers often have a clear explanation for the possibly lower results of their students (e.g., prior knowledge is too weak, insufficient effort), which are based on beliefs and an existing framework often accepted by and shared with direct colleagues. Seeing the link between lower scores and a possible need to adjust teaching and assessment approaches, let alone acknowledging a lack of specific competencies to be able to realize this, doesn't happen immediately (Coburn 2009; Earl and Timperley, 2008; Little et al., 2003; Little, 2012). Therefore, we assume that in a first phase—and step by step thereafter—a sensitivity to using data will have to be developed. We further assume that this sensitivity can be based on a growing insight into learning processes and their consequences on the role and tasks of a teacher (e.g., related to differentiation).

Therefore, in this first phase, it will be important for the teachers involved to be better aware of the goals they set in relation to the learning position of their students (Timperley, 2009). Analyzing the possible discrepancy between these goals and the current situation will be central to understanding what is desired and what is required (Muijs et al., 2014). The first focus, therefore, relates to better positioning the actual learning needs of the students for which specific data—in the broad sense—will have to be gathered, confronted, and pieced together. Teachers will not only have to become aware of the students' results on tests, but also of teaching and

evaluation variables defining these results. Therefore, more important than comparing with data on a macro level (e.g., results of students in comparable schools)
will be the gathering of "data" specifically linked to the teachers' own teaching
practice on a micro level. The first phase will be about starting to reflect, and from
there, describing their own teaching practice in a more objective way, based on
growing frameworks related to learning and teaching processes (Little and Curry,
2009). However, to reach this apparently simple goal, preliminary professional
development processes will be needed, which teachers are not always able to realize
in an individual way (Timperley, 2009). We come back to this when we discuss
the need for creating learning communities as a necessary platform for professional
development in Section 3.4.

We further expect teachers to confront these objective descriptions—
"snapshots"— of their teaching practice with broader frameworks on learning and
teaching, to decide which learning and developmental goals they want to set for
themselves. An essential part of the process, for those unable to be specific on their
professional development goals, is to learn how to collect the relevant evidence
(Muijs et al., 2014). We represent this interaction between a professional development process (on learning and teaching processes) and a gradual increase in the
integrated use of data in Figure 3.3. The cyclical and self-reinforcing character,
starting with setting feasible learning goals, is represented by the arrows.

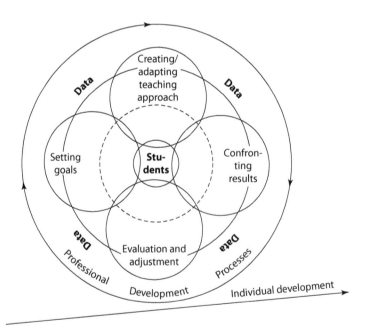

**Figure 3.3   Relationship between a professional development process and a
gradual increase in the use of data.**

The second part of the cycle presented by Timperley et al. (2007) (see Figure 3.2) asks teachers to identify what knowledge and skills they already have, and what new areas of understanding they need, in order to meet the goals they have identified for their students. This kind of analysis usually requires evidence of teachers' existing competencies and teaching practice and the assistance of someone with specific expertise in this particular area of inquiry. In this way, teachers are assisted to develop greater metacognitive awareness of their learning processes and become self-regulated in their approaches to their own learning (Muijs et al., 2014). In most school contexts, however, teachers have to reflect and decide on possible professional development needs in a self-regulated way (Hargreaves and Fullan, 1992), and this context has not changed much (OECD, TALIS, 2013). Perhaps this would be facilitated by the support of a process coach with a view on the individual competencies of the teacher. In this case, there would also be a need for a data system in which this information could be gathered in an effective way. These data and data system would have to be fed by someone with specific expertise and would have to be used as integrated parts of school policy. School leaders could be well placed to play this role, but they often lack time, subject-specific expertise in secondary education, and expertise in creating this interaction between data and professional development approaches. Therefore, identifying and mapping these professional development needs will best be embedded in a feasible way into the school organization. In Section 3.4.2, we focus on how (different forms of) learning communities can be implemented as a method to reach this goal.

3.3.2 Creating and/or Adapting the Teaching Approach

The third dimension of the cycle of deepening professional knowledge and refining skills (see Figure 3.2) is where traditional approaches to professional development usually begin. Often, the problem with these traditional approaches is that the need to know something new is identified by someone external to the group of teachers, without the participating teachers necessarily understanding the reason why it is important to know it, or being committed to start learning it. Under these circumstances, the goals belong to others who are taking responsibility for promoting the professional learning. Teachers can choose to engage or to resist (Muijs et al., 2014). In our model, we assume that professional development processes must begin with the needs that teachers experience as most urgent, directly linked to the daily practice of the curriculum they have to follow (Schelfhout et al., 2015). Teachers have to learn to determine these needs, which isn't easy. Based on our research into learning communities, we notice that a joint determination of these needs and learning goals can support this process. By means of a focused approach by a process coach—always with the consent of the group—a gradually stronger didactical elaboration of concrete teaching materials can be reached, which can address the needs of improved teaching materials as well as the specific learning needs of the teachers (Schelfhout et al., 2015).

3.3.3 Confronting with Results

Feedback is just as important for teachers as for those they teach. Feedback on the effectiveness of processes to reach particular goals or to promote self-regulated learning has greater impact than other kinds of feedback (Hattie and Timperley, 2007). For teachers, one of the most powerful sources of feedback comes from how students respond to the changes they make to their practice, so the next two dimensions of the cycle involve engaging students in new learning experiences, with teachers subsequently checking their impact on the original challenge or problem (Muijs et al., 2014). Confronting the trial of newly developed teaching material, based on specific underlying frameworks, with "data" in the broad sense (e.g., macro data and examples of good teaching practices stemming from other schools.), together with "data" as a direct consequence of this trial (students' results and students' comments on the teaching method), can foster this learning process (Timperley, 2011). The mere confrontation with the results of a teaching approach isn't sufficient in itself as a basis for a critical self-evaluation to which the necessary adjustments will be linked. Data introduced into learning communities will not automatically be integrated into the learning process of the teachers (Little, 2002, 2012). It is important, therefore, that when building new professional knowledge and refining skills, teachers are assisted to make these connections. A learning community can offer an organizational structure to support a process of learning to deal with data as gradually developing quality criteria (Schildkamp et al., 2016).

3.3.4 Data-Driven Group Development

This approach to professional learning and development has implications both for what it means to be a professional in a school organization and for the role of school leaders. In the framework of Timperley et al. (2007), the need for intense cooperation between teachers and between teachers and school leaders, and the need to transcend school borders, is stressed. Teachers need to be placed in a situation where they (1) are willing to question their teaching practices, (2) are supported to be able to question these practices, and (3) are supported to search for ways to improve their practices. We assume that (different forms of) learning communities in schools will be able to create a practical approach to support reaching these goals, because in these communities, opportunities for school leaders arise to help create a degree of "dissonance" between existing teaching practice and relevant new ideas and theory as a basis for school and professional development (Timperley, 2011). However, a number of conditions—also related to the use of data—have to be met in order to make this a successful professional development strategy. We will discuss this in the next section.

3.4 Learning Communities as Platforms for Integrating Data Use

3.4.1 *Learning Dynamics in Teacher Teams and the Role of the Process Coach*

Different strategies of professional development are needed to answer the challenges in the field of professional development of teachers in secondary education (Muijs et al., 2014; Timperley, 2011; van Veen et al., 2010). The concept of PLCs seems to be able to make a difference here (Stoll et al., 2006; van Keulen, 2015; Verbiest, 2008). However, PLC in the educational context has become a kind of ill-defined *container concept*. There are a number of corresponding initiatives/concepts that, however, also differ on a number of essential aspects. These concepts include *communities of practice* (e.g., Wenger, 1998), *professional development schools* (e.g., Abdal-Haqq, 1998), *networked learning communities* (e.g., Coenders and de Laat, 2010; Goodyear, 2005; Katz and Earl, 2010), *teacher communities* (e.g., Admiraal et al., 2012), *lesson study* (e.g., Coenen, 2014; Goei and Verhoef, 2015), *innovative teams* (e.g., Meirink et al., 2010), and *teacher design teams* (Becuwe et al., 2016; Binkhorst et al., 2015). Furthermore, PLC can be related to more overarching concepts, such as *collaborative continuing professional development* (e.g., Cordingley et al., 2003) and *team learning* (e.g., Decuyper et al., 2010), which can also be applied to an educational context. This proliferation of concepts persuaded Vangrieken et al. (2015) to search for a structure in which these different concepts could be framed—using a number of typical dimensions—under the overarching term *teacher teams*. Collaboration was perceived here as a continuum, ranging from mere aggregates of individuals to strong team collaboration. This continuum reflects the degree of "team entitativity," which is conceptualized as the degree to which a team of individuals meets certain team criteria: being an intact social entity, being a cohesive unit, and having members who need each other to perform their tasks and reach the team goal. This makes it possible to extend team learning research to various types of teams, including teacher teams.

What is the essence of a *learning community* as a form of teacher team in education? It is about "making teachers learn from and with each other in a group, with the following basic features: the rise of a group identity, linked to a common teaching context, with shared goals and repertoire for interaction" (Admiraal et al., 2012). The research strand related to "team learning" (e.g., Decuyper et al., 2010) can form a first, well-informed basis for creating a model for understanding learning dynamics in learning communities. It is important to understand which processes in learning communities can support learning outcomes and which factors can influence the occurrence of these processes (Edmondson, 1999). These conditions can be influenced by specific structures, actions, and supporting means that can be provided and attended to deliberately. In the model of Decuyper et al. (2010), variables are divided on a general level into three categories: supra-system variables, system variables, and subsystem variables. The *supra-system* variables category contains all variables on the level of the embedding context of the team (on the level of the culture, organizational structures, and strategies of participating *schools*, communities of schools, pedagogical coaching services, other educational structures, and institutions involved). To enrich this level with more specific knowledge on embedding teacher collaborative initiatives into broader school systems, the literature on collaboration between schools (Muijs et al., 2011a,b) or on networked learning (Hodgson et al., 2014) is inspiring, because focused research has been done on embedding cooperation into a broader school system level and on conditions, mechanisms, and burdens to connect teachers on a cross-school level. The *system* variables category contains all variables on the level of the team, such as task cohesion, team culture, and shared mental models. Finally, the *subsystem* variables category contains variables that are situated at the level of the individual, such as prior knowledge and motivation. For an *overview of the model*, we refer to Figure 3.4.

In the model of Decuyper et al. (2010), the variables influencing team learning found in the literature were divided into five categories: inputs, processes, interpersonal conditions, outputs, and development. A similar categorization was used earlier by authors such as Mathieu et al. (2008) and Ilgen et al. (2005), to review and model the concept of teamwork. Their *inputs* category contains "generic variables that exist within individuals, groups and organizations; they become conditions that affect learning when they are particularized to specific situations" (Dechant et al., 1993, p. 7). The input variables were grouped into three major clusters: inputs at the level of the organization, inputs at the level of the team, and inputs at the level of the team members. The inputs form an integrative part of the model in three ways: as teachers' features that contribute to/obstruct the development of learning communities and their learning outputs; as intermediate interpersonal conditions within the learning communities that will determine its further progress; and as implicit attributes of the school policy influencing the learning communities and the teachers involved. The input of the model is thus situated at the level of the teachers (subsystem), the learning communities (system), and school policy (supra-system).

The *processes* category in the model contains variables that embody interactions between the different stakeholders in the learning process. Without these processes there is no learning. Applied to learning communities, the processes in this research are threefold: the processes on the learning communities level that are necessary to induce teacher team learning (e.g., sharing, co-construction, constructive conflict); the processes of influencing, supporting, and stimulating that (consciously or not) occur on the learning communities level (e.g., team activity, team reflexivity, boundary crossing, storage and retrieval); and finally, the processes within the learning communities that can be steered by an overarching school policy (e.g., team leadership, team structure). To get a better understanding of team activity and leadership processes, we also look to the literature on continuous learning

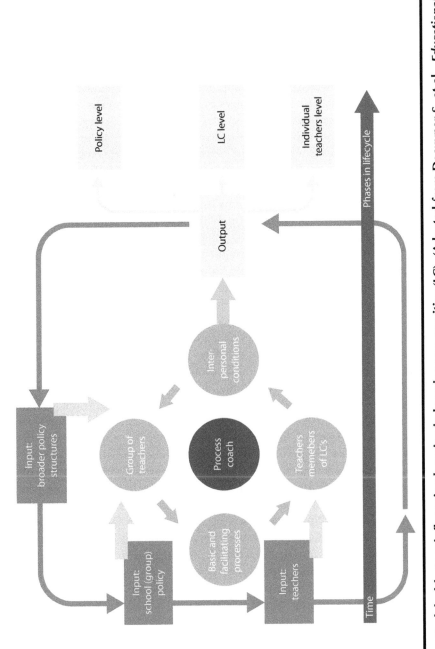

Figure 3.4 Model of factors influencing learning in learning communities (LC). (Adapted from Decuyper S. et al., *Educational Research Review*, **5(2), 111–133, 2010.)**

in organizations within broader organizational perspectives (Sessa and London, 2008). Figure 3.4 shows the complexity of these different processes by representing them in a circular way, where the arrows describe the progressive interaction between teachers (members of learning communities) and the functioning of the learning communities (consisting of the group of teachers involved).

Certain processes within the learning communities will induce particular changes within the teachers. These changes can manifest themselves in the emergence of *interpersonal conditions*. In the team-learning model, this category contains variables that do not embody concrete interactive processes themselves, but are closely connected to the team learning process, since they grow from team learning processes and directly catalyze or reinforce them. Marks et al. (2001) and Mathieu et al. (2008, p. 414) used a similar category in their models of team effectiveness and described it as influencing mechanisms that are to be conceived as cognitive, motivational, or affective states in the team. In this way, *interpersonal conditions* can be considered as important features of the group level of the learning communities that can have an impact on learning and functioning of the individual teachers, but also as a kind of output that should be realized in order to achieve other results related to the tasks the teachers are expected to do. Hence, these interpersonal conditions can also be considered as an output of the team dynamics that are unconsciously achieved or even consciously strived for.

As part of this model on processes in learning communities, we also stress the role of a number of organizational variables, including team leadership, team structure, and time-related variables, in interaction with the output of the learning communities and the learning communities' dynamics. We assume an important role for the process coach in defining these steering mechanisms (Edmondson, 1999; Heikkinen et al., 2012; Schelfhout et al., 2015). Furthermore, the role of the process coach is essential in order to bring (a group of) teachers to a sufficiently deep level of learning, whereby they transcend the mere exchange of existing teaching materials and grow toward a level where new insights are gained and new teaching approaches are developed, thus providing a basis for putting new insights into practice, gaining competencies for tackling challenges related to the realization of the curriculum, and acquiring competence in learning to embed external knowledge (through, e.g., books, chapters, training) in the continuous improvement of one's educational practice. A *time category* is also added to the model to gather variables that express the dynamic or developmental dimension of developing and learning within learning communities, constituting typical and distinguishable phases in a life cycle (e.g., Arrow and Cook, 2008; Dechant et al., 1993; Ellis et al., 2003; Engeström and Sannino, 2010; Kozlowski and Bell, 2008; Senge, 1990). In Figure 3.4, this has been visualized by means of the arches going right, accompanied by a certain (positive, negative, or non-existent) output. Based on our research, it became clear that the entire approach would have to be adapted over time to changing contexts and phases in the life cycle of learning communities (Schelfhout et al., 2015).

The variables and processes in this model for learning within learning communities (Figure 3.4) are further connected to professional development conditions that have been proved to induce these learning processes in the specific context of education in the most optimal way, as described by Timperley et al. (2007), and as schematically represented in Figure 3.5. By bringing teachers together in a deliberate way (steered by a process coach), a stronger platform arises for the exchange of insights, experiences, and ideas as a basis to formulate new and more challenging learning goals than within individual professional development approaches (Phase 1). This leads to an *increase in learning opportunities*. By linking the concrete development of teaching materials to the learning goals, as chosen by the group, optimal opportunities for the basic learning processes of team learning—*sharing, co-construction, and constructive conflict*—will be created (Phase 2). In learning communities, existing frameworks and beliefs can be questioned in a more focused way than as part of an individual trajectory, at least if a number of conditions are met (Schelfhout et al., 2015). For instance, the role of a process coach will be essential (see Section 3.4.3). In a next phase, by clearly expecting the newly elaborated teaching materials to be put into practice by different members in the group, concrete *opportunities for evaluating results* will appear (Phase 3). We assume that, based on these discussions, information on these results will reach the status of data accepted by the group, and as a consequence that these can be used as a kind of evaluation benchmark by the members of the group. A learning community will

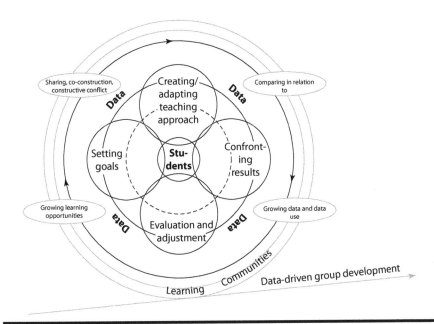

Figure 3.5   Relationship between learning communities as platforms for professional development process and a gradual increase in the integrated use of data.

then gradually go through a process to gather more concrete data—if possible, also external data—but always related to their own teaching practice, making the data more meaningful and motivating. Based on this motivation, opportunities arise to extend this data gathering toward external data, because we assume that, linked to a growing openness and sensitivity for general as well as subject-specific professional development, an understanding of the broader educational context and theoretical frameworks related to learning and teaching can develop. In this way, a focus on *gathering more data and also using these data* may originate (Phase 4). These newly collected data can then be part of a next *professional development cycle,* in which new teaching and professional development goals will be set, predicated upon a broader and better informed database.

3.4.2 Which Kind of Learning Communities Do We Need in Education?

As argued at the start of Section 3.4.1, there is a proliferation of different concepts related to collaborative learning between teachers. A number of these concepts correspond to existing teacher teams in education (e.g., teacher subject groups). However, an important difference is that there are informed efforts to apply the principles of effective team learning in these groups. Based on the professional development goals we deliberately strive for, a number of conditions related to the approach within learning communities can be determined (Schelfhout et al., 2015). A clear starting point is the goal-oriented character of the broader professional development policy. This has consequences; developing learning communities in school contexts as well as participating in learning communities cannot remain open- ended. Expectations will have to be set for participating teachers. However, developing these learning communities will also make demands on school leadership related to supporting and embedding the initiatives in school policy in the longer term. Furthermore, the specific context of secondary education will have implications for designing these learning communities. One context factor, for example, is the frequently occurring situation in which teachers are alone in teaching a specific curriculum without direct colleagues. This then could lead to a growing (professional) isolation. To successfully respond to this complex reality in secondary education, we assume that different forms of (focused) teacher teams will have to be developed on different levels in the school system. Without being exhaustive, we distinguish the following major (existing) forms (see Table 3.1) of consultative and/or cooperative teacher groups, which could be structured in such a way that they become focused teacher teams. We start with informal forms of consultation and/or cooperation between teachers (which teachers are often most familiar with) and end with complex forms of cooperation that pass well over the limits of individual schools. We start with a general definition of the teacher groups in the first column. In the second column, we briefly indicate some advantages of

Table 3.1 Different Forms of Teacher Groups in Secondary Education, Advantages and Challenges

Forms of Teacher Groups	Some Advantages	Some Challenges
Informal cooperation Teachers finding each other, cooperating in an informal, self-regulated way—often one to one—on specific self-chosen subjects.	Obviously a very strong means of cooperation. Good collegiality remains essential.	Are the self-chosen subjects sufficient to ensure and/or improve quality? Is it sufficiently knowledge- and data-driven? Are other colleagues also sufficiently involved?
Co-teaching Teachers creating a more formal cooperation on teaching, usually developing a (specific part of a) curriculum together.	More formal pressure to strive for quality and improve existing approaches, to test these new approaches in practice, and adjust them.	Does the small group of teachers involved (from the same school) possess an appropriate background (didactical knowledge, supportive data) to ensure quality? Is there sufficient boundary crossing? Is there transfer to other teachers? Is it payable?
Subject groups Typical in secondary education is the formal grouping of teachers according to the different subjects they teach. There is a growing number of initiatives to improve team learning in these groups.	To some degree, these teachers share common subject-specific goals, there is no burden of distance to work, and these subject groups can be supported by school-specific data. This creates opportunities for professional development if a number of conditions are met.	Often subject groups consist of teachers teaching different curricula. This gives a weak basis for shared goal-orientation. There is a chance of stagnation if the group can't transcend existing habits, knowledge, goals, or even patterns of oppressive interaction. Often, there is no process coach with either the skills to support the aimed-at learning processes, or the school policy-embedded mandate to do so.

(Continued)

Table 3.1 (Continued)   Different Forms of Teacher Groups in Secondary Education, Advantages and Challenges

Forms of Teacher Groups	Some Advantages	Some Challenges
Teacher work groups Teachers working together on cross-curricular subjects ranging from didactical topics (ICT—integration, evaluation, differentiation) to organizational topics (school trips).	The same advantages as for subject groups. Especially for well delineated topics there is shared goal-orientation. Another advantage is that cooperating in these groups can lead to learning processes with a possible transfer to other teacher grouping forms (e.g., subject groups).	The same challenges as for subject groups hold, especially for didactical topics. Where the quality of subject group decisions is mostly influenced by the curriculum to be taught (which is the same for many schools), the stronger influence of (different) school policies in cross-curricular topics has to be taken into account and responded to.
Teacher class councils' intervision Until now too often forgotten as an essential teacher team with direct impact on the core processes of a school. All teachers from different subject fields have to decide together on how to support the learning processes of their pupils and on (end) evaluation.	This form of teacher team holds great potential to (a) create a shared focus (pupils learning processes and gains), (b) bring in data that can be discussed in group, with (c) possible and objectively enforceable teacher actions to be taken (related to remediation, but possibly also differentiation, evaluation, even teaching methods).	In many schools, the possible benefits of class councils as a form of learning communities are not achieved because (a) there is no process coach who supports working on these different goals and (b) to be able to work on these goals there is a need to embed this approach in an appropriate supportive form of school policy and leadership, based on a focused data-gathering.

(Continued)

Table 3.1 (Continued)   Different Forms of Teacher Groups in Secondary Education, Advantages and Challenges

Forms of Teacher Groups	Some Advantages	Some Challenges
Subject-specific learning communities (SLCs) SLCs are groups of teachers from different schools, teaching the same curriculum, who are brought together face to face. The explicit goal is to discuss and improve their teaching practice, aiming to optimize the learning processes of the students. These cross-school learning communities can also be developed on cross-curricular topics.	Shared subject-specific teaching goals. Avoiding professional isolation if no colleagues teach the same curriculum in the teacher's school. Opening new perspectives and ideas. Creating concrete teaching methods directly applicable to teaching practice. Dividing the work load. Possibilities for intensive didactical learning if certain conditions are met.	Challenge of distance between schools, making teachers lesson-free if SLCs are during lesson hours. Risk of permissiveness if no goal-oriented expectations are created. Risk of superficial learning if team learning processes are not supported, sometimes directed by a competent process coach (able to integrate data). Too temporary if not embedded in a broader school policy.
Online teacher communities or networks Online communities and networks for teacher professional development can be hosted in a variety of digital environments that	The asynchronous nature of online communities and networks, the shared knowledge, and the immediacy of responses make these environments a suitable space for enhancing teacher professional development. The opportunity to share their own	One of the main problems is the gradual lack of engagement that occurs over time, which results in reduced user participation and eventually in member dropout. Evidence from other studies indicates reluctance to participate in online communities because of a fear of being criticized, lack of experience, insecurity in

(Continued)

Table 3.1 (Continued)   Different Forms of Teacher Groups in Secondary Education, Advantages and Challenges

Forms of Teacher Groups	Some Advantages	Some Challenges
mainly depend on the resources, skills, and means of the creators. The terms community and network are used interchangeably. In the columns on advantages and challenges, we refer to the interesting overview of Macià and García (2016).	experiences helps teachers to think about what they do in their daily routine as a result of the contributions or the questions posed by other teachers and also the effect that writing about the experience has on the creation of new understanding. However, a number of conditions have to be met in order to create these advantages.	sharing own ideas, miscommunication, as well as concerns about copyright, ownership or misuse of the published material. Another burden is "peripheral participation," which reflects those people who benefit from the created content but rarely manifest themselves.

these groups, while in the third column some important limitations and challenges are described to which an answer should be given by means of

1. A more focused process coaching of the group, and/or
2. Resolving specific limitations of one teacher group by using another grouping form.

3.4.3 Delineating (Data) Goals of Learning Communities: Subject-Specific Learning Communities as One Example

As indicated in Table 3.1, we argue that existing teacher groups and forms of consultation in secondary education are not sufficient for supporting professional development and school development related to the educational core processes. Within each of these teacher groups, there will be a need to optimize the approach, for which expertise stemming from the research on communities of practice, teacher teams, learning communities, and team learning can be used. For instance, the consultative processes within the traditional subject groups could be steered in a more focused way toward more intense subject-specific didactical learning by a process coach who responds to group dynamic and learning processes (Visscher and Witziers, 2004). As part of this coaching, the process coach can support the group in searching for, creating, and using data, as described in Section 3.4.1 and Figure 3.5, as a means to strengthen the learning process in a group (Lomos et al., 2011). Further specific limitations of one teacher team can be resolved by the characteristics of another grouping form. Initiatives to support subject-specific learning communities (SLCs), cross-school work groups, and online teacher communities or networks, as described in Table 3.1, can feed schools as learning organizations with the necessary external ideas to lead to boundary crossing (Akkerman and Bakker, 2011). In the following, we will further describe the SLC concept, to illustrate the position of these cross-school initiatives compared to other forms of teacher collaboration and the specific and promising use of data in this concept (Schelfhout et al., 2015).

3.4.4 Shared Subject-Specific Teaching Goals

SLCs will have as an explicit goal to contribute to the teachers' professional development (cf. Watson, 2005), to the school's professional development policy, and to the development of the schools involved (cf. Meirink et al., 2010). Consequently, participating in an SLC requires a basic commitment toward a number of goals as known by the participating teachers and the supporting school leaders. In that way, there will exist a focus on creating a common goal that is more in keeping with the "formal work group" concept than with the "informal network" concept, as aptly rendered in Blankenship and Ruona's (2009) research. Within their "tacit–explicit continuum," we situate SLCs rather on the "explicit" side, as a kind of strategic community with even features of "project teams" and "formal work groups," because there are clear output expectations related to developing new teaching materials and putting these into practice. Related to the framework of Vangrieken et al. (2013) on "team entitativity," and based on the work of Cohen and Bailey (1997) on "teamness," a consequence is that, as part of SLCs, there will be a growing dimension of interdependency in tasks and shared responsibilities for outcomes, which can become the consequence of a (growing) joint goal orientation (Meirink et al., 2010). We consider this essential, because research into group learning indicates that merely bringing together a group of teachers is not sufficient to make them learn (Little, 2003; Meirink etal., 2010; Van den Bossche et al., 2006). To reach a common sense of purpose in a learning community, it helps that the teachers involved share similar educational goals that have to be strived for (Akkerman et al., 2008) as part of their daily professional practice (Agterberg et al., 2010). Blankenship and Ruona (2009, p. 295) denominate these specifying features that can hold a group together as "glue." Because a huge number of teachers in secondary education do not have direct subject-specific colleagues in their own school, a first starting point for the SLC concept is the need to bring together teachers from different schools teaching the same (or at least a very similar) curriculum in face-to-face settings as a possible basis for subject-specific professional development (Hofman and Dijkstra, 2010; McConnell et al., 2013). Subject-specific teaching challenges and problems shared from daily practice can serve for creating a "deep level similarity" (van Emmerik et al., 2011) between the members as a basis for a common sense of purpose. Clearly defining different aspects of these shared problems will constitute meaningful data. Data situate on the level of defining, for instance, (1) which parts of teaching the curriculum are problematic, (2) which teaching approaches are currently used by the different teachers participating in the SLC, (3) where these approaches are similar and where they differ, and (4) which approaches correlate with better students results and vice versa. These data will then form the basis from which to work in a very concrete way.

3.4.5 Focused Organization and Support of Didactical Learning

Creating SLCs in face-to-face settings can contribute to a targeted exchange of knowledge and teaching materials. However, just bringing teachers together also runs the risk that this exchange remains too open-ended, and that the knowledge base remains too different between the teachers at the beginning of an SLC to support self-regulated and new didactical learning (Little, 2002, 2003). Therefore, another principle of the SLC concept is that a structural focus on learning results should be built into the SLC organization. Therefore, the SLC concept also entails aspects of what Blankenship and Ruona (2009) define as "strategic communities," which are learning- and product-oriented in an open and rather self-regulated way, as aspects of "team learning" in which more formal learning structures are elaborated (see e.g., Decuyper et al., 2010; Vrieling et al., 2014), and in which the group cooperates in a focused way on a shared goal (Dechant et al., 1993). As part of the SLC concept, an essential task will be given to a process coach in this regard. An important role of this person is to organize and support the necessary learning processes that the different teachers have to pass through (Zaccaro et al., 2008). Also, a growing body of research into different forms of learning communities in educational contexts points to the role of a kind of process coach, for instance, within PLCs (DuFour and DuFour, 2013), teacher communities (Pareja Roblin et al., 2014), teacher networks and (digital) networked learning (Hanraets et al., 2011), and in data teams (Bolhuis et al., 2016). Also, in research on communities of practice, in which, at the outset, the self-regulative character of the group of teachers has been stressed (Wenger, 1998), we notice growing attention on the role of a facilitator (MacPhail et al., 2014). Because the teachers in an SLC often don't know each other beforehand, the initial role of a process coach will be to help the group to indicate common challenges to be tackled and to help the group to concretize these challenges by means of rich descriptions and other data (Schelfhout et al., 2015). Furthermore, the process coach will have to find an appropriate balance between a rather focused steering of the group and supporting and encouraging the group toward learning based on activities that the group choose in a self-regulated way (Meirink et al., 2010; Schelfhout et al., 2015; Silberstang and Diamante, 2008).

Our conception of teachers learning in teams and the underlying theory of learning is based on what Hammerness et al. (2005) call the "innovative dimension of teacher learning," in which teachers are encouraged to change old routines and existing conceptions on teaching based on interesting, sometimes even confrontational data (Schelfhout et al., 2015). Based on research into team learning, a number of processes are taken as a basis for learning in the group. It is about creating dialogical space between the group members, in which such communicative processes as "sharing," "co-construction," and "constructive conflict" are encouraged (Decuyper et al., 2010). Comparable to the goal of fostering active and self-regulated student learning, we regard teacher learning as an ongoing process of engagement in activities informed by data that result in changes in teacher practices and changes in teacher beliefs regarding teaching and learning (Barak et al., 2010; Engeström and Sannino, 2010; Meirink et al., 2010; Putnam and Borko, 1997). However, we also stress the sociocultural aspects of teacher learning in groups (Wenger, 1998). Changes in participation by the teachers in these learning communities will be mirrored by changes in their collective framing practices of a problem salient to their joint enterprise over time (Bannister, 2015; Horn and Little, 2010). Furthermore, a balance will have to be found between individual goals and a (growing) perception among the group members that they can reach their individual goals if the other members can also reach their goals (Hornby, 2009). Based on research into developmental phases in social learning (e.g., Arrow and Cook, 2008; Drath et al., 2008; Ellis et al., 2003; Knapp, 2010; Kozlowski and Bell, 2008; Verbiest, 2008; Zaccaro et al., 2008), a number of general stages in the formation and development of SLCs can be determined (Schelfhout et al., 2015).

3.4.6 *Deliberate Embedding of SLCs in School Policy*

A last dimension of SLCs as we aim to delineate the concept is the need for a structural embedding of the learning community into a broader school policy (Muijs et al., 2011a,b). We assume that for its successful development and further continuity, an SLC should be embedded in an appropriate way into the daily operation of the school organization (Chapman and Harris, 2004; Huffman et al., 2014). In terms of team entitativity (Vangrieken et al., 2013), we expect an SLC to develop as a basic social entity (the group of teachers who are experts in teaching a specific subject responsible for getting the best results possible with the students involved) embedded in a social system (the class council, the school), managing their relationships across organizational boundaries (e.g., the interaction between the SLC and external schooling initiatives, pedagogical counselors) (Cohen and Bailey, 1997). SLCs will have as specific tasks and responsibilities qualitative instruction, learning, innovation, and school reform (Vangrieken et al., 2013). Therefore, as we

Table 3.2 Defining the SLC Concept

Shared subject-specific teaching goals
SLCs are groups of teachers from different schools, with the same subject-specific background and teaching the same curriculum, who are brought together face to face. The explicit goal is to discuss, question, and improve their own professional practice, aiming to optimize the learning processes of the students.
Focused organization and support of didactical learning
The group of teachers starts by exchanging and sharing knowledge, ideas, and existing teaching materials, and evolves toward a concrete and practice-oriented elaboration of new teaching approaches, with didactical learning that will be put into practice as a goal. To reach this goal, the group will be deliberately supported by a) a process coach, b) the school leaders, and c) the pedagogical coaches involved.
Deliberate embedding of SLCs in school policy
SLCs are aiming for continuous professional development of the group of teachers in the long run, and are structurally embedded in the school policy of the (group of) schools involved.

delineate the SLC, the concept is not aiming for the short term, for instance, by bringing together a group of teachers to elaborate on one specific teaching method or assignment. One of the goals is that teachers will gradually form a group that can map its own professional development needs and looks for suitable solutions in a more self-regulated way (Vanblaere and Devos, 2016). During this process, more active periods will alternate with periods of reduced activity, but there will always be an aspect of sustainability. Therefore, we assume that the approach of the SLC will have to be supported in a structural way by the school leaders involved (Stoll et al., 2006). One of the school leaders' tasks will be, on the one hand, to provide the SLCs with relevant data, and, on the other hand, to follow up the SLCs in an encouraging way by expecting concrete data on results (Schelfhout et al., 2015). We will further discuss this in Section 3.5. We presume that without embedding SLCs in school policy, most SLCs will fail in the longer term (Muijs et al., 2011a,b; van Veen et al., 2010; Wahlstrom and Louis, 2008). Based upon the former general principles, we delineate the SLC concept as indicated in Table 3.2.

3.5 Shared Instructional Leadership, Learning Communities, and Data Use

Research has shown that PLCs (Stoll et al., 2006) and other forms of teacher teams (Vangrieken et al., 2015) do not arise naturally. In fact, many secondary school teachers seem to prefer working on an individual basis than working together

(Goldberg and Proctor, 2000). This is not an evident starting position for developing this kind of initiative, especially when different schools are involved, as in the case of SLCs. As discussed, we assume that the successful development of different forms of learning communities will depend on the way that school leaders embed these initiatives in their school policy and school structures (Stoll et al., 2006). Hargreaves (1995) argued that the expected presence of collegiality in learning communities specifically invokes an institutional base and specific structural conditions, which emphasize the organizational context. As a starting point for a model on supportive/obstructive school policy conditions, the research strand on creating PLC is informative. Research on PLC points both to the link between teacher involvement and a fundamental shift in the habits of mind that teachers bring to their daily job (Lomos et al., 2011a; Stoll et al., 2006; van Veen et al., 2010; Vescio et al., 2008). There is a need for deliberate support of this endeavor (e.g., Edwards, 2011; Heikkinen et al., 2012). Based on research by Verbiest and Timmerman (2008, p. 21) on the role of the school leader in the development of PLCs, a large number of interventions can be grouped into three roles: "The role of 'culture developer' means disseminating and strengthening of certain values, views and standards in the service of a commonly supported professional learning culture. The role of 'educator' means fostering the intensity and quality of the individual and collective learning processes of team members, so that profound learning takes place. And the role of 'architect' means building structures, sources and systems in schools that enhance personal and interpersonal capacity development." In Table 3.3, we summarize the school policy factors that have a clear impact on the development of PLC as put forward by Stoll et al. (2006) and Stoll (2011), based on their review studies. We organize the whole using the three categories as proposed by Verbiest and Timmerman (2008).

Shaping this kind of professional development policy cannot be done within a traditional top-down view on leadership. The arguments and evidence presented on how to promote professional learning in ways that have positive impacts on outcomes for students challenge traditional ideas about professional development policy (Muijs et al., 2014). As discussed in Section 3.3, the cycle of inquiry and knowledge-building has at its core the notion of teachers as adaptive experts, alert to situations where previous routines are not working well and seeking different kinds of solutions. This conceptualization of professionalism and development as one of adaptive expertise is gaining considerable currency among the research and professional community (Bransford et al., 2005; Hammerness et al., 2005; Hatano and Oura, 2003). As Muijs et al. argue,

> This requires more than individual teachers understanding how they need to think and act differently. It also requires that schools become places for deliberate and systematic professional learning, where leaders are vigilant about the impact of school organization, leadership, and teaching on student's engagement, learning, and well-being. Schools

Table 3.3   School Policy Factors on Creating PLCs

The role of "culture developer" • Principals have to be committed to create professional learning communities (Mulford and Silins, 2003). • Principals will have to create a learning culture (Fullan, 1992; Schein, 1985, Shulman, 1997). • Trust and positive working relationships (Louis et al., 1995; Nias et al., 1989)
The role of "educator" • Principals will have to focus on learning on all levels (Law and Glover, 2000; Leithwood et al., 1999; Louis et al., 1995). • Interacting and drawing on external agents. There are strong arguments that schools cannot "go it alone" and need connections with outside agencies (Fullan, 1993).
The role of "architect" • Time: To facilitate exchange between teachers, the research suggests that the school needs to be organized to allow time for staff to meet and talk regularly (Louis et al., 1995; Stoll et al., 2003). • Space: Opportunities for professional exchange appear to be further facilitated by physical proximity (Dimmock, 2000; McGregor, 2003). • To promote, sustain and extend PLCs, schools appear to need external support, networking, and other partnerships (Anderson and Togneri, 2003; Leithwood et al., 1998; Rosenholtz, 1989).

Source: Adapted from Stoll, L., in J. Robertson and H. Timperley (Eds.), *Leadership and Learning*, pp. 103–117, 2011, Sage, London; Stoll, L. et al., *Journal of Educational Change*, 7, 221–258, 2006.

organized for learning in this way are usually referred to as having high adaptive capacity (Staber and Sydow, 2002).

(Muijs et al., 2014, p. 249)

To reach this goal as a school leader, it will be important to deliberately create conditions for collaborative inquiry, because effective professional learning happens when teachers are supported to investigate, challenge, and extend their current views. Teachers cannot meet new challenges in teaching and learning alone, so everyone who has a place in the chain of influence from policy to practice needs to ensure that the right conditions for professional learning are in place (Muijs et al., 2014). To be able to reach this goal, a specific kind of leadership is expected from principals who (1) have a strong focus on improving the core educational processes which take place in their schools as a basis for constant school development (Hallinger, 2003) and (2) use participatory processes to get a better grip on these educational processes by delegating tasks, sharing responsibility, and creating more involvement of teachers in well-defined work groups (Hazel and Allen, 2013).

As discussed, we assume that different forms of teacher teams and their deliberate interaction, for instance, created within teacher departments (Lomos et al., 2011b; Visscher and Witziers, 2004), could contribute to these goals. We assume that in each of these forms of teacher teams, the process coach can become a kind of "liaison officer" for the school leader. We assume that this will happen in two directions. First, these process coaches will gradually start to encourage a group of teachers to work on and improve certain aspects of their educational tasks in an informed way, based on data. To a high degree, this can happen in a self-regulated way, because the group decides together which topics they will work on. Another aspect, however, is that a shared sense of purpose will also be deliberately created by the process coach, in which certain expectations will be set and monitored. We hypothesize that process coaches not only have encouraging roles, but also coordinating roles, and sometimes even steering tasks. Second, these process coaches can become important contact persons for the school leaders. The school leaders will be able (1) to ask the process coaches for advice on specific (and growing) expertise in a certain field (as elaborated in the SLC and the subject group, another kind of teacher team); (2) to monitor the progress made in these teacher teams based on results and data on these results, as jointly developed in the teacher teams; (3) to take into account the results and conclusions represented by the data stemming from the different teacher teams, and to discuss with the process coaches new initiatives to be taken in the teacher teams in line with school policy and school development; and (4) to coordinate the interaction between the different forms of teacher teams.

In this way, we gradually arrive at a concrete elaboration of the concept of "shared instructional leadership," as put forward by Marks and Printy (2003). In this concept, different subsequent lines of thought related to school leadership converge: the concept of instructional leadership, in which the school leader is focused on steering the primary educational processes as realized by the teachers (e.g., Hallinger, 2003), but which was quite directive and top-down, has been broadened and deepened with insights from the research on transformational leadership (Leithwood et al., 1996) and shared leadership (e.g., Gronn, 2003; Harris et al., 2008). With the concept of transformational leadership, the school leader creates a vision which can inspire the school staff. He or she focuses on optimizing individual and collective processes of problem solving and learning. He or she tries to create a culture of professional collaboration in which teachers are encouraged toward continuing professional development and common problem solving (Leithwood et al., 1996). Therefore, transformational leadership is more focused on capacity building for school development and less on direct coordination, control, and supervision of the instructional processes (Verbiest, 2010). Criticisms of the concept of transformational leadership are its lack of attention to the processes of mutual influencing as part of a shared leadership (Gronn, 2003) and that a transformational leader misses an explicit focus on the primary processes of teaching and learning. Strongly transformation-oriented leaders could therefore even hinder their teachers in their teaching tasks (Marks and Printy, 2003). In shared leadership, the school leader will realize leadership activities in an interactive web of leaders and followers in different situational constellations (Gronn, 2003a, b; Hargreaves, 2003; Spillane, 2006; Harris et al., 2008). Marks and Printy (2003) integrated these different lines of research on school leadership into an overarching concept called "shared instructional leadership." Verbiest (2010, p. 4) indicates that, in this form of leadership,

> the school leader on the one hand works transformational: (s)he stimulates the involvement and development of teachers. On the other hand (s)he co-operates with teachers to optimize the primary process. (S)he is not the only one leading this primary process, but rather gives guidance to the teachers that lead the primary process.

There is a growing body of research on dimensions of shared instructional leadership (Goddard et al., 2015; Lee et al., 2012; Neumerski, 2013; Urick, 2016) and the impact on teachers' organizational commitment (Hulpia et al., 2012). However, specific research on how to deliberately create conditions within schools to foster shared instructional leadership and the interaction with different forms of learning communities as platforms for professional development—within schools and in cross-school contexts—remains scarce. Recent research by Vanblaere and Devos (2016) on the interaction between school leadership and perceived PLC characteristics gives insight into how instructional and transformation leadership and PLCs are intertwined. Vanblaere and Devos (2016) found, for instance, that how teachers perceived the instructional leadership in their school was related to their participation in de-privatized practice and their participation in reflective dialogue, and that teachers' perceptions of transformational leadership were associated with participation in reflective dialogue and the presence of collective responsibility. The question is then how this kind of leadership can deliberately be connected to implementing different forms of teacher teams and their interaction (Schelfhout et al., 2015). An essential feature of teacher teams, which we will try to create, is a collective responsibility for qualitative education, which will gradually be concretized by (1) helping each other as teachers to develop supportive teaching methods, but also by (2) creating conditions in which individual teaching will be de-privatized by means of, for instance, discussing (but also criticizing) teaching methods within the group. The role of a process coach, essentially supported by the school leaders' policy, will be to foster conditions in which teachers start to be concerned with each other's teaching and resulting student learning, which will create an incentive to engage in meaningful collaborative behaviors (Newmann and Wehlage, 1995). In the case of cross-school collaboration that is pursued in SLCs or cross-school work groups, the level of school group policy will also play an important role (Muijs et al., 2011a,b).

This interaction between the role of process coaches in different learning communities, instructional leadership, and participatory school development is schematically represented in Figure 3.6. Linked to the growing use of data in learning communities, a clear need to deliberately support this through school policy and

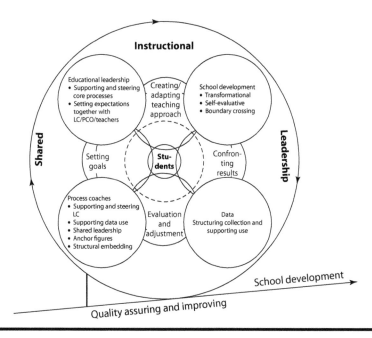

Figure 3.6 Relationship between professional and school development, learning communities, the role of process coaches, shared instructional leadership, and data use.

organization will arise. A growing demand for data use will encourage the gathering and processing of these data in a more structured way and the delivery of these data in an efficient way to the teachers involved. From there, a need for a data system related to the core educational processes—for example, results on tests and exams, results of remediation, and well-being—will arise (Wohlstetter et al., 2008). As discussed here, in line with a growing openness to critical self-evaluation of individual teaching practices, gathering these "traditional" output data can be deepened by a more systematic mapping of process data: teaching approaches during classes, specific remediating approaches, student reviews of these teaching and remediating approaches, and so on, in order to link these to the output data. As a consequence, possibilities to evaluate these core processes in a data-driven way will grow (Poortman and Schildkamp, 2011). It is clear that this will not happen automatically, and that structures will have to be created to deliver these data. We assume that this should gradually grow from the teacher teams in a bottom-up way, but also in interaction with an educational leadership that dares to set (feasible but expanding) expectations. The school leader will have to function as a key agent in influencing other key players in data use (Levin and Datnow, 2012). Furthermore, it will be necessary to logistically invest in the data system and to professionalize the teachers learning to handle it (Wayman and Cho, 2009).

Starting from the gradual consolidation of a school-intern data system, a growing demand for relevant external data will arise (Lee and Kirby, 2016; Honig and Venkateswaran, 2012), related to reliable output data such as regionally defined benchmarks and/or comparative data. This brings us to the last level within our model on data use: the need for a relevant and well-structured interaction with external macro educational structures and stakeholders.

3.6 Shared Instructional Leadership, Data Use, and External Macro Educational Structures

In the preceding section, we discussed why a successful shared instructional leadership should gradually be based on clear and sound data. For the school leaders, as well as process coaches and teachers within learning communities, it is important to be able to make well-informed decisions. Furthermore, being involved in successfully developing learning communities will foster a growing need to dispose of relevant data. This brings us to the role of external stakeholders in designing the complex interaction between individual teachers, different forms of teacher teams as effective platforms for professional development, and shared instructional leadership. In fact, delivering the needed data is not easy. Therefore, a qualitative gathering (and elaboration) can—however partially—be supported by educational structures on a higher level. These institutions can take a broad view, and are in a position to gather data from the different schools involved, which they can elaborate in such a way that schools and teachers can use the data in a focused way, deliberately aiming for school quality development. A number of stakeholders are well placed to gather these data: for instance, the educational networks and/or the school group (or other forms of partnership) to which the school belongs, the governmental education department, and school inspection services. As argued in the previous section, there is a need not only for sound output data, but also for reliable process data related to the interaction between teachers and students as well as the interaction between school policy and teachers. It is exactly the process of confronting output and underlying teaching processes that can provide significant information on where the best chances on quality improvement lie (Schildkamp and Ehren 2013). However, as school effectiveness research shows, gathering in-depth process data is quite a challenge (Scheerens 1990; Reynolds et al., 2014). Gathering process data in a sufficiently large sample will be necessary to create reliable comparative data. Because school inspectorates are expected to control quality in a reliable way and with enough depth (on the level of policy as well as implementation) in all schools, they could be well placed to deliver this kind of information by cooperating with school effectiveness researchers.

To create and deliver reliable data as a basis for data-driven decision making is important, but forms only one side of the coin. In our model for data use, creating and fostering a school culture in which these data will actually be used is at least equally important. The macro educational structures previously discussed expect schools to assure and improve their quality. They therefore have every interest in the schools implementing forms of shared instructional leadership, because these form a solid basis for capacity building and school development: self-evaluation will start to form part of these school cultures, whereby a self-reinforcing interaction with deploying concrete data can arise. Research by Vanlommel et al. (2016) demonstrates that the quality of teachers' motivation for using data is a key element in promoting data use in schools. They found that teachers who feel autonomously motivated will make greater use of data than teachers with a controlled motivation, but that this was also influenced by the degree of supportive relationships within the school and the reflective capacity of the school team, which in turn lead to an increase in teachers' autonomous motivation for using data. This supports our model, in which we assume the need to create new forms of professional development policy in schools as a preliminary condition for implementing in-depth data use. We assume that this bottom-up approach can be reinforced by setting top-down expectations, on the condition that these expectations are developed in a participatory and feasible way.

In recent research by Ehren et al. (2015), different inspection models were compared in terms of their impact on school improvement and the mechanisms that each of these models generate to have such an impact. Their results indicate that inspectorates of education that use a differentiated model (in addition to regular visits), in which they evaluate both educational practices and outcomes of schools, and publicly report the inspection findings of individual schools, are the most effective. These changes seem to be mediated by improvements in the schools' self-evaluations and the schools' stakeholders' awareness of the findings in the public inspection reports. As a consequence, during their school visits, inspectorates should pay significant investigative attention to the degree to which schools are able to assess and adjust their own quality in a self-regulated way (Ehren et al., 2015). Therefore, for an inspectorate to be able to assess this, it remains important to judge the educational quality delivered, taking into account input and context features, but it will also be important to judge whether the broader conditions for school development are present. In that context, "traditional" forms of top-down leadership or a "refresher course—professional development policy" will not suffice (Brennan and Shah, 2000). This means that, as part of school inspections, attention will have to be paid to forms of shared instructional leadership, which in their turn go together with forms of data-driven professional development. This brings us to a second consequence: inspection systems will have to be shaped to encourage schools to work in a self-regulated way on these forms of leadership, professional development, and data use as a basis for their quality improvement approaches (de Volder, 2012; Ehren et al., 2013, 2015; Wilkins, 2015). In schools proven to deliver high quality and to protect and further develop this quality, inspection can limit itself over the longer term to less far-reaching quality audits. In other schools, however—and possibly to different degrees—inspection has to keep on judging a number of quality aspects in a formal way. Based on these judgments, the school can then deliberately be encouraged to elaborate, first, on systems of self-evaluation based on gathering feasible data, and second, on subsequent quality improvement approaches. Depending on the severity of specific shortages, inspection can grant a shorter or longer period of time in which the schools can work on these challenges. We refer to Ehren et al. (2015, p. 395) who indicate that "An increasingly accepted theory is that inspection systems tend to be adapted when education systems mature. Maturity in this sense refers, according to Barber (2004), to the self-evaluation literacy and innovation capacity of schools and their stakeholders to improve on their own, and to the availability of high-quality data (e.g., from national student achievement tests) to inform school-level evaluation and improvement. According to this hypothesis, mature systems have a diminished need for top-down, standards-based inspections, and instead rely increasingly on the profession to review and develop their own quality."

An important condition for reducing this "top-down" inspecting is that schools have sufficiently proven themselves capable of protecting and improving their quality in a self-regulated way. Therefore, inspections should investigate this, and should have a clear framework—communicated to the schools—on which quality aspects this judgment can be based. We like to refer to the important work that has been done by the Flemish inspection who created—in cooperation with the educational networks and pedagogical counseling services—a joint framework as a basis for defining quality in schools (www.onderwijsinspectie.be). Furthermore, this also requires an adequate participatory approach to inspection (Park, 2013) and an openness of all stakeholders toward developing collaborative partnerships and networks between teachers, schools, and groups of schools, as well as between inspectors, schools, pedagogical counseling services, and educational networks (Gray, 2014). As Ehren et al. (2016) states,

> Networks as the dominant form of organizing and social coordination reflect the idea that one single government (such as in a hierarchical model) does not have all the knowledge required to solve complex, diverse, and dynamic problems, and that no single actor has the overview necessary to employ all the instruments needed to make regulation effective.

If such a basis of mutual trust has been installed as a feature of these networks, data can start to be developed on a broader and better informed macro educational level, and can start to be shared in a focused way, fostering systems of self-evaluation and quality improvement. This collaborative interaction with external stakeholders is represented in Figure 3.7 as an integral part of our model on data use.

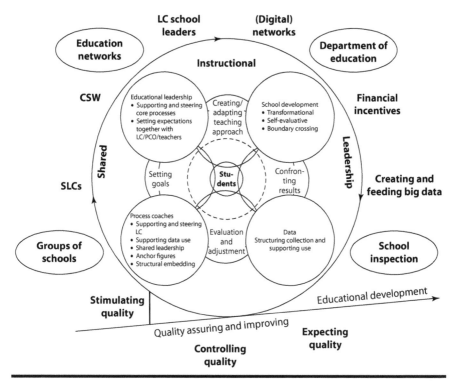

Figure 3.7 A model of "data for development" together with external stakeholders.

3.7 Conclusion

In this contribution, we aimed to define a holistic model of "data for development," in which the use of data will gradually be encouraged and implemented in a bottom-up way, starting from the core processes and concerns of schools and teachers. We argued that schools and teachers are not open to data use because essential conditions for starting to integrate data use into daily practice are not met in many schools. There is a lack of an effective professional development policy that deliberately links data use to continuous reflection on, and improvement of, daily teaching practice. We argued that developing different forms of learning communities—in focused interaction—will constitute a platform for starting to remedy these challenges and needs. Process coaches, who facilitate developing these learning communities, can become anchor figures within an ongoing interaction between the teachers and the school leaders, focused on the core learning and teaching processes. As part of this growing shared instructional leadership, there should be a focus on gradually increasing the use of data. We foresee a need for learning how to gather specific process data on teaching practices in interaction with school internal output data. We believe that school leaders will have to support this in a deliberate way, but also—given the complexity of this endeavor—that they will have to be supported by other educational structures. In the first place, by partnerships between groups of schools, but also by external stakeholders such as education networks, governmental education departments, and school inspection. A number of essential guidelines on different levels can be deduced:

On the level of the teachers:

- Integrate professional development as a normal and ongoing part of teaching during school hours.
- Be open to gathering reflective critical data on your teaching processes.
- Start to share your strengths, teaching practices, and reflections, but also needs and concerns with your colleagues.
- Be open to cooperation. Understand that teaching is a joint endeavor and that within these shared goals it is perfectly normal that best practices are shared with colleagues who can make use of this expertise to—in their turn—further improve the learning processes of their students.

On the level of the school leaders:

- Expect cooperation and results from cooperation.
- Support cooperation in a structural way, by means of, for instance, creating regular moments for consultation during school hours, encouraging the development of learning communities, supporting the work of the process coaches who have been mandated by the group, and so on.
- Gather rich output data (based on internal self-evaluations).
- Encourage teachers to gather process data (e.g., on teaching methods used, on forms of remediation) and to bring these data together in a growing database.
- Make teachers and learning communities reflect on the interaction and correlation between process and output data. Understand that the quality of learning processes is one of the core businesses of a school and therefore is an essential responsibility of a school leader.
- Understand that you cannot be an expert on all teaching subjects, but that you should be an expert in delegating (setting expectations, granting autonomy, following up in a motivating way) the educational core processes to (different forms of) learning communities and to their process coaches, who can become anchor figures in your growing shared instructional leadership.
- Be open to cooperation with other schools. A lot of professional development processes can better be done and/or complemented by teacher teams/learning communities on the level of a group of schools.

On the level of macro educational structures

- Support cooperation between teachers to become self-sufficient by means of creating school structures and school staff regulations that grant time and space for continuous consultation, in school as well as cross-school.
- Support developing cross-school learning communities and networks.
- Support developing rich output data, importantly together with rich process data, to be able to compare/interpret these data in a meaningful way.

A number of the conclusions and hypotheses that we have described are based on ongoing longitudinal research in two Flemish regions (Antwerp and Louvain) within 18 SLCs (Schelfhout et al., 2015). Based on this research, a number of conditions for implementing SLCs could already have been deduced. However, there is still a huge lack of research into the conditions for the successful implementation of different kinds of learning communities (and their interaction) in school contexts. Also, specific research on cross-school learning communities remains very scarce, while the importance of schools working together within larger entities is clear. Furthermore, there is a need for in-depth research into how exactly learning communities can support didactical learning in combination with the use of data. There is a need for further research on the role of a process coach in creating favorable conditions, encouraging and helping to integrate data use, especially if an explicit goal of a learning community is to support the continuous professional development of a group of teachers, while structurally embedded in school policy in the long run. We hypothesize the need for "shared instructional leadership" as a basis to create these conditions. Research into the interaction between leadership and professional development by means of learning communities and data use seems to be of great importance and will be highly innovative.

References

Abdal-Haqq, I. (1998). *Professional Development Schools: Weighing the Evidence.* Thousand Oaks, CA: Corwin Press.

Admiraal, W., Lockhorst, D., and van der Pol, J. (2012). An expert study of a descriptive model of teacher communities. *Learning Environments Research*, 15(3), 345–361.

Agterberg, M., Van Den Hooff, B., Huysman, M., and Soekijad, M. (2010). Keeping the wheels turning: The dynamics of managing networks of practice. *Journal of Management Studies*, 47(1), 85–108.

Akkerman, S., Petter, C., and de Laat, M. (2008). Organising communities-of-practice: Facilitating emergence. *Journal of Workplace Learning*, 20(6), 383–399.

Akkerman, S. F., and Bakker, A. (2011). Boundary crossing and boundary objects. *Review of Educational Research*, 81(2), 132–169.

Arrow, H., and Cook, J. (2008). Configuring and reconfiguring groups as complex learning systems. In V. Sessa and M. London (Eds.), *Work Group Learning. Understanding, Improving and Assessing How Groups Learn in Organizations*, 45–72, Mahwah, NJ: Lawrence Erlbaum Associates.

Avalos, B. (2011). Teacher professional development in Teaching and Teacher Education over ten years. *Teaching and Teacher Education*, 27(1), 10–20.

Ballet, K., Colpin, H., März, V., Baeyens, C., De Greve, H., and Vanassche, E. (2010). *Evaluatie van het professionaliseringsbeleid van basis-en secundaire scholen* (onderzoeksrapport OBPWO 07.01). Centrum voor Onderwijsbeleid en-vernieuwing KU Leuven, Leuven.

Bannister, N. A. (2015). Reframing practice: Teacher learning through interactions in a collaborative group. *Journal of the Learning Sciences*, 24(3), 347–372.

Barak, J., Gidron, A., and Turniansky, B. (2010). 'Without stones there is no arch': A study of professional development of teacher educators as a team. *Professional Development in Education*, 36(1–2), 275–287.

Barber, M. (2004). The virtue of accountability: System redesign, inspection, and incentives in the era of informed professionalism. *The Journal of Education*, 185(1), 7–38.

Becuwe, H., Tondeur, J., Pareja Roblin, N., Thys, J., and Castelein, E. (2016). Teacher design teams as a strategy for professional development: The role of the facilitator. *Educational Research and Evaluation*, 22(3–4), 141–154.

Binkhorst, F., Handelzalts, A., Poortman, C. L., and van Joolingen, W. R. (2015). Understanding teacher design teams: A mixed methods approach to developing a descriptive framework. *Teaching and Teacher Education*, 51, 213–224.

Birman, B. F., Desimone, L., Porter, A. C., and Garet, M. S. (2000). Designing professional development that works. *Educational Leadership*, 57(8), 28–33.

Blankenship, S. S., and Ruona, W. E. A. (2009). Exploring knowledge sharing in social structures: Potential contributions to an overall knowledge management strategy. *Advances in Developing Human Resources*, 11(3), 290–306.

Bolhuis, E. D., Schildkamp, K., and Voogt, J. M. (2016). Improving teacher education in the Netherlands: Data team as learning team? *European Journal of Teacher Education*, 39(3), 320–339.

Borko, H. (2004). Professional development and teacher learning: Mapping the terrain. *Educational Researcher*, 33(8), 3–15.

Brennan, J., and Shah, T. (2000). Quality assessment and institutional change: Experiences from 14 countries. *Higher Education*, 40(3), 331–349

Chapman, C., and Harris, A. (2004). Improving schools in difficult and challenging contexts: Strategies for improvement. *Educational Research*, 46(3), 219–228.

Coburn, C. E., Touré, J., and Yamashita, M. (2009). Evidence, Interpretation, and Persuasion: Instructional Decision Making at the District Central Office. *Teachers College Record*, 111(4), 1115–1161.

Coenders, M. J., and de Laat, M. F. (2010). *Netwerkleren in het onderwijs: professionalisering vanuit de praktijk*. Alphen aan den Rijn: Kluwer.

Coenen, T. (2014). *Professionele ontwikkeling van docenten in een Lesson Study team: de aanpak van telproblemen*. Enschede: UTwente.

Cohen, S. G., and Bailey, D. E. (1997). What makes teams work: Group effectiveness research from the shop floor to the executive suite. *Journal of Management*, 23(3), 239–290.

Cordingley, P., Bell, M., Rundell, B., and Evans, D. (2003). *The Impact of Collaborative Continuing Professional Development (CPD) on Classroom Teaching*. London: EPPI Centre.

Cornbleth, C. (2002). What constrains meaningful social studies teaching?. *Social Education*, 66(3), 186–191.

Dechant, K., Marsick, V. J., and Kasl, E. (1993). Towards a model of team learning. *Studies in Continuing Education*, 15(1), 1–14.

Decuyper, S., Dochy, F., and Van den Bossche, P. (2010). Grasping the dynamic complexity of team learning: An integrative model for effective team learning in organisations. *Educational Research Review*, 5(2), 111–133.

de Volder, I. (2012). *Externe Schoolevaluaties. Een Vergelijkend Onderzoek*. Antwerpen: Maklu.

de Vries, S., van de Grift, W. J., and Jansen, E. P. (2013). Teachers' beliefs and continuing professional development. *Journal of Educational Administration*, 51(2), 213–231.

Drath, W. H., McCauley, C. D., Palus, C. J., Van Velsor, E., O'Connor, P. M. G., and McGuire, J. B. (2008). Direction, alignment, commitment: Toward a more integrative ontology of leadership. *The Leadership Quarterly*, 19, 635–653.

DuFour, R., and DuFour, R. (2013). *Learning by Doing: A Handbook for Professional Learning Communities at Work TM*. Bloomington, IN: Solution Tree Press.

Earl, L. M. and Timperley, H. (2008). *Professional Learning Conversations: Challenges in Using Evidence for Improvement*. New York, NY: Springer.

Edmondson, A. C. (1999). Psychological safety and learning behaviour in work teams. *Administrative Science Quarterly*, 44(2), 350–383.

Edwards, C. H. (2011). *Educational Change: From Traditional Education to Learning Communities*. Lanham, MD: RandL Education.

Ehren, M. C., Altrichter, H., McNamara, G., and O'Hara, J. (2013). Impact of school inspections on improvement of schools: Describing assumptions on causal mechanisms in six European countries. *Educational Assessment, Evaluation and Accountability*, 25(1), 3–43.

Ehren, M. C., and Shackleton, N. (2015). Mechanisms of change in Dutch inspected schools: Comparing schools in different inspection treatments. *British Journal of Educational Studies*, 64(2), 185–213.

Elchardus, M., Huyge, E., Kavadias, D., Siongers, J., and Vangoidsenhoven, G. (2010). Leraars. Profiel van een beroepsgroep. Leuven: LannooCampus, 192 p. *Tijdschrift voor Sociologie*, 1, 83.

Ellis, A. P. J., Hollenbeck, J. R., Ilgen, D. R., Porter, L. H., West, B. J., and Moon, H. (2003). Team learning: Collectively connecting the dots. *Journal of Applied Psychology*, 88, 821–835.

Engeström, Y., and Sannino, A. (2010). Studies of expansive learning: Foundations, findings and future challenges. *Educational Research Review*, 5(1), 1–24. doi:10.1016/j.edurev.2009.12.002

Evans, L. (2011). The "shape" of teacher professionalism in England: Professional standards, performance management, professional development and the changes proposed in the 2010 White Chapter. *British Educational Research Journal*, 37(5), 851–870.

Firestone, W. A., and Gonzalez, R. A. (2007). Culture and processes affecting data use in schools. In P. A. Moss (Ed.), *Evidence and Decision Making*, 132–154. Malden, MA: Blackwell.

Flinders, D. J. (1988). Teacher isolation and the new reform. *Journal of Curriculum and Supervision*, 4(1), 17–29.

Fullan, M. (2004). *Leading in a Culture of Change: Personal Action Guide and Workbook*. San Francisco, CA: Jossey-Bass.

Goddard, R., Goddard, Y., Kim, E. S., and Miller, R. (2015). A theoretical and empirical analysis of the roles of instructional leadership, teacher collaboration, and collective efficacy beliefs in support of student learning. *American Journal of Education*, 121(4), 501–530.

Goei, S. L., and Verhoef, N. (2015). Lesson study as a tool for teacher learning: the context of combinatorial reasoning problems. Retrieved from: http://doc.utwente.nl/

Goldberg, P. E., and Proctor, K. M. (2000). *Teacher Voices 2000: A Survey on Teacher Recruitment and Retention*, October 2000. *Scholastic.*

Goodyear, P. (2005). Educational design and networked learning: Patterns, pattern languages and design practice. *Australasian Journal of Educational Technology*, 21(1), 82–101.

Gray, A. (2014). *Supporting School Improvement: The Role of Inspectorates across Europe*. Brussels: SICI. Retrieved from: http://www.sici-inspectorates.eu.

Grissom, J. A., Loeb, S., and Master, B. (2013). Effective instructional time use for school leaders longitudinal evidence from observations of principals. *Educational Researcher*, 0013189X13510020.

Gronn, P. (2003a). *The New Work of Educational Leaders: Changing Leadership Practice in an Era of School Reform*. London: Paul Chapman Publishers.

Gronn, P. (2003b). Leadership's place in a community of practice. In: Brundrett, M., Burton, N., and Smith, R. (Eds.), *Leadership in Education*, pp. 23–35. London: Sage Publishers.

Hallinger, Ph. (2003). Leading educational change. Reflections on the practice of instructional and educational leadership. *Cambridge Journal of Education*, 33(3), 329–351.

Hammerness, K., Darling-Hammond, L., and Bransford, J. (2005). How teachers learn and develop. In *Preparing Teachers for a Changing World: What Teachers Should Learn and Be Able to Do*, pp. 358–389. New York: Jossey Bass.

Hanraets, I., Hulsebosch, J., and de Laat, M. (2011). Experiences of pioneers facilitating teacher networks for professional development. *Educational Media International*, 48(2), 85–99.

Hargreaves, A. (2003). *Teaching in the Knowledge Society*. London: Open University Press.

Hargreaves, A., and Fullan, M. G. (1992). *Understanding Teacher Development*. New York, NY: Teachers College Press.

Hargreaves, D. H. (1995). School culture, school effectiveness and school improvement. *School Effectiveness and School Improvement*, 6(1), 23–46.

Harris, A., Leithwood, K., Day, C., Sammons, P., and Hopkins D. (2008). Distributed leadership and organizational change: Reviewing the evidence. *Journal of Educational Change*, 8, 337–347.

Haycock, K. (1998). Good teaching matters … a lot. *Magazine of History*, 13(1), 61–63.

Hazel, C. E., and Allen, W. B. (2013). Creating inclusive communities through pedagogy at three elementary schools. *School Effectiveness and School Improvement*, 24(3), 336–356.

Hodgson, V., de Laat, M., McConnell, D., and Ryberg, T. (Eds.). (2014). *The Design, Experience and Practice of Networked Learning*. London: Springer.

Hofman, R. H., and Dijkstra, B. J. (2010). Effective teacher professional development in networks? *Teaching and Teacher Education*, 26(4), 1031–1040.

Honig, M. I., and Hatch, T. C. (2004). Crafting coherence: How schools strategically manage multiple, external demands. *Educational Researcher*, 33(8), 16–30.

Honig, M. I., and Venkateswaran, N. (2012). School–central office relationships in evidence use: Understanding evidence use as a systems problem. *American Journal of Education*, 118(2), 199–222

Hoogendijk, R. W. (2013). *Het verschil in schoolleidershandelingen op goede en zwakke basisscholen*. Utrecht University.

Horn, I. S., and Little, J. W. (2010). Attending to problems of practice: Routines and resources for professional learning in teachers' workplace interactions. *American Educational Research Journal*, 47(1), 181–217.

Hornby, G. (2009). The effectiveness of cooperative learning with trainee teachers. *Journal of Education for Teaching: International Research and Pedagogy*, 32(5), 161–168.

Houtveen, A. A. M., Versloot, B., and Groenen, I. (2006). De begeleiding van startende leraren: in het voortgezet onderwijs en het basisonderwijs. SBO.

Hubbard, L., Datnow, A., and Pruyn, L. (2014). Multiple initiatives, multiple challenges: The promise and pitfalls of implementing data. *Studies in Educational Evaluation*, 42, 54–62.

Huffman, J. B., Hipp, K. A., Pankake, A. M., and Moller, G. (2014). Professional learning communities: Leadership, purposeful decision making, and job-embedded staff development. *Jsl*, 11(5), 11, 448.

Hulpia, H., Devos, G., Rosseel, Y., and Vlerick, P. (2012). Dimensions of distributed leadership and the impact on teachers' organizational commitment: A study in secondary education. *Journal of Applied Social Psychology*, 42(7), 1745–1784.

Ikemoto, G. S., and Marsh, J. A. (2007). Cutting through the data-driven mantra: Different conceptions of data-driven decision making. In P.A. Moss (Ed.), *Evidence and Decision Making*, 105–131, Malden, MA: Blackwell.

Ilgen, D. R., Hollenbeck, J. R., Johnson, M., and Jundt, D. (2005). Teams in organizations: From input–process–output models to IMOI models. *Annual Review of Psychology*, 56, 517–543.

Jimerson, J. B. (2014). Thinking about data: Exploring the development of mental models for "data use" among teachers and school leaders. *Studies in Educational Evaluation*, 42, 5–14.

Katz, S., and Dack, L. A. (2014). Towards a culture of inquiry for data use in schools: Breaking down professional learning barriers through intentional interruption. *Studies in Educational Evaluation*, 42, 35–40.

Katz, S., and Earl, L. (2010). Learning about networked learning communities. *School Effectiveness and School Improvement*, 21(1), 27–51.

Kehoe, R. R., and Wright, P. M. (2013). The impact of high-performance human resource practices on employees' attitudes and behaviors. *Journal of Management*, 39(2), 366–391.

Knapp, R. (2010). Collective (team) learning process models: A conceptual review. *Human Resource Development Review*, 9(3), 285–299.

Kozlowski, S. W., and Bell, B. S. (2008). Team learning, development and adaptation. In V. Sessa and M. London, (Eds.), *Work Group Learning. Understanding, Improving and Assessing How Groups Learn in Organizations*, 15–44. Mahwah, NJ: Lawrence Erlbaum Associates.

Lee, M., Hallinger, P., and Walker, A. (2012). A distributed perspective on instructional leadership in International Baccalaureate (IB) schools. *Educational Administration Quarterly*, 48(4), 664–698.

Lee, M., and Kirby, M. M. (2016). The promises and perils of school leadership for accountability: Four lessons from China, Hong Kong, and India. In J. Easley and P. Tulowitzki (Eds.), *Educational Accountability: International Perspectives on Challenges and Possibilities for School Leadership*, 129–141, Abingdon: Routledge.

Leithwood, K., Tomlinson, D., and Genge, M. (1996). Transformational school leadership. In K. Leithwood, J. Chapman, D. Corson, Ph. Hallinger, and A. Hart, (Eds.), *International Handbook of Educational Leadership and Administration* Vol. II, 785–840, Dordrecht: Kluwer Academic Publishers.

Leithwood, K. A., and Riehl, C. (2003). *What We Know about Successful School Leadership.* Nottingham: National College for School Leadership.

Levin, J. A., and Datnow, A. (2012). The principal role in data-driven decision making: Using case-study data to develop multi-mediator models of educational reform. *School Effectiveness and School Improvement,* 23(2), 179–202.

Lewis, W. D., and Young, T. V. (2013). The politics of accountability: Teacher education policy. *Educational Policy,* 27(2), 190–216.

Little, J. (2003). Inside teacher community: Representations of classroom practice. *The Teachers College Record,* 105(6), 913–945.

Little, J. W. (2002). Locating learning in teachers' communities of practice: Opening up problems of analysis in records of everyday work. *Teaching and Teacher Education,* 18(8), 917–946.

Little, J. W. (2012a). Professional community and professional development in the learning-centered school. In M. Kooy and K. van Veen (Eds.), *Teacher Learning that Matters: International Perspectives,* 22–46, New York, NY: Routledge.

Little, J. W. (2012b). Understanding data use practice among teachers: The contribution of micro-process studies. *American Journal of Education,* 118(2), 143–166.

Little, J. W., and Curry, M. W. (2009). Structuring talk about teaching and learning: The use of evidence in protocol-based conversation. In L. M. Earl and H. Timperley (Eds.), *Professional Learning Conversations: Challenges in Using Evidence for Improvement,* 29–42, Dordrecht: Springer Netherlands.

Little, J. W., Gearhart, M., Curry, M., and Kafka, J. (2003). Looking at student work for teacher learning, teacher community, and school reform. *Phi Delta Kappan,* 83(November), 184–192.

Lomos, C., Hofman, R. H., and Bosker, R. J. (2011a). Professional communities and student achievement: a meta-analysis. *School Effectiveness and School Improvement,* 22(2), 121–148.

Lomos, C., Hofman, R. H., and Bosker, R. J. (2011b). The relationship between departments as professional communities and student achievement in secondary schools. *Teaching and Teacher Education,* 27(4), 722–731.

Macià, M., and García, I. (2016). Informal online communities and networks as a source of teacher professional development: A review. *Teaching and Teacher Education,* 55, 291–307.

MacPhail, A., Patton, K., Parker, M., and Tannehill, D. (2014). Leading by example: Teacher educators' professional learning through communities of practice. *Quest,* 66(1), 39–56.

Marks, H., and Printy, S. (2003). Principal leadership and school performance. An integration of transformational and instructional leadership. *Educational Administration Quarterly,* 39(3), 370–397.

Marks, M. A., Mathieu, J. E., and Zaccaro, S. J. (2001). A temporally based framework and taxonomy of team processes. *Academy of Management Review,* 29(3), 356–376.

Marshall, K. (2013). *Rethinking Teacher Supervision and Evaluation: How to Work Smart, Build Collaboration, and Close the Achievement Gap.* New York, NY: John Wiley and Sons.

Marzano, R. J. (2012). *Wat Werkt op School. Research in Actie.* Meppel: Printsupport4U.

Matena, S. (2013). *Cognities en Handelen van Schoolleiders in het Voortgezet Onderwijs in Nederland ten aanzien van Goed Schoolleiderschap. Kennis, Ideaalbeeld, Zelfbeeld, en Docentbeeld.* Utrecht University.

Mathieu, J., Maynard, M. T., Rapp, T., and Gilson, L. (2008). Team effectiveness 1997–2007: A review of recent advancements and a glimpse into the future. *Journal of Management*, 34, 410–476.

McConnell, T. J., Parker, J. M., Eberhardt, J., Koehler, M. J., and Lundeberg, M. A. (2013). Virtual professional learning communities: Teachers' perceptions of virtual versus face-to-face professional development. *Journal of Science Education and Technology*, 22(3), 267–277.

Means, B., Chen, E., DeBarger, A., and Padilla, C. (2011). *Teachers' Ability to Use Data to Inform Instruction: Challenges and Supports*. Washington, DC: U.S. Department of Education, Office of Planning, Evaluation, and Policy Development.

Meirink, J. A., Imants, J., Meijer, P. C., and Verloop, N. (2010). Teacher learning and collaboration in innovative teams. *Cambridge Journal of Education*, 40(2), 161–181.

Muijs, D., Ainscow, M., Chapman, C., and West, M. (2011a). Leading networks. In *Collaboration and Networking in Education*, 159–165, Dordrecht: Springer Netherlands.

Muijs, D., Ainscow, M., Chapman, C., and West, M. (2011b). Widening opportunities? A case study of school-to-school collaboration in a rural district. In *Collaboration and Networking in Education*, 103–114, Dordrecht: Springer Netherlands.

Muijs, D., Kyriakides, L., van der Werf, G., Creemers, B., Timperley, H., and Earl, L. (2014). State of the art–teacher effectiveness and professional learning. *School Effectiveness and School Improvement*, 25(2), 231–256.

Musgrove, F., and Taylor, P. H. (2012). *Society and the Teacher's Role*. London: Routledge.

Neumerski, C. M. (2013). Rethinking instructional leadership, a review what do we know about principal, teacher, and coach instructional leadership, and where should we go from here? *Educational Administration Quarterly*, 49(2), 310–347.

Newmann, F. M., and Wehlage, G. G. (1995). *Successful School Restructuring: A Report to the Public and Educators*. Madison, WI: Center on Organization and Restructuring of Schools.

OECD (Ed.). (2009). *Creating Effective Teaching and Learning Environments: First Results from TALIS*. Paris: OECD Publishing. http://dx.doi.org/10.1787/978926 4068780-en.

OECD (Ed.). (2013). *TALIS Technical Report*. Paris: OECD Publishing. http:// dx.doi. org/10.1787/ 9789264079861-en.

Pareja Roblin, N. N., Ormel, B. J., McKenney, S. E., Voogt, J. M., and Pieters, J. M. (2014). Linking research and practice through teacher communities: a place where formal and practical knowledge meet? *European Journal of Teacher Education*, 37(2), 183–203.

Park, J. (2013). *Detoxifying School Accountability: The Case for Multi-Perspective Inspection*. Retrieved from http://dera.ioe.ac.uk/23199/1/Detoxifying_School_Accountability

Poortman, C. L., and Schildkamp, K. (2011). Alternative quality standards in qualitative research? *Quality and Quantity*, 46(6), 1727–1751.

Putnam, R. T., and Borko, H. (1997). Teacher learning: Implications of new views of cognition. In: *International Handbook of Teachers and Teaching*, 1223–1296. The Netherlands: Springer.

Reynolds, D., Sammons, P., De Fraine, B., Van Damme, J., Townsend, T., Teddlie, C., and Stringfield, S. (2014). Educational effectiveness research (EER): A state-of-the-art review. *School Effectiveness and School Improvement*, 25(2), 197–230.

Rivers, J. C., and Sanders, L. (2002). *Teacher Quality and Equity in Educational Opportunity: Findings and Policy Implications*. Stanford, CA: Hoover Institution Press.

Scheerens, J. (1990). School effectiveness research and the development of process indicators of school functioning. *School Effectiveness and School Improvement*, 1(1), 61–80.

Schelfhout, W., Bruggeman, K., and Bruyninckx, M. (2015). Vakdidactische leergemeenschappen, een antwoord op professionaliseringsbehoeften bij leraren voortgezet onderwijs? *Tijdschrift voor lerarenopleiders*, 36(4), Themanummer PLG.

Schelfhout, W., Dochy, F., Janssens, S., Struyven, K., Gielen, S., and Sierens, E. (2006). Towards an equilibrium model for creating powerful learning environments. Validation of a questionnaire on creating powerful learning environments. *European Journal for Teacher Education*, 29(4), 471–503.

Schildkamp, K., and Ehren, M. (2013). From "intuition"- to "data"-based decision making in Dutch secondary schools? In K. Schildkamp, M. K. Lai, and L. Earl (Eds.), *Data-Based Decision Making in Education*, 49–67, New York, NY: Springer Netherlands.

Schildkamp, K., Karbautzki, L., Breiter, A., Marciniak, M., and Ronka, D. (2013). The use of data across countries: Development and application of a data use framework. In D. Passey, A. Breiter, A. Visscher (Eds.), *Next Generation of Information Technology in Educational Management*, 3–14, Heidelberg: Springer Verlag.

Schildkamp, K., Karbautzki, L., and Vanhoof, J. (2014). Exploring data use practices around Europe: Identifying enablers and barriers. *Studies in Educational Evaluation*, 42, 15–24.

Schildkamp, K., and Kuiper, W. (2010). Data-informed curriculum reform: Which data, what purposes, and promoting and hindering factors. *Teaching and Teacher Education*, 26(3), 482–496.

Schildkamp, K., Poortman, C. L., and Handelzalts, A. (2016). Data teams for school improvement. *School Effectiveness and School Improvement*, 27(2), 228–254.

Schleicher, A. (2012). *Preparing Teachers and Developing School Leaders for the 21st Century: Lessons from around the World*. Paris: OECD Publishing.

Seddon, T., and Levin, J. (2013). *Educators, Professionalism and Politics: Global Transitions, National Spaces and Professional Projects*. London: Routledge.

Senge, P. (1990). *The Fifth Discipline: The Art and Science of the Learning Organization*. New York: Currency Doubleday.

Sessa, I. V., and London, M. (2008). Group learning: An introduction. In V. Sessa and M. London (Eds.), *Work Group Learning. Understanding, Improving and Assessing How Groups Learn in Organizations*, 1–14, Mahwah, NJ: Lawrence Erlbaum Associates.

Silberstang, J., and Diamante, T. (2008). Phased and targeted interventions: Improving team learning and performance. In V. I. Sessa and M. London (Eds.), *Work Group Learning: Understanding, Improving, and Assessing How Groups Learn in Organizations*, 347–364, Mahwah, NJ: Lawrence Erlbaum.

Spillane, J. (2006). *Distributed Leadership*. San Francisco, NJ: Jossey-Bass.

Staman, L., Visscher, A. J., and Luyten, H. (2014). The effects of professional development on the attitudes, knowledge and skills for data-driven decision making. *Studies in Educational Evaluation*, 42, 79–90.

Stoll, L. (2011). Leading professional learning communities. In J. Robertson and H. Timperley (Eds.), *Leadership and Learning*, 103–117, London: Sage.

Stoll, L., Bolam, R., McMahon, A., Wallace, M., and Thomas, S. (2006). Professional learning communities: A review of the literature. *Journal of Educational Change*, 7, 221–258.

Supovitz, J. (2010). Knowledge-based organizational learning for instructional improvement. In A. Hargreaves, A. Lieberman, M. Fullan, D. Hopkins (Eds.), *Second International Handbook of Educational Change* 707–723, New York, NY: Springer.

Timperley, H. (2009). Evidence-informed conversations making a difference to student achievement. In L. Earl and H. Timperley (Eds.), *Professional Learning Conversations: Challenges in Using Evidence for Improvement*, 69–79, Dordrecht: Springer.

Timperley, H., Wilson, A., Barrar, H. and Fung, I. (2007). *Teacher Professional Learning and Development. Best Evidence Synthesis Iteration [BES]*. Wellington: Ministry of Education.

Timperley, H. S. (2011). *Realizing the Power of Professional Learning*. Maidenhead: Open University Press.

Urick, A. (2016). Examining US principal perception of multiple leadership styles used to practice shared instructional leadership. *Journal of Educational Administration*, 54(2), 152–172.

Vanblaere, B., and Devos, G. (2016). Relating school leadership to perceived professional learning community characteristics: A multilevel analysis. *Teaching and Teacher Education*, 57, 26–38.

Van den Bossche, P., Gijselaers, W., Segers, M., and Kirschner, P. A. (2006). Social and cognitive factors driving teamwork in collaborative learning environments. Team learning beliefs and behaviors. *Small Group Research*, 37(5), 490–521.

van Emmerik, H., Jawahar, I. M., Schreurs, B., and De Cuyper, N. (2011). Social capital, team efficacy and team potency: The mediating role of team learning behaviors. *Career Development International*, 16(1), 82–99.

Vangrieken, K., Dochy, F., and Raes, E. (2015). Team learning in teacher teams: Team entitativity as a bridge between teams-in-theory and teams-in-practice. *European Journal of Psychology of Education*, 31(3), 275–298.

Vangrieken, K., Dochy, F., Raes, E., and Kyndt, E. (2013). Team entitativity and teacher teams in schools: Towards a typology. *Frontline Learning Research*, 2, 86–98.

Vangrieken, K., Dochy, F., Raes, E., and Kyndt, E. (2015). Teacher collaboration: A systematic review. *Educational Research Review*, 15, 17–40.

Vanhoof, J., and Schildkamp, K. (2014). From "professional development for data use" to "data use for professional development." *Studies in Educational Evaluation*, 42, 1–4.

van Keulen, H., Voogt, J., van Wessum, L., Cornelissen, F., and Schelfhout, W. (2015). Professionele leergemeenschappen in onderwijs en lerarenopleiding. *Tijdschrift voor lerarenopleiders*, 36(4), Themanummer PLG.

van Veen, K., Zwart, R., Meirink, J., and Verloop, N. (2010). *Professionele ontwikkeling van leraren. Een reviewstudie naar effectieve kenmerken van professionaliseringsinterventies van leraren*. [Teacher professional development. A review of studies on effective characteristics of teacher professional development interventions.] Leiden: ICLON/ Expertisecentrum Leren van Docenten.

Van de Werfhorst, H. G. (2014). Changing societies and four tasks of schooling: Challenges for strongly differentiated educational systems. *International Review of Education*, 60(1), 123–144.

Vanlommel, K., Vanhoof, J., and Van Petegem, P. (2016). Data use by teachers: The impact of motivation, decision-making style, supportive relationships and reflective capacity. *Educational Studies*, 42(1), 36–53.

Verbiest, E. (2008). *Scholen duurzaam ontwikkelen. Bouwen aan professionele leergemeenschappen.* Antwerp/Apeldoorn: Garant.

Verbiest, E. (2010). Op weg naar Nieuw Onderwijskundig Leiderschap. *School en begeleiding: Personeel en Organisatie,* 25, 17–37.

Verbiest, E., and Timmerman, N. (2008). Professionele Leergemeenschappen: Wat en Waarom? In E. Verbiest (Red.), *Scholen duurzaam ontwikkelen. Bouwen aan professionele leergemeenschappen,* 41–53). Antwerpen/Apeldoorn: Garant.

Vescio, V., Ross, D., and Adams, A. (2008). A review of research on the impact of professional learning communities on teaching practice and student learning. *Teaching and Teacher Education,* 24(1), 80–91.

Visscher, A. J., and Witziers, B. (2004). Subject departments as professional communities? *British Educational Research Journal,* 30, 785–800.

Vrieling, E., Van den Beemt, A., and de Laat, M. (2014). What's in a name: Dimensions of social learning in teacher groups. *Teachers and Teaching: Theory and Practice,* 22(3), 273–292.

Wahlstrom, K., and Louis, K. S. (2008). How teachers experience principal leadership: The roles of professional community, trust, efficacy, and shared responsibility. *Educational Administration Quarterly,* 44(4), 458–495.

Watson, S. T. (2005). Teacher collaboration and school reform: distributing leadership through the use of professional learning teams (Doctoral dissertation). University of Toronto.

Wayman, J. C., Jimerson, J. B., and Cho, V. (2012). Organizational considerations in establishing the data-informed district. *School Effectiveness and School Improvement,* 23(2), 159–178.

Wayman, J. C., and Stringfield, S. (2006). Data use for school improvement: School practices and research perspectives. *American Journal of Education,* 112(4), 463–468.

Wei, R. C., Darling-Hammond, L., and Adamson, F. (2010). *Professional Development in the United States: Trends and Challenges.* Dallas, TX: National Staff Development Council.

Wenger, E. (1998). *Communities of Practice: Learning, Meaning and Identity.* New York, NY: Cambridge University Press.

Wilkins, A. (2015). Professionalizing school governance: The disciplinary effects of school autonomy and inspection on the changing role of school governors. *Journal of Education Policy,* 30(2), 182–200.

Wohlstetter, P., Datnow, A., and Park, V. (2008). Creating a system for data-driven decision-making: Applying the principal-agent framework. *School Effectiveness and School Improvement,* 19(3), 239–259.

Young, V. M. (2006). Teachers' use of data: Loose coupling, agenda setting, and team norms. *American Journal of Education,* 112, 521–548.

Zaccaro, S. J., Ely, K., and Shuffler, M. (2008). The leader's role in group learning. In V. Sessa, and M. London (Eds.), *Work Group Learning. Understanding, Improving and Assessing How Groups Learn in Organizations,* 15–44, Mahwah, NJ: Lawrence Erlbaum Associates.

Chapter 4

The Impact of Fraudulent Behavior on the Usefulness of Learning Analytics Applications: The Case of Question and Answer Sharing with Medium-Stakes Online Quizzing in Higher Education

Silvester Draaijer and Chris van Klaveren

Contents

4.1 Introduction

An important objective of online quizzing in higher education is to prepare students for upcoming summative tests. Online quizzes serve as moments of practice in acquiring knowledge and skills. In order to increase their participation rates in these online quizzes, students may receive an incentive of extra grade points if they pass. Anecdotal reports (Hambelton, 2002; Kibble, 2007) indicate that fraudulent student behavior such as sharing answers on social media does occur, as students try to game the system. However, no empirical evidence has yet been provided regarding the extent of the impact of this behavior.

Fraudulent behavior is a serious threat. First, it means that outcomes can no longer be regarded as completely valid representations of student knowledge (Kibble, 2007; SURF, 2015). Second, fraudulent behavior undermines the preparatory objective of these online quizzes, since students may be more focused on passing these quizzes than on the actual process of practicing. Third, fraud can induce problems regarding the credibility of an institution's diplomas and degrees. It is therefore not surprising that there is widespread media coverage when student fraud is detected (*Algemeen Dagblad*, 2014), which in turn has a negative influence on the educational institution, as when boards of directors are held publicly accountable or student enrollment decreases. Finally, and of chief interest for this volume, fraudulent behavior can cause learning analytics applications using data retrieved from online quizzing to be less reliable or useful for valid predictions of measures such as study success.

To the best of our knowledge, this is the first study that provides empirical evidence that examines the extent of the effects of fraudulent student behavior. Information was used from first-year law students who were enrolled in the VU University Amsterdam law program in 2013 and who took weekly online quizzes with direct feedback showing the correct answers. To identify the presence of fraudulent behavior and its impact on quiz scores, we exploited exogenous variation in the feedback procedure. Exogenous variation was induced because a sudden change in the feedback procedure occurred: the display of feedback was delayed until all students had completed the test, instead of appearing immediately to a student once that student had submitted answers. This exogenous variation resulted in a temporary reduction in the average score on the quizzes. The main conclusion of this finding is that fraudulent behavior inflated quiz scores by 1.5 points on a scale of 0–10. A unique feature of this study is that it had access to discussion data and files exchanged in two closed Facebook groups composed of students who had started the law education program under study. This gave additional insight into the process of fraudulent behavior.

This chapter is structured as follows. In Section 4.2, the literature on online quizzing, fraudulent behavior, and test validity is briefly discussed. In Section 4.3, the descriptive statistics of our sample and information originating from the Facebook groups are presented. In Section 4.4, we detail the estimation strategy regarding fraud's impact on scores and discuss our main findings. Finally, the results are discussed in Section 4.5, along with implications for practice and research.

4.2 Literature

4.2.1 Online Quizzing and Learning Analytics

Online quizzes in higher education serve as an important feedback tool that provides valuable information to both students and teachers about knowledge and skills acquired as courses progress (Angus and Watson, 2009; Kibble, 2011; Tempelaar et al., 2014). The feedback provided gives students information that they can use to reinforce their acquisition of knowledge of specific topics (Bälter et al., 2013; Butler and Roediger, 2008; Butler et al., 2008; Karpicke and Blunt, 2011; Nicol, 2007; Roediger and Karpicke, 2006) and to establish further progress in mastering the course material (Cracolice and Roth, 1996; Kulik et al., 1974; Maki and Maki, 2001).

Many empirical studies show that there is a positive correlation between online quiz participation and quiz achievement with course achievement (Angus and Watson, 2009; Bouwmeester et al., 2013; Carrillo-de-la-Peña and Pérez, 2012; De Kleijn et al., 2013; Gier and Kreiner, 2009; Haak et al., 2011; Johnson and Kiviniemi, 2009; Johnson, 2006). As such, online quizzes can be powerful data sources in learning analytics applications. The term *assessment analytics on the basis of assessment data* has already been coined for this area of study (Ellis, 2013; Tempelaar et al., 2013). This assessment data can inform groups and individual learners, teachers, and institutions about the chances of future success in a course of study or on specific topics. It can also be used to provide learners with targeted support and guidance to study more intensely or more effectively, or to focus on specific subjects. This information can be particularly useful in learning analytic dashboards (Arnold and Pistilli, 2012; Duval, 2011; Verbert et al., 2013) to inform individuals and teachers.

4.2.2 *Fraudulent Student Behavior and Test Validity*

It has been shown that students participate more frequently in online quizzes as quizzes' stakes become higher (Kibble, 2007). The stakes go up if, for example, students can earn extra course credit by participating in or achieving some minimum standards on such quizzes. Teachers may use this mechanism to motivate students to engage actively with the course materials. Anecdotal reports, however, suggest that fraudulent behavior by students increases with the stakes of online quizzes (Hambelton, 2002; Kibble, 2007). By fraudulent behavior, we refer to circumstances in which students have access to and exploit a source—a person, a file, an Internet site, a communication archive, and so on—that possesses quiz answers before or during the quiz. Current wireless communication possibilities even allow students to share and distribute information, such as the answers on online quizzes, in real time. If these anecdotes reflect reality, the validity of achieved online quiz scores may be threatened, as these scores would no longer be a valid and reliable reflection of students' knowledge and skills. Fraud might only be an issue involving some isolated individuals, limiting its impact on learning analytic applications. However, fraud may also be widespread in large groups of individuals, which would mean a more significant impact. If the obtained quiz data is distorted and does not reflect actual student effort or achievement regarding the course knowledge and skills, learning analytics applications and providing feedback regarding course success chances or study guidance will be compromised, perhaps seriously. Therefore, establishing the extent to which quizzing data is distorted and compromises validity for use in learning analytics applications needs careful consideration. However, there are no known empirical studies estimating the extent of the effects of fraudulent student behavior with respect to higher-stakes quizzes.

The study in this chapter therefore presents a case regarding medium-stakes online quizzes and the effects of fraud on quiz scores. In this case, online quizzes using multiple-choice questions (MCQs) were administered to first-year students in the VU University Amsterdam law program. In the first year, two courses ran simultaneously. During the first year of the program, students had to take 8 courses over 5 periods that lasted a total of 28 weeks. In these 5 periods, 55 quizzes were administered to students before the start of weekly lectures and tutorial groups. The central idea was that these quizzes would help students prepare for lectures, tutorial groups, and ultimately, achievement tests. As an incentive, students could earn extra credits if they answered 9 or 10 out of 10 questions correctly. An overview of the quizzes and courses is shown in Table 4.2. Based on Draaijer and Klinkenberg (2015), 10 quiz questions were randomly drawn for each individual student from a pool of 30–50 items each week for each quiz. Students did not receive information about how quizzes were constructed or about the size of the actual pool of test items from which questions were drawn. The probability was low that students received identical quizzes, because the questions were randomly chosen. Additionally, a copyright notice was displayed for each question, stating that copying and distributing any question or answer was forbidden. However, students students received immediate feedback with the correct answers and students had the opportunity to share those answers with their peers before they took the quizzes, perhaps through social media. In this study, we show that students, despite the randomization and copyright notice, shared correct answers on the quizzes and boosted overall quiz scores. Detailed information about the online quizzes considered in this study is provided in Section 4.3.

4.3 Data and Descriptive Statistics

This study uses the registered data of a sample of 480 first-year law students at VU University Amsterdam for the academic year beginning in 2013. All were active participants in the courses from the beginning of the program and 3 weeks before and after the change in feedback policy. This sample selection, to a large extent, rules out differences in achieved quiz scores by students who left the program, who could be among the lowest-performing students. Quiz score data was retrieved from the institution's Learning Management System (LMS: Blackboard), with which the online quizzes were developed and administered. Most student data was obtained from a survey that was administered to students who visited a pre-university introduction meeting, with additional data extracted from national records on upper secondary school GPA scores.

4.3.1 Student Data and Quiz Data

Table 4.1 shows the background characteristics of the students in the sample: the first-year law students were predominantly female and averaged 22 years of age. We note that the age distribution of the law students was skewed to the right, although 64 students did not supply their age. While most students were between 18 and 22 (62%), a substantial percentage were between 22 and 24 (14%) or even older (i.e., 10%). The average GPA was 6.51, which is roughly comparable to the average Dutch student's GPA. Further, students can enter university programs in the Netherlands if they pass an exam in upper secondary school or by successfully finishing the first year of higher vocational education. This explains, first, why the minimum value of the GPA is higher than 5.5, as it reflects the fact that students who scored at least 5.5 points on the exam were given a passing grade. Second, it explains why there are relatively more missing values for GPA, because a large proportion of first-year students enrolled in the program after finishing the first year of higher vocational education (27%). Finally, the quiz performance shows that, on average, students answered 8.54 of the 10 questions correctly. We show later in the

Table 4.1   Descriptive Statistics of the Participants

	N	Mean	Std. dev.	Min	Max
Total number of students	480				
Gender (Man)	416	0.33	0.47	0	1
Age	416	22.31	4.71	18	58
GPA	269	6.51	0.41	5.8	8.5
Quiz Performance	480	8.54	1.48	1	10

text that the average quiz performance is not a valid representation of student skills because it partly reflects the effects of fraudulent student behavior.

Table 4.2 represents an overview of the weekly courses and quizzes that students could take. The course duration was 7 weeks, at the end of which students took an achievement test. We note that no quizzes were offered for the courses in Periods 3 or 5.

Each week, students could take a quiz featuring 10 MCQs on the subject matter of the upcoming week. The questions were largely factual in nature, with the objective of guiding students through the main concepts of the material. In any given week, an online quiz was available from 6:00 p.m Thursday to 6:00 p.m Sunday. Once students began the quiz, they had 30 min to answer the 10 questions, though they could submit their answers as soon as they wished after starting the quiz. After 30 min, answers were submitted automatically, and the correct answers were immediately revealed to the students. Students were rewarded if they performed well on the quizzes, receiving 0.1 extra credits if 9 of the 10 items were correctly answered and 0.2 extra credits if all the questions were answered correctly. Students could receive a total of 1.0 bonus points for each course. This was a substantial inducement, given that students could receive a grade on the achievement test between 0 and 10, and pass that exam by scoring 5.5 points or higher. The first week of each course featured a dummy quiz for which no bonus points were awarded.

4.3.2 Facebook Data

A distinctive feature of the present study is the use of Facebook data from two student-controlled, closed Facebook groups (Figure 4.1) that were intended for students who started their programs in the academic year 2013 (*VU Rechten 2013–2016*) or in the academic year 2012 (*VU Rechten 2012–2015*). Each group had about a thousand members; most students who began law school became a member of their year's group.

Table 4.2   Overview of Quizzes and Courses During the First 28 Weeks of the Educational Program

Period	Course Week	Week Number	Submission Deadline	Quiz Related to Courses	
1	Week 1	1	1-Sep-13	IntrL_wk 01	FoCiL_wk 01
1	Week 2	2	8-Sep-13	IntrL_wk 02	FoCiL_wk 02
1	Week 3	3	15-Sep-13	IntrL_wk 03	FoCiL_wk 03
1	Week 4	4	22-Sep-13	IntrL_wk 04	FoCiL_wk 04
1	Week 5	5	29-Sep-13	IntrL_wk 05	FoCiL_wk 05
1	Week 6	6	6-Oct-13	IntrL_wk 06	FoCiL_wk 06
1	Week 7	7	13-Oct-13	IntrL_wk 07	
2	Week 1	8	27-Oct-13	FoCrimL_wk 01	IntrPropL_wk 01
2	Week 2	9	3-Nov-13	FoCrimL_wk 02	IntrPropL_wk 02
2	Week 3	10	10-Nov-13	FoCrimL_wk 03	IntrPropL_wk 03
2	Week 4	11	17-Nov-13	FoCrimL_wk 04	IntrPropL_wk 04
2	Week 5	12	24-Nov-13	FoCrimL_wk 05	IntrPropL_wk 05
2	Week 6	13	1-Dec-13	FoCrimL_wk 06	IntrPropL_wk 06
2	Week 7	14	8-Dec-13	FoCrimL_wk 07	IntrPropL_wk07
4	Week 1	15	2-Feb-14	Ency_wk 01	IntrContrL_wk 01
4	Week 2	16	9-Feb-14	Ency_wk 02	IntrContrL_wk 02
4	Week 3	17	16-Feb-14	Ency_wk 03	IntrContrL_wk 03
4	Week 4	18	23-Feb-14	Ency_wk 04	IntrContrL_wk 04

(Continued)

Table 4.2   (Continued) Overview of Quizzes and Courses During the First 28 Weeks of the Educational Program

Period	Course Week	Week Number	Submission Deadline	Quiz Related to Courses	
4	Week 5	19	2-Mar-14	Ency_wk 05	IntrContrL_wk 05
4	Week 6	20	9-Mar-14	Ency_wk 06	IntrContrL_wk 06
4	Week 7	21	16-Mar-14	Ency_wk 07	IntrContrL_wk 07
5	Week 1	22	30-Mar-14	FoEurL_wk 01	HoL_wk 01
5	Week 2	23	6-Apr-14	FoEurL_wk 02	HoL_wk 02
5	Week 3	24	13-Apr-14	FoEurL_wk 03	HoL_wk 03
5	Week 4	25	20-Apr-14	FoEurL_wk 04	HoL_wk 04
5	Week 5	26	27-Apr-14	FoEurL_wk 05	HoL_wk 05
5	Week 6	27	4-May-14	FoEurL_wk 06	HoL_wk 06
5	Week 7	28	11-May-14	FoEurL_wk 07	HoL_wk 07

Note: IntrL = Introduction to Legal Sciences, FoCiL = Fundamentals of Civil Law, FoCrimL = Fundamentals of Criminal Law, IntrPropL = Introduction to Property Law, Ency = Encyclopedia of Law, IntrContL = Introduction to Contract Law, FoEurL= Fundamentals of European Law, HoL = History of Law.

Because closed Facebook groups do not allow for automated data extraction, it is not possible to obtain logged student data or retrieve other data automatically. However, the timeline of the Facebook group contains a complete history of posts and uploaded documents, so those that were relevant to the quizzes could be traced by using the Facebook search function. Collapsed posts were expanded so that all posts could be grabbed from each screen and pasted into other software for later analysis. The same method was applied to finding and retrieving documents.

KEEP
CALM
AND
JUST
GRADUATE
VU Rechten 2013 - 2016
Closed Group
Joined
Share
Notifications
Discussion
Members
Events
Photos
Files
Search this group

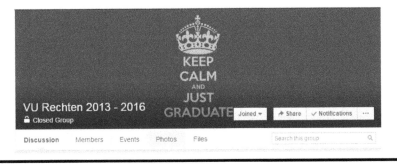

Figure 4.1 Home page of the Facebook group of the 2013–2016 class.

The content of student conversations in these groups confirmed the impact of changing the feedback procedure. Figure 4.2 shows the first occurrence of sharing questions and answers on Facebook (February 9, 2014): a student posted all the questions and answers for the first graded quiz. Interestingly, students only began to share their answers through Facebook in February 2014, which appears rather late, as that was more than four months after the start of the program. One possible explanation for this is that students considered sharing quiz information through Facebook to be more dangerous than through text messaging or other means. However, Facebook sharing may be more efficient, and it is therefore not surprising that after this first occurrence, many more sharing actions occurred.

Figure 4.3 illustrates two examples of sharing questions and answers on Facebook. Panel (a) shows that students who received Blackboard feedback on a quiz pasted that feedback into an MS Word document and shared it with the

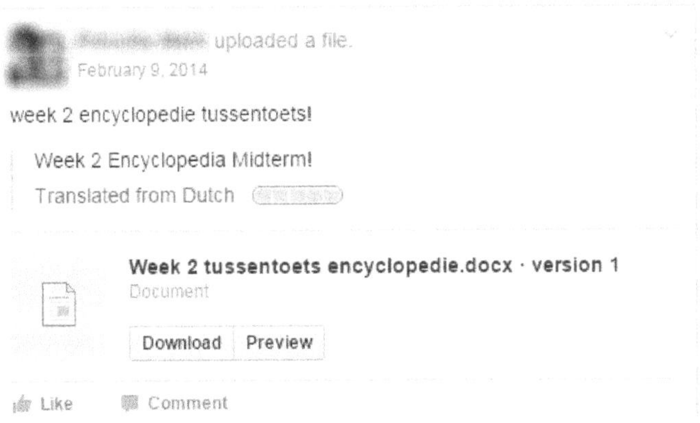

uploaded a file.
February 9, 2014
week 2 encyclopedie tussentoets!
Week 2 Encyclopedia Midterm!
Translated from Dutch
Week 2 tussentoets encyclopedie.docx · version 1
Document
Download
Preview
Like
Comment

Figure 4.2 First occurrence of sharing quiz questions and answers on Facebook (February 9, 2014).

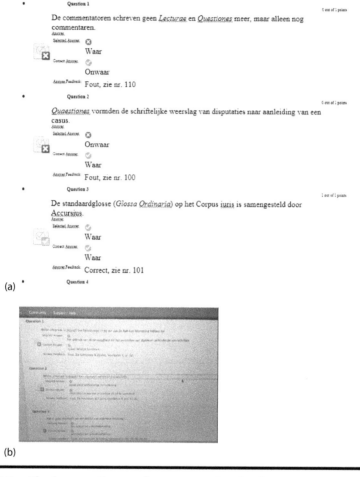

(a)

(b)

Figure 4.3   Sharing questions and answers on Facebook.

group. The feedback received included their own answers, the correct answers, and guidance on where students could find more information in the textbook on the various questions. Panel (b) shows that students also took photos with their phones of the correct answers and posted them directly into the Facebook group.

As a compelling reason to change the feedback policy, in April 2014, a trustworthiness problem of online quizzes for a first-year statistics course at another Dutch university surfaced in the media (*Algemeen Dagblad*, 2014). In that course, students could earn a credit of 0.5 points for their final course grade, which was on a 1–10 scale, and students could open two browser windows for the same attempt at a given quiz. As a result, they could answer questions in one browser, receive immediate feedback on whether this answer was correct, and then fill in the correct answers in the other browser window and submit only those answers. This flaw

Figure 4.4 Facebook posts on media reports regarding fraud at another university.

was first discovered by a small number of students, but soon many students used it to answer quizzes. In both the mainstream and social media worlds, this episode garnered a great deal of negative publicity for that university.

On April 15, 2014, as this problem surfaced, messages like those shown in Figure 4.4 appeared in the Facebook groups used in the present study. These messages reveal that students were aware of the situation at the other university and of their own opportunistic fraudulent behavior. The left panel shows a Facebook post from the 2012–2015 student group, which demonstrates awareness of students' opportunistic behavior by referring to a form of online test fraud that had been detected. The main message states, "kuch kuch," which translates literally as "cough, cough" and serves as a discreet warning to the other students. Panel (a) shows that the 2013–2016 students began discussing new and better methods to share their questions and answers more efficiently.

The communication pattern in the Facebook groups provides clear evidence of the fraudulent behavior of many students and their awareness that they acted fraudulently.

4.4 Estimation Strategy and Findings

4.4.1 Estimation Strategy

Exogenous variation in receiving immediate feedback on quiz answers was exploited by applying a regression discontinuity (RD) analysis (Angrist and Pischke, 2009; Imbens and Lemieux, 2008) to test whether students' scores were inflated. In particular, we estimated the relationship between quiz achievement (A) when receiving no feedback on quiz answers after Week 24 and a flexible continuous function that measured the distance in weeks between the week in which the quiz was taken and the week in which students no longer received quiz answers (i.e., after Week 24, the cutoff week). The distance in weeks is the running variable used in the RD analysis. The following estimation model was used to gauge this relationship:

$$A_i = \alpha_0 + \alpha_1 NF_i + g(w_i) + \beta' x_i + \varepsilon_i \tag{4.1}$$

The quiz score achieved in a given week by student i is represented by A_i. The variable NF indicates that, without warning, no immediate feedback was received on the quiz taken, with the value of this variable represented by the following deterministic and discontinuous function of the covariate week:

$$NF_i = \begin{cases} 1 \text{ if } w_i \geq c \\ 0 \text{ if } w_i < c \end{cases} \tag{4.2}$$

In this function, w represents the quiz week and c equals 24, which refers to the threshold level of 24 weeks, after which immediate feedback was no longer given.

The function $g(w_i)$ represents a linear trend relationship of the forcing variable w_i with the quiz scores achieved on either side of the cutoff.

4.4.2 Findings

We first illustrate the impact of sharing questions and answers while running the program and then the effect of suddenly disabling feedback with correct answers after quizzes were submitted. Figure 4.5 plots the average quiz scores achieved and 95% confidence intervals over time. The y-axis represents the quiz scores achieved, while the x-axis represents the distance in weeks to the cutoff of feedback.

A steady increase in average weekly quiz scores can clearly be observed. Notably, the observed increase in average quiz scores achieved during the first 24 weeks was not caused by selective quiz participation, as illustrated in Appendix 1; the participation rate of the group of 480 students remained relatively stable. Considering the confidence intervals at the cutoff, Figure 4.5 clearly shows that quiz scores dropped significantly as soon as feedback was disabled, which is the main point of interest for this chapter.

Interestingly, the figure illustrates that average quiz scores returned to their inflated level after only 3 weeks. This could indicate that students found new ways of distributing answers to the questions or that students adapted their study behavior. It was noticed from the Facebook group data that students went into a mode of asking for correct answers for individual questions. It might also be possible that students started to use more real-time communication channels to share

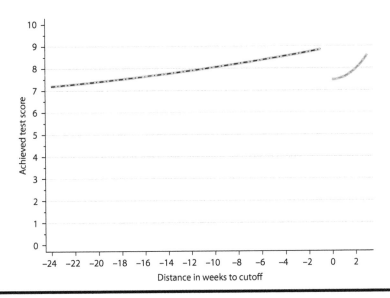

Figure 4.5   **Average quiz scores during the run of the first-year program.**

information (such as WhatsApp, SnapChat, Skype, or TeamViewer). However, no data for these channels was available.

Table 4.3 shows the baseline estimation results. Model (1) shows the effect on the quiz scores of suddenly receiving no feedback, if only the control variables that estimate the linear trend relationship of the forcing variable are included. The estimated effect can be viewed as the Wald estimator. In Models (2) and (3), student- and program-level control variables were subsequently included. The student-level control variables included refer to gender, age, and GPA, while the program-level control variables refer to the type of program in which students were enrolled (general law, notary law, or criminology) and the year of enrollment of the individual student at VU University Amsterdam (2012 or earlier, in 2013, or 2014). The estimation results of Model (1) indicate that the scores achieved on the quizzes dropped by 1.5 points after immediate feedback was disabled. The estimation results of Models (2) and (3) show that the estimated impact did not change when

Table 4.3 Baseline Estimation Results

	(1)		(2)		(3)	
	Coeff	*SE*	*Coeff*	*SE*	*Coeff*	*SE*
No feedback	−1.469	(0.077)***	−1.477	(0.076)***	−1.469	(0.078)***
Trend before cutoff	0.072	(0.004)***	0.071	(0.004)***	0.075	(0.004)***
Trend after cutoff	0.373	(0.028)***	0.365	(0.027)***	0.362	(0.027)***
Constant	8.83	(0.061)***	7.43	(0.886)***	7.02	(0.890)***
Student-level controls	No		Yes		Yes	
Program-level controls	No		No		Yes	
N	15002		15002		15002	
# Student clusters	480		480		480	
R²	0.062		0.075		0.078	

Note: SEs are clustered at the student level.

*, **, *** denote significance at 10%, 5%, 1% level (two-sided).

student- and program-level control variables were included, which confirms that the sudden change in feedback was indeed a source of exogenous variation.

Table 4.4 shows how the impact of disabling feedback on quiz scores varied with gender, age, and GPA. For a more convenient interpretation of the results, we centered the variables age and GPA such that they reflected distances from the average. With respect to the impact, the values of the heterogeneous model were within the extent of the standard error. Analyzing heterogeneous effects by including the interaction between the impact and student-level factors also did not result in significant effects at the 5% level. This is an indication that the impact was independent of student-level and program-level factors, and thus that the effects of students' fraudulent behavior on quiz scores achieved was independent of the

Table 4.4   Heterogeneous Treatment Effects

	Male		Age (centered)		GPA (centered)	
	Coeff	SE	Coeff	SE	Coeff	SE
No feedback	−1.421	(0.084)***	−1.453	(0.078)***	−1.465	(0.078)***
(No feedback) *(interaction variable)	−0.126	(0.104)	0.022	(0.013)*	0.117	(0.013)
Interaction variable	0.063	(0.089)	−0.005	(0.016)	0.237	(0.128)*
Trend before cutoff	0.075	(0.004)***	0.075	(0.004)***	0.075	(0.004)***
Trend after cutoff	0.362	(0.027)***	0.363	(0.027)***	0.362	(0.027)***
Constant	7.01	(0.889)***	8.64	(0.113)***	7.01	(0.890)***
Student-level controls	Yes		Yes		Yes	
Program-level controls	Yes		Yes		Yes	
N	15002		15002		15002	
# Student clusters	480		480		480	
R²	0.078		0.078		0.078	

Note: SEs are clustered at the student level. In each model, we also included a variable that interacts *NF* with a dummy that indicates that the interaction characteristic of interest was missing. These interaction terms are not shown, as they were not significant.

*,**,*** denote significance at 10%, 5%, 1% levels (two-sided).

student-level variables of gender, age, and GPA and of the program-level variables of study program and year of enrollment.

4.4.3 Discussion

In this chapter, a study was presented that provides empirical evidence that supports anecdotal reporting on fraudulent student behavior with respect to online quizzes. What had only been a matter of conjecture, however plausible, has been enriched in this study by estimations of the extent of fraud's effects on quiz scores at the cohort level and over a longer time frame. To identify the effect of fraud, we considered a sample of first-year VU University Amsterdam law students who took weekly online quizzes over a 28-week period. We used exogenous variation in quiz feedback procedures to estimate the magnitude of fraud's effects. More precisely, the feedback procedure was changed during the run of this first-year educational program *without prior notice* to the students. This change in procedure was that the *immediate* display of the correct answers to the questions in online quizzes after submission by each student was changed to a *delayed* display of the correct answers after all students had answered the quiz. As a result, correct answers, as displayed directly on screen for an individual student, could no longer be immediately shared by the students through social media.

This study shows that fraudulent behavior had a large and significant effect on online quiz scores. Average quiz scores dropped by 1.5 points on a scale of 1–10 after the feedback procedure was changed. These results, first, support the anecdotal evidence regarding fraudulent behavior in online quizzing provided by Kibble and others (Kibble, 2007; SURF, 2015) and the concerns that fraudulent behavior can influence quiz scores of whole groups. Fraud may therefore threaten the preparation and practice objectives of online quizzing. A second empirical result of this study is that the size of fraud's effect on quiz scores is independent of the student-level background characteristics of age, gender, and GPA in upper secondary education. A third empirical result is that the average quiz score rebounded quickly after the change in feedback procedure, which may be due to the ability of students to find new ways of distributing their answers or to students' adapting their study behavior.

The findings of this study send out a worrying message. In the current information era, the speed of the flow of information between great numbers of individuals is constantly increasing, and students can use this high-speed information flow to game the testing system. Curriculum designs that use online systems in which students can acquire extra credits in their courses can be vulnerable to opportunistic and fraudulent behavior. Students can use modern communication means and social media very quickly and effectively, with the objective of securing a superficial outcome, bypassing the actual objective of the learning opportunity.

With respect to the use of scores of online quizzes in learning analytic application settings, incorporating medium-stakes quizzes may compromise the intended use of this data. Compromised data is ineffective, for example, in providing feedback regarding achievement, any extra effort needed to master course materials, or study success predictions. Incorporating and combining this compromised data with other data further lowers the predictive power of these systems. This is an important finding for the future development and research of learning analytic analysis and applications.

In view of this study's findings, it is important that learning analytics applications incorporate monitoring activity of scores for online activities in general, but especially when tests are administered in unsupervised circumstances that allow students to game the system. The analysis in this chapter has shown that exogenous variation, such as a sudden change in the policy of providing feedback to students, can reveal if and to what extent students demonstrate opportunistic fraudulent behavior. Given this reality, it may be necessary to establish policies in which such changes are carefully planned and built into the program in order to protect and improve the accuracy of learning analytics applications. For example, by "accidentally" providing less feedback to students, introducing different credit rules, providing questions from a much larger item pool in a particular week, or providing questions in which deliberately incorrect answers are marked as correct may all discourage the practice and limit the unwelcome effects of fraud. The data that is generated in this way can be used to identify and make estimations about the inflation in scores by estimating change in average scores. Further research into the effects of the exogenous variation generated could reveal important insights into the mechanisms and effects of the impact on scores on medium-stakes online quizzes and other online learning activities for which students can obtain course credit.

References

Algemeen, Dagblad (2014, April 15). Grootschalige fraude door eerstejaars economie UvA [Large scale fraud by freshmen Economics University of Amsterdam]. *Algemeen Dagblad*. Retrieved from http://www.ad.nl/ad/nl/1012/Nederland/article/detail/3635930/2014/04/15/Grootschalige-fraude-door-eerstejaars-economie-UvA.dhtml

Angrist, J. D. and Pischke, J. (2009). Getting a little jumpy: Regression discontinuity designs. In *Mostly Harmless Econometrics: An Empiricist's Companion*, 251–268. Princeton, NY: Princeton University Press.

Angus, S. D. and Watson, J. (2009). Does regular online testing enhance student learning in the numerical sciences? Robust evidence from a large data set. *British Journal of Educational Technology*, 40(2), 255–272. https://doi.org/10.1111/j.1467-8535.2008.00916.x

Arnold, K. E. and Pistilli, M. D. (2012). Course signals at Purdue: Using learning analytics to increase student success. In *Proceedings of the 2nd International Conference on Learning Analytics and Knowledge*, 267–270. New York, NY: ACM. https://doi.org/10.1145/2330601.2330666

Bälter, O., Enström, E. and Klingenberg, B. (2013). The effect of short formative diagnostic web quizzes with minimal feedback. *Computers and Education*, 60(1), 234–242. https://doi.org/10.1016/j.compedu.2012.08.014

Bouwmeester, R. A., De Kleijn, R. A., Freriksen, A. W., Van Emst, M. G., Veeneklaas, R. J., Van Hoeij, M. J., Spinder, M., Ritzen, M. J., Ten Cate, O. J. and Van Rijen, H. V. (2013). Online formative tests linked to microlectures improving academic achievement. *Medical Teacher*, 35(12), 1044–1046.

Butler, A. C. and Roediger, H. L. (2008). Feedback enhances the positive effects and reduces the negative effects of multiple-choice testing. *Memory and Cognition*, 36(3), 604–616. https://doi.org/10.3758/MC.36.3.604

Butler, M., Pyzdrowski, L., Goodykoontz, A. and Walker, V. (2008). The effects of feedback on online quizzes. *International Journal for Technology in Mathematics Education*, 15(4), 131–136.

Carrillo-de-la-Peña, M. T. and Pérez, J. (2012). Continuous assessment improved academic achievement and satisfaction of psychology students in Spain. *Teaching of Psychology*, 39(1), 45–47. https://doi.org/10.1177/0098628311430312

Cracolice, M. S. and Roth, S. M. (1996). Keller's "old" personalized system of instruction: A "new" solution for today's college chemistry students. *The Chemical Educator*, 1(1), 1–18. https://doi.org/10.1007/s00897960004a

De Kleijn, R. A., Bouwmeester, R. A., Ritzen, M. M., Ramaekers, S. P. and Van Rijen, H. V. (2013). Students' motives for using online formative assessments when preparing for summative assessments. *Medical Teacher*, 35(12), 1644–1650.

Draaijer, S. and Klinkenberg, S. (2015). A practical procedure for the construction and reliability analysis of fixed-length tests with randomly drawn test items. In E. Ras and D. J. Brinke (Eds.), *Computer Assisted Assessment. Research into E-Assessment* 47–60. Springer International Publishing. Retrieved from http://link.springer.com/chapter/10.1007/978-3-319-27704-2_6

Duval, E. (2011). Attention please!: Learning analytics for visualization and recommendation. In *Proceedings of the 1st International Conference on Learning Analytics and Knowledge* 9–17. New York, NY: ACM. Retrieved from http://dl.acm.org/citation.cfm?id=2090118

Ellis, C. (2013). Broadening the scope and increasing the usefulness of learning analytics: The case for assessment analytics. *British Journal of Educational Technology*, 44(4), 662–664. https://doi.org/10.1111/bjet.12028

Gier, V. S. and Kreiner, D. S. (2009). Incorporating active learning with PowerPoint-based lectures using content-based questions. *Teaching of Psychology*, 36(2), 134–139. https://doi.org/10.1080/00986280902739792

Haak, D. C., HilleRisLambers, J., Pitre, E. and Freeman, S. (2011). Increased structure and active learning reduce the achievement gap in introductory biology. *Science*, 332(6034), 1213–1216. https://doi.org/10.1126/science.1204820

Hambelton, R. K. (Ed.). (2002). *New CBT Technical Issue: Developing Items, Pretesting, Test Security, and Item Exposure*. London: Lawrence Erlbaum Associates.

Imbens, G. W. and Lemieux, T. (2008). Regression discontinuity designs: A guide to practice. *Journal of Econometrics*, 142(2), 615–635. https://doi.org/10.1016/j.jeconom.2007.05.001

Johnson, B. C. and Kiviniemi, M. T. (2009). The effect of online chapter quizzes on exam performance in an undergraduate social psychology course. *Teaching of Psychology*, 36(1), 33–37. https://doi.org/10.1080/00986280802528972

Johnson, G. M. (2006). Optional online quizzes: College student use and relationship to achievement. *Canadian Journal of Learning and Technology/La Revue Canadienne de L'apprentissage et de la Technologie*, 32(1), 105–108. Retrieved from http://cjlt.csj.ual-berta.ca/index.php/cjlt/article/viewArticle/61

Karpicke, J. D. and Blunt, J. R. (2011). Retrieval practice produces more learning than elaborative studying with concept mapping. *Science*, 331(6018), 772–775. https://doi.org/10.1126/science.1199327

Kibble, J. D. (2007). Use of unsupervised online quizzes as formative assessment in a medical physiology course: Effects of incentives on student participation and performance. *Advances in Physiology Education*, 31(3), 253–260.

Kibble, J. D. (2011). Voluntary participation in online formative quizzes is a sensitive predictor of student success. *Advances in Physiology Education*, 35(1), 95–96. https://doi.org/10.1152/advan.00053.2010

Kulik, J. A., Carmichael, K. and Kulik, C.-L. (1974). The Keller plan in science teaching: An individually paced, student-tutored, and mastery-oriented instructional method is evaluated. *Science*, 183(4123), 379–383. https://doi.org/10.1126/science.183.4123.379

Maki, W., and Maki, R. (2001). Mastery quizzes on the web: Results from a web-based introductory psychology course. *Behavior Research Methods*, 33(2), 212–216. https://doi.org/10.3758/BF03195367

Nicol, D. (2007). E-assessment by design: Using multiple-choice tests to good effect. *Journal of Further and Higher Education*, 31(1), 53–64. https://doi.org/10.1080/03098770601167922

Roediger, H. L. and Karpicke, J. D. (2006). Test-enhanced learning. *Psychological Science*, 17(3), 249–255. https://doi.org/10.1111/j.1467-9280.2006.01693.x

SURF. (2015, March 18). Verslag symposium: Fraudepreventie bij digitaal toetsen [Symposium report: Fraud and fraud prevention in computer based testing]. Retrieved May 3, 2016, from https://www.surfspace.nl/artikel/1785-verslag-symposium-fraude-preventie-bij-digitaal-toetsen/

Tempelaar, D. T., Heck, A., Cuypers, H., Van der Kooij, H. and Van de Vrie, E. (2013). Formative assessment and learning analytics. In *Proceedings of the Third International Conference on Learning Analytics and Knowledge*, 205–209. New York, NY: ACM. Retrieved from http://dl.acm.org/citation.cfm?id=2460337

Tempelaar, D. T., Rienties, B. and Giesbers, B. (2014). Computer assisted, formative assessment and dispositional learning analytics in learning mathematics and statistics. In *Computer Assisted Assessment. Research into E-Assessment*, 67–78. Basel: Springer. Retrieved from http://link.springer.com/chapter/10.1007/978-3-319-08657-6_7

Verbert, K., Duval, E., Klerkx, J., Govaerts, S. and Santos, J. L. (2013). Learning analytics dashboard applications. *American Behavioral Scientist*, 57(10), 1500–1509.

Appendix A

The appendix shows that the impact on students' quiz scores of changing from immediate to delayed feedback *was not significantly related to quiz participation*. Figure 4.6 plots which proportion of students participated in the quizzes each week. The 95% confidence intervals around these student proportions show that the difference around the cutoff was not significant.

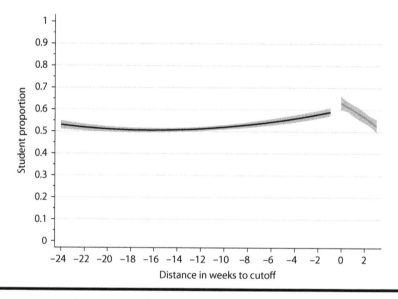

Figure 4.6   Participation rate for answering quizzes for each week in the sample of the student population.

DATA ANALYTICS TO MEASURE PERFORMANCE

Chapter 5

Disentangling Faculty Efficiency from Students' Effort

Cristian Barra, Sergio Destefanis,
Vania Sena, and Roberto Zotti

Contents

5.1 Introduction

In most European countries, the evaluation of universities is a key mechanism for the improvement of the educational services provided by these universities. Every year, students' performance is analyzed by several stakeholders, including governmental agencies and the media. At the same time, advances in information and communication technology (ICT) and data analysis techniques allow schools and universities to make use of massive amounts of data in their daily management. This chapter focuses on the use of data on students' performance to benchmark universities, and illustrates the potential contribution of data analytics to the improvement of universities' processes.

The emergence of new types of data, more granular than those previously available, and experience from the private sector, which has shown that data exploitation can generate tangible benefits to an organization, have led to a change in the attitude of the public sector toward the data it stores. While data have traditionally been considered by-products of the sector's core activities, the sector accepts that their data represent a critical resource that can yield insights into their users and internal processes. For example, information on traffic flows in a large city, which is routinely collected by closed-circuit television (CCTV) cameras, can be used to identify not only bottlenecks in the traffic flows but also where future investment in infrastructure is needed.*

Within the public sector, higher education institutions (HEIs) are well positioned to benefit from the exploitation of their own data. Like other large institutions, HEIs produce very granular data on their students, staff, and outreach activities. These data can be used for many purposes. For example, they can help in understanding how services can be delivered to staff and students in a cost-effective way, or to improve the students' experiences and monitor their current performance so that corrective actions to improve their final results can be implemented. At the same time, increasing public scrutiny and shrinking budgets mean that HEIs have to operate in a smart way, by developing integrated intelligence that would allow them to monitor their current activities and forecast future demand. All this has led to the development of learning analytics, a set of techniques and procedures having in common the idea of converting educational data into useful actions to foster learning.

In this chapter, as a novel example of learning analytics in a university setting, we present an empirical methodology that can be used to monitor the current performance of university students using data that are routinely produced and stored by universities. The key advantage of this procedure is that it allows disentangling the portion of the students' academic achievement affected by the institutions' activities from the portion directly influenced by the students' own effort. Our analysis can offer novel insights into the performance of universities, usefully supplementing information from the standard league tables. The methodology relies on data envelopment analysis (DEA). We follow the procedure suggested by Portela and Thanassoulis (2001) and Thanassoulis and Portela (2002), and use DEA to decompose the academic performance of students into a student-specific effect (directly

---

* The U.S. Department of Transportation has started to use cameras and license plate recognition to monitor traffic flow so as to identify where investment is needed (Smart Data Collective, 2015).

linked to their effort and capabilities) and a faculty-specific effect (which detects the efficiency with which faculties manage teaching resources and their impact on the students' academic performance).

Our procedure is applied to a sample of 37,459 first-year students from a large university in the South of Italy from academic year 2004–2005 to academic year 2010–2011. Using student-level data allows us to control for the ability of the students and other socio-economic characteristics known to influence students' performance at university. Furthermore, by focusing on data from one university only, we reduce the role of unobserved heterogeneity in our data. As we explain in greater detail in the text (Section 5.4), our statistical information combines three datasets: (1) an administrative dataset provided by the statistical office of the university under analysis; (2) a second dataset, relying on the university and faculty official reports; and (3) data on the Programme for International Student Assessment (PISA). Combining these datasets allows a better specification of our DEA model, and a deeper assessment of the correlates of the efficiency scores.

The chapter is organized in the following way. Section 2 introduces the topic of learning analytics in higher education, while Section 5.3 more specifically summarizes the main literature on how the performance of HEIs is traditionally measured (particularly through league tables). Section 5.4 describes the empirical approach, the production set, and the data we use. Results are presented in Section 5.5, and some comments about their managerial relevance are made in Section 5.6. Section 5.7 offers some concluding remarks.

5.2 Learning Analytics in Higher Education

In the era of big data, HEIs are able to collect a large amount of data related to their students and their educational process, making use of several sources such as the admission files, library records, online community environment, surveys, and questionnaires, and by tracking students' behaviors.

As the volume of the available data has increased, university administrators, faculty boards, and policy makers have been strongly attracted by the possibility of analyzing these data to improve decision making and resource allocations. Techniques such as educational data mining, academic analytics, and learning analytics have become increasingly widespread among universities in order to address issues such as improving student retention, measuring teaching quality, increasing graduation rate, and making employment placement more effective (Arnold and Pistilli, 2012; Dawson, 2011; Kovacic, 2012).

Unlike educational data mining (focused more on how to extract related data from these big sets of learning [Ferguson, 2012]), and academic analytics (more concerned with aspects of institutional business [Sclater, 2014]), learning analytics is more focused on the aspect of learning and on the learning processes and behaviors (Greller and Drachslrer, 2012; Jones, 2012). Siemens (2010) defines learning analytics as the use of learner-produced data and analysis models to assess and predict learning. More formally, and following the principles established in the First International Conference on Learning Analytics and Knowledge, learning analytics is the measurement, collection, analysis, and reporting of data about learners and their context, for the purposes of understanding and optimizing the environment in which learning occurs (Long et al., 2011). The main goals of learning analytics, according to Arnold and Pistilli (2012), are to predict which students might be falling behind and guide them in their use of the supporting resources.

All the different definitions of learning analytics have in common the idea of converting educational data into useful actions to foster learning. The applications of learning analytics in higher education have expanded in the last few years, due to the combination of big datasets, large-scale online learning, and political concerns regarding educational standards. HEIs have been counting on methods from learning analytics to make decisions about learners, academic progress, and performance predictions. Learning analytics is seen by universities as a way of enhancing teaching, giving students more detailed information on their progress and on what they have to do to improve their educational goals and to build better relationships between students and staff (Sclater et al., 2014). It can help faculties to improve teaching and learning opportunities for students (Hrabowski et al., 2011; Mattingly et al., 2012), to detect undesirable learning behaviors such as dropping out and academic failure (Verbert et al., 2012; Baker et al., 2006), and to be aware of the gaps in knowledge displayed by their students (Greller and Drachslrer, 2012). In other words, faculties have an important tool to deal with student underperformance and to provide helpful feedback. Moreover, their position in league tables can also be improved (Arnold, 2010).

The data for learning analytics come from student activity in online community environments such as viewing timetables, assessments, and course information; accessing learning materials and submitting assignments; from the students' use of computer applications; and from the student information system, which contains information on socio-economic status (i.e., financial situation), preenrollment characteristics (type of high school and grades), individual characteristics (age, gender, ethnicity) and grades obtained (i.e., credits acquired, exams passed).

A straightforward example of learning analytics is predictive modeling (Essa et al., 2012). By taking advantage of the whole information set known before students enroll in the university (i.e., previous educational experience) and known during the course of study (i.e., grades), this technique produces estimates of student success and retention, which can be used by universities' boards to design interventions in order to improve those outcomes (Olmos and Corrin, 2012; Smith et al., 2012). More precisely, one can estimate the probability that a student will drop out or identify at-risk students and use this information to support students and improve their completion rate (Dekker et al., 2009; Guruler et al., 2010; Wolff and Zdrahal, 2012). One can also predict learning performances through knowledge, scores, and learning grades (Lárusson and White, 2012; Romero and Ventura,

2007; Huang and Fang, 2013; Moridis and Economides, 2009; Pardos et al., 2013; Romero-Zaldivar et al., 2012). Such predictions might be used by more advanced tutoring systems to support students in solving problems and to argue for increased funding to support student preparation for a course of study.

In this chapter, we broadly move within the ambit of learning analytics. Our aim is not, however, to predict learning performance. Rather, elaborating on some DEA models available in the literature (Portela and Thanassoulis, 2001; Thanassoulis and Portela, 2002), we attempt to identify two different sources of students' performance: one ascribable to the institutions' capabilities and another directly influenced by the students' own efforts. Furthermore, in order to better understand the sources of differences in performance among the students, we correlate individual and faculty characteristics with both components of the efficiency scores.

5.3 On the Universities' Performances and League Tables: A Short Survey

The fierce public budget constraints and the new funding mechanism of the university system in Italy* have brought back to the center of academic and political debates the assessment of universities' performance. The allocation of resources from the government has been increasingly based on a formula-based mechanism and, as a consequence, (public) funds to HEIs are now linked to university-based performance indicators. Therefore, in recent years, measuring how well universities perform has become a topic of great interest, and has prompted the production of several league tables.

Several rankings have been published in newspapers or otherwise made available. Despite many criticisms, these rankings are influential. They help to collect useful information regarding HEIs that can be easily interpreted. Students and their families can then make thoughtful decisions when looking for the right university or subject of study. These rankings have a significant impact on individuals' performance on the labor markets (see Clarke, 2007; Harvey, 2008a,b; Stella and Woodhouse, 2006). Rankings have a strong impact on academic decision making and behavior, and on the structure of the institutions (Hazelkorn, 2007). Governments also use academic rankings in the process of allocating public funding to HEIs (Bernardino and Marques, 2010; Tofallis, 2012).

Some league tables are formal research-based rankings, as their indicators are all related to research activities, and a weight is assigned to several academic indicators of performance (i.e., Academic Ranking of World Universities by Shanghai

---

* In 2007, Law 544/2007 reduced the transfer of resources from central government to universities. In 2008, Law 133/2008 was approved, slowing down the turnover of academic staff across the whole university system. These measures achieved a significant reduction in the financial resources devoted nationally to higher education.

Jiao Tung University; the Performance Ranking of Scientific Papers for Research Universities published by the Higher Education Evaluation and Accreditation Council of Taiwan), such as the number of highly cited researchers, the number of papers published, staff of an institution winning the Nobel Prize and Fields Medal, and some bibliometric indicators. Alternatively, individual indicators are separately considered (e.g., the Leiden Ranking produced by the Centre for Science and Technology Studies at Leiden University). Other league tables also take into account other objectives pursued by the universities, and composite indicators are considered by weighting, along with the academic research reputation, the web presence and visibility of the institutions (i.e., Webometrics Ranking of World Universities by the Cybermetrics Lab), employer reputation, proportion of international students and of international faculty (i.e., the World's Best Universities Ranking provided by Quacquarelli Symonds), innovation activities, and teaching quality (i.e., the World University Ranking by Times Higher Education). There are also rankings that, although using a large number of indicators, do not produce a league table, but present instead the results of individual indicators or groups of indicators (i.e., CHE Ranking).

In many cases, these rankings produce very conflicting results (see De Witte and Hudrlikova, 2013 for a detailed discussion). Universities' performance strongly depends on the set of variables considered and on the methods of analysis employed. Institutions with distinct goals and missions cannot be compared. Moreover, universities have different internal structures, and may be very hard or even impossible to be measured as a whole (Bowden, 2000). University quality may be measured by a variety of indicators and methodologies, depending on the perspective of the ranking's creators. Another big issue is represented by the exogenous environmental variables reflecting the context in which the institutions operate. Characteristics such as government rules and decisions and labor market conditions—to mention a few—may influence the academic performance of students and the final ranking. Furthermore, the rankings reflect reputational factors only loosely linked to the quality of the institutions (see Taylor and Braddok, 2007 and Marginson, 2007 on this point). Another common problem is that institutions are ranked even where differences in the data are not statistically significant (Van der Wende, 2008). Although institutions may not actually change in a significant way, ratings can fluctuate from year to year as rankers change the weight assigned to different indicators (Salmi and Saroyan, 2006). The arbitrariness of these weights has been criticized in the literature (Stella and Woodhouse, 2006). Furthermore, these weights cannot satisfy the Berlin Principle on Ranking of Higher Education Institutions (IREG, 2006), according to which rankings should make allowance for differences in national conditions and education systems. In order to obviate these problems, De Witte and Hudrlikova (2013) propose an endogenous weighting mechanism assigning different weights to different universities, which is consistent with the Berlin Principle.

This survey suggests that the currently available league tables should at least be complemented by other kinds of information. An obvious way to provide this information is by using benchmarking methods that allow comparison of the performance of institutions against similar ones. An example of such benchmarking methodologies is DEA proposed by Charnes et al. (1978) and extended by Banker et al. (1984). More specifically, DEA makes it possible to compare similar units, and deals very easily with the multiple input–output nature of production in universities. In DEA, there is no need to set weights in advance, as the method applies a linear weighting scheme computed endogenously: these weights are not arbitrary, but are chosen in such a way that the outputs of the institution under evaluation are equivalent to the outputs of the benchmark institutions, while inputs are minimized (or, vice versa, inputs are made equivalent to the inputs of the benchmark institutions, while outputs are maximized). Arguably, DEA leads to a more realistic approach to benchmarking, and is especially adequate to evaluate the efficiency of non-profit entities, as it allows using non-monetary measures of outputs and inputs.

DEA has been commonly used to compare the performance of universities and departments within different universities (Abbott and Doucouliagos, 2003; Flegg et al., 2004; Agasisti and Johnes, 2010; Johnes and Johnes, 1995; Thursby, 2000; Tomkins and Green, 1988; Sarrico and Dyson, 2000; Kao and Hung, 2008; Tyagi et al., 2009; Halkos et al., 2012; Moreno and Tadepalli, 2002). Studies that make use of data aggregated at the university level provide straightforward efficiency rankings, but lose important information. It becomes impossible to disentangle the effect of students' effort from that of the institution to which they belong. Johnes (2006a) analyzes the performance of English universities in 1993, controlling for their subject mix, while Johnes (2006b) focuses on the teaching efficiency of British economic departments in 1993. Her evidence suggests that the rankings of universities derived from individual-level data differ from the rankings derived from the same data aggregated at university level.

In this chapter, data limitations prevent us from carrying out a comparison of efficiency across universities. Rather, we use a rich administrative dataset for a single university in order to correlate student and faculty characteristics with the components of efficiency respectively linked to the institutions' activities and to the students' own efforts. This allows us to better understand the potential sources of differences in performance among the faculties of the university we analyze, and is propaedeutic to an analysis taking into account different universities. Some of the factors behind the current league tables are then unveiled and their relative importance is assessed.

5.4 Empirical Set-Up

5.4.1 Framework of Empirical Analysis: DEA Applied to Individual-Level Data

Our procedure builds on the methodology developed in the context of British schools by Portela and Thanassoulis (2001) and Thanassoulis and Portela (2002).

We adapt their procedure to the higher education context, and apply DEA to decompose the academic performance of university students into a student-specific effect (assumed to be correlated with the students' efforts) and a faculty-specific effect. The original methodology has been modified to take into account the variations in the subject mix across different faculties. Following the guidelines of the Italian Department of Education, we group faculties into three main areas: Social Sciences (including Faculty n. 1 and Faculty n. 2), Humanities (including Faculty n. 3, Faculty n. 4, and Faculty n. 5), and Pure and Applied Sciences (including Faculty n. 6, Faculty n. 7, and Faculty n. 8).

The efficiency scores are computed in three stages. First, we compute an efficiency score that captures the performance of each student against the student population in the same subject area. Second, we construct a measure that captures the performance of each student in relation to a frontier computed for the student population in the same faculty. Finally, the ratio between the two measures allows the computation of the faculty-dependent efficiency measure, which reflects the component of the students' performance affected by the extent to which the faculty is efficient in organizing its teaching resources.

The frontiers against which the academic performance of each student is measured are computed by using DEA, first proposed by Charnes et al. (1978, 1981). DEA is a well-established methodology for the measurement of efficiency. It does not require a specific functional form, although it imposes some assumptions about the production technology (for more details on DEA, see Coelli et al., 1998; or Cooper et al., 2004). Following Johnes (2006a,b) and Barra and Zotti (2016), we focus on technical efficiency, computed by using an output-oriented* DEA model with variable returns to scale (DEA-VRS)[†] using the benchmarking package from freeware R. In order to understand the sources of variation in performance among the students, we then correlate the individual characteristics of the students with the efficiency scores calculated in the preceding section.

---

* Agasisti and Dal Bianco (2009, p. 487) claim that "as Italian universities are increasingly concerned with reducing the length of studies and improving the number of graduates, in order to compete for public resources, the output-oriented model appears the most suitable to analyse higher education teaching efficiency." According to Johnes (2006a, p. 91), "in a given year, once an individual student is at university, his characteristics (both social and academic) are fixed, and therefore his efficiency (in terms of academic achievement at university) is maximised by maximizing outputs subject to his given level of inputs."

[†] DEA-VRS is to be preferred in our case, as suggested by Agasisti (2011, p. 205), who argues that the assumption of constant returns to scale is restrictive in a university setting because it is reasonable to assume that the "dimension (number of students, amount of resources, etc.) plays a major role in affecting the efficiency." Johnes (2006a, pp. 91–92) also points out that "measurement scales of attainment are arbitrary in the educational context, and if one student's A level score is n times another's, and if both students are efficient, then there is no reason to expect that the degree result of the first student will also be n times that of the second."

5.4.2 Production Set and the Data

The specification of our production set (see Table 5.1) follows the main empirical literature in this field (Johnes, 2006a; Barra and Zotti, 2016).

Knowledge and skills when entering tertiary education are important determinants of students' performance as higher ability lowers their educational costs and increases their motivation. Many studies show that the type of high school and the final grade are correlated with students' performance at university (Boero et al., 2001; Smith and Naylor, 2001; Des Jardins et al., 2002; Di Pietro, 2004; Arulampalam et al., 2004; Di Pietro and Cutillo, 2008; Lassibille, 2011). Therefore, the first input is the grade that each student has obtained at the national exam held at the end of the high school cycle (HSG); the second input is the mean score for the type of secondary school track (academic oriented or lyceum; technical high school; professional high school) obtained in the PISA 2006 survey* (HST).

Furthermore, it is well known that other personal characteristics (mainly income of the family, gender, and age; see Montmarquette et al., 2000; Smith and Naylor, 2001; McNabb et al., 2002) are related to students' academic performance. We use two of these variables, gender (GEN) and the level of self-reported household income (INC), for sorting students in smaller groups; in this way, we are able to define more homogeneous subsets of students and then apply DEA separately to each subgroup (see Thanassoulis, 1999; Portela and Thanassoulis, 2001; Thanassoulis and Portela, 2002; Johnes, 2006a,b; Barra and Zotti, 2016, for a similar choice).

Table 5.1 Specification of Outputs and Inputs in DEA

Inputs	Output
HSG; HST; GEN[a]; INC[a]	CREDITS
Legend:	INC: Income class (binary variable differentiating low from middle-high incomes)
HSG: high school grades HST: PISA average student score by type of high school track GEN: gender	CREDITS: sum of credits at the end of the first year

[a] Gender (GEN) and household income (INC) are not proper inputs but are used to categorize the observations so that DEA can be run on the separate subgroups (Thanassoulis, 1999).

---

* The Programme for International Student Assessment (PISA) is a triennial international survey aimed at evaluating education systems worldwide by testing the skills and knowledge of 15-year-old students.

Our measure of output is the number of credits obtained at the end of the first year (CREDITS). We follow here the main literature on student performance (Smith and Naylor, 2001; Boero et al., 2001; Bratti et al., 2010), Moreover, the choice of this variable is also strictly related to the institutional background of Italian universities. Indeed, as a consequence of the reforms implemented in the Italian higher education system in the 1990s and at the beginning of the 2000s, both quantitative and qualitative indicators were developed to evaluate teaching productivity. The quality of education was meant to increase by urging students to acquire a number of credits and exams as close as possible to those theoretically obtainable in a given year and to obtain the degree in a time as close as possible to the one legally established by the degree course regulations. In this framework, the credits obtained at the end of the first year are among the quality assessments according to which universities have started to receive public funding.*

We rely on a unique administrative dataset of 37,459 first-year students enrolled in a large public university in southern Italy for each academic year starting from 2004/2005 until 2010/2011. The analysis has been carried out only on first-year students in order to incorporate the critical elements and weaknesses of the Italian higher education system, such as the high dropout rate at the end of the first year and the consistent amount of students who do not take any exam in the first year of study; indeed, the performances of first-year students have been considered as a proxy of the regularity of the educational path and a good predictor of the probability of getting a degree on time (CNVSU, 2011).

More specifically, the empirical investigation has been performed using three datasets. Firstly, we processed an administrative dataset provided by the statistical office of the university under analysis. These data are collected through a student record system that gathers information at the individual level on prior educational qualifications, ethnicity, gender, age, socio-economic status, courses and modules in which students are enrolled, as well as assessment results. Although the data available correspond to what can be referred to as *structured data*, a large amount of work has been done in order to make the enormous quantity of information amenable to analysis. Students had to be assigned to the corresponding course of study and faculty of enrollment, and assessment results had to be reorganized in order to obtain useful information on the number of exams passed and on the number of credits associated with the corresponding exams. Secondly, we built another

---

* We recall that the main parameters that the Italian Ministry of Education has been using in the teaching quality assessment include (a) the share of students enrolled in the second year, having already obtained a given number of credits in the first year, and (b) the share of students who do not obtain any credits or pass any exam (i.e., inactive students) at the end of the first year (Ministerial Decree 18 October 2007, n. 506; CNVSU, DOC 07/2009).

dataset, relying on the university and faculty official reports, in order to construct consistent information for each faculty on the number of full professors, associate professors, and lecturers, and on the expenses allocated to teaching activities. Finally, we used a third source of data, PISA, a triennial international survey aimed at evaluating education systems worldwide by testing the skills and knowledge of 15-year-old students. Here, we collected information on the mean score obtained by Italian students for broad types of secondary school track (non-vocational, technical, or professional).

By merging these three datasets, we aimed to combine information both for individual student characteristics and for some indicators of faculty resources. This allows us to explore whether the student's academic achievement is affected by his or her own characteristics or by the institution's capabilities and, equally, to investigate the effects on faculty effectiveness attributable to the faculties' own resources or to student effort.

In summary, our overall dataset gathers information on student demographics such as gender, age, educational background, and preenrollment characteristics (type of high school attended and grade gained at the high school final exams), the class of family's self-declared income, and general information regarding university careers and performance, such as exams passed and credits acquired. There is also information on the structural characteristics of the faculties, such as the professor to student ratio (the ratio between the sum of full and associate professors and the number of first-year students). We give some descriptive statistics in Table 5.2. The data labels are all self-explanatory but for gap time, which is a binary variable equal to one for students who have not enrolled in university immediately after the end of their secondary studies.

It is also appropriate to provide some information regarding the university in which the students are enrolled. It is an institution of medium to large size. About 40,000 students were registered on average over the sample years. In the period under consideration, the university was organized into departments and faculties, with departments overseeing research, and faculties in charge of teaching provision and management. On average, about 900 full professors, associate professors, and lecturers were teaching in nine faculties.* Regarding the financial commitment of the institution, in the last decade about €90,000,000 has been invested every year on both academic and non-academic resources. The total university turnover has been fluctuating in the same period at around €100,000,000. It is a state-funded university. Fees, dependent on the income of the student's family, are quite low (on average, across the time span considered in the analysis, the highest fees are generally around €1000 per year). The main campus of the

---

* In 2007, faculties of law throughout Italy decide to introduce a separate regime for the credit system. Subsequently, all these faculties (including the one in our university) were excluded from our administrative dataset from 2007 onward. In the empirical analysis of this chapter, we chose to exclude the faculty of law altogether from our sample.

Table 5.2 Descriptive Statistics

Females (n, %)	20,521	54.8%
Males (n, %)	16,938	45.2%
High school grade (mean value)	78.97	
High school grade (F) (mean value)	80.46	
High school grade (M) (mean value)	77.15	
Non-vocational high school (lyceum and others) (PISA mean score, 2006)	517.67	
Vocational high school: Technical (PISA mean score, 2006)	467.67	
Vocational high school: Professional (PISA mean score, 2006)	402	
Non-vocational high school (scientific lyceum) (n, %)	13,093	35.0%
Non-vocational high school (classical lyceum) (n, %)	3,689	9.8%
Non-vocational high school (linguistic lyceum) (n, %)	2,121	5.7%
Vocational high school (technical institute) (n, %)	10,566	28.2%
Vocational high school (professional institute) (n, %)	3,156	8.4%
Vocational high school (other institutes) (n, %)	4,834	12.9%
Household income (low—median value €7,000)—(n, %)	9,542	25.5%
Household income (medium-high—median value €21,500)—(n, %)	27,917	74.5%
Gap time = 1 (n, %)	6,658	18.0%
Gap time = 0 (n, %)	30,801	82.0%
Professor to student ratio (%)		8.4%
Credits (mean)	23.72	

Note: All data have been sourced from the Ufficio Statistico dell'Università degli Studi.

university has its headquarters a few kilometers east of the main city in the area, to which it is well connected through a motorway. The institution can thus be considered a quasi-urban university, close to a city whose population is slightly above 100,000 inhabitants with a relative income of about €22,300 (lying around the national mean value).

5.5 Empirical Results

Using an output-oriented DEA-VRS model,* we have computed a within-faculty efficiency score measure of student performance, comparing each student's achievement at the end of the first year with the performance of other students registered in the same faculty (WFEFF). Secondly, a student-level measure of performance computed has been calculated by comparing a student's attainment at the end of the first year to the performance of the other first-year students registered in the same academic area (EFF). The ratio of these two efficiencies provides a measure of the faculty-dependent effect (FDEFF, a student-level measure of under-attainment due to the underperformance of the student's faculty with respect to the other faculties in the same subject area).

In order to gain some knowledge about the determinants of FDEFF and WDEFF, we examine the distribution of the efficiency scores calculated across various sample cuts. In order to see whether students' and faculties' characteristics affect the faculty-dependent efficiency score performance of first-year students, we first examine the values for mean, standard deviation, median, and interquartile range of FDEFF and WDEFF scores across faculties. Then, controlling for faculty-specific effects, we provide mean, standard deviation, median, and interquartile range across various student types. In order to control for faculty-specific effects, we calculated the values for mean, standard deviation, median, and interquartile range of efficiency scores across student characteristics (female vs. male, etc.) within each faculty. Then, in Tables 5.3 and 5.4, we show the mean (median) values across faculties for the resulting means and standard deviation (medians and interquartile ranges). Notice that one variable, the professor to student ratio, is uniform within each faculty but varies over time. For this variable, and the other continuous variable, the high school grade, we constructed two categories for the purposes of statistical analysis: below and above the sample mean value. We begin by examining the behavior of FDEFF scores. A final remark is that we do not allow for ethnic background or nationality in the following analysis, as Italians make up the overwhelming majority of our sample (99.5%).

The faculty effects observed in Table 5.3 are interesting. The mean and median values of Faculty n. 6 and Faculty n. 7 are strongly below those of the other faculties. The opposite holds for Faculty n. 2, and especially Faculty n. 8. As a consequence, we find considerable heterogeneity within Social Sciences and Pure and Applied Sciences, while the performance within Humanities is more uniform.

Turning to the individual characteristics of first-year students, there is evidence in favor of the importance of some personal features. Females yield FDEFF scores higher than males, and the same is true for students with a low household income

---

* Before computing our DEA scores, we tested for the presence of outliers in the sample by relying on the concept of super-efficiency. Since we did not find any anomalous observation, we proceeded to the estimation of DEA models on the full sample.

Table 5.3   Some Correlates of the FDEFF Scores from DEA

	n	*Mean*	*s.d.*	*Median*	*in.r.*
Total	*37,459*	**0.85**	*0.17*	**0.92**	*0.24*
Differences Across Faculties					
Faculty					
1	7,711	**0.87**	0.10	**0.87**	0.11
2	2,935	**0.94**	0.09	**1.00**	0.10
3	6,838	**0.86**	0.14	**0.85**	0.23
4	2,582	**0.93**	0.12	**0.97**	0.08
5	6,105	**0.90**	0.13	**0.98**	0.20
6	357	**0.66**	0.19	**0.67**	0.29
7	5,874	**0.57**	0.12	**0.54**	0.09
8	5,057	**0.99**	0.04	**1.00**	0.00
Differences Across Time. Controlling for Faculty Effects					
Below mean PSR	22,349	**0.84**	0.12	**0.92**	0.11
Above mean PSR	15,110	**0.85**	0.12	**0.93**	0.10
Differences Across Students' Characteristics. Controlling for Faculty Effects					
Female	20,521	**0.85**	0.09	**0.91**	0.04
Male	16,938	**0.80**	0.11	**0.87**	0.14
Low income	9,542	**0.87**	0.11	**0.97**	0.10
Medium-high income	27,917	**0.83**	0.11	**0.95**	0.11
Below mean hi-sch. grade	21,598	**0.83**	0.13	**0.93**	0.16
Above mean hi-sch. grade	15,861	**0.85**	0.08	**0.91**	0.09
Scient. lyc.	13,093	**0.82**	0.11	**0.82**	0.16
Class. lyc.	3,689	**0.82**	0.11	**0.82**	0.16
Ling. lyc.	2,121	**0.83**	0.10	**0.82**	0.10
Techn. inst.	10,566	**0.82**	0.11	**0.83**	0.14

(Continued)

Table 5.3 (Continued)   Some Correlates of the FDEFF Scores from DEA

	n	*Mean*	*s.d.*	*Median*	*in.r.*
Prof. inst.	3,156	**0.87**	0.14	**0.92**	0.14
Others	4,834	**0.87**	0.12	**0.89**	0.14
Gap time = 1	6,658	**0.85**	0.13	**0.95**	0.14
Gap time = 0	30,801	**0.84**	0.11	**0.93**	0.10

Note: n = number of observations; *s.d.* = standard deviation; *in.r.* = interquartile range; PSR = professor to student ratio.

(vs. those with a medium-high household income). As for the other preenrollment characteristics, having received higher high school grades has no clearly discernible effect on faculty-specific efficiency. On the other hand, the school type is highly significant, in the sense that professional and other institutes are associated with much higher FDEFF performance (other institutes offer various pathways to artistic and educational high school degrees with a large vocational content). Finally, the gap time and professor to student ratio do not appear to matter very much. This suggests that increasing the number of professors per first-year students has little effect on faculty-specific efficiency.

Is the within-faculty efficiency score component of the academic performance of first-year students also affected by the individual student characteristics, and faculty-related variables? To be able to test this hypothesis, we repeat the same exercise for WFEFF scores. For the ease of the reader, we provide again all the values for the number of observations in the overall sample and in each sample cut.

In general, mean and median values are much lower than in Table 5.3, while dispersion of the scores is much higher. The faculty-specific values for WFEFF scores are relatively low for Faculty 1, Faculty n. 2, Faculty n. 7, and Faculty n. 8, suggesting that the performances of first-year students in these faculties are particularly problematic. The opposite holds, instead, for Faculty n. 3, Faculty n. 4, Faculty n. 5 and Faculty n. 6. Turning to the individual characteristics, the contribution of the preenrollment information is even clearer than before. Having a higher high school grade has a positive effect on the within-faculty efficiency score performance of first-year students. Moreover, having obtained a high school diploma in a vocational school (technical and professional institutes specialized in providing students with skills needed in order to perform the task of a particular job) has a detrimental effect on the WFEFF performance of first-year students. The relative effects for females and low-income students are even stronger than for their FDEFF homologues (still abiding by the same pattern). The gap time is now highly relevant: students not enrolling in university immediately after the end of their secondary studies are much less efficient. The professor to student ratio matters even less than before, as central value differences are small and the dispersion of scores is very high.

Table 5.4 Some Correlates of the WFEFF Scores from DEA

	n	*Mean*	*s.d.*	*Median*	*in.r.*
Total	*37,459*	*0.23*	*0.20*	*0.21*	*0.38*
Differences Across Faculties					
Faculty					
1	7,711	**0.22**	0.19	**0.22**	0.36
2	2,935	**0.19**	0.22	**0.13**	0.33
3	6,838	**0.27**	0.21	**0.27**	0.36
4	2,582	**0.27**	0.21	**0.27**	0.36
5	6,105	**0.25**	0.21	**0.24**	0.40
6	357	**0.28**	0.23	**0.25**	0.35
7	5,874	**0.18**	0.17	**0.15**	0.31
8	5,057	**0.20**	0.20	**0.14**	0.33
Differences Across Time. Controlling for Faculty Effects					
Below mean PSR	22,349	**0.24**	0.21	**0.21**	0.36
Above mean PSR	15,110	**0.24**	0.21	**0.23**	0.35
Differences Across Students' Characteristics. Controlling for Faculty Effects					
Female	20,521	**0.27**	0.22	**0.27**	0.36
Male	16,938	**0.19**	0.19	**0.14**	0.29
Low income	9,542	**0.28**	0.25	**0.28**	0.46
Medium-high income	27,917	**0.22**	0.19	**0.22**	0.32
Below mean hi-sch. grade	21,598	**0.19**	0.19	**0.15**	0.31
Above mean hi-sch. grade	15,861	**0.29**	0.21	**0.31**	0.32
Scient. lyc.	13,093	**0.25**	0.20	**0.24**	0.31
Class. lyc.	3,689	**0.25**	0.20	**0.24**	0.34
Ling. lyc.	2,121	**0.22**	0.19	**0.21**	0.32
Techn. inst.	10,566	**0.19**	0.19	**0.15**	0.31

(Continued)

Table 5.4 (Continued) Some Correlates of the WFEFF Scores from DEA

	n	*Mean*	*s.d.*	*Median*	*in.r.*
Prof. inst.	3,156	**0.20**	0.24	**0.11**	0.35
Others	4,834	**0.25**	0.25	**0.19**	0.41
Gap time = 1	6,658	**0.18**	0.21	**0.11**	0.31
Gap time = 0	30,801	**0.24**	0.20	**0.24**	0.35

Note: n = number of observations; *s.d.* = standard deviation; *in.r.* = interquartile range; PSR = professor to student ratio.

5.6 Managerial Relevance of the Evidence

Over the last decade or so, European universities have become increasingly concerned with how to allocate their dwindling resources in such a way that the efficiency of their departments is enhanced without adversely affecting the students' performance. The latter has become a key variable in order to obtain public funding as well as support from private households (both in terms of enrollment and donations). So far, however, no analytical techniques have been systematically used to disentangle the students' own performance from the performance of the faculties. University administrators have had to rely on qualitative methodologies (questionnaires) to collect this type of data. The technique proposed in this chapter allows the collection of quantitative information on the performance of students and departments in a transparent way, while providing administrators with a clear understanding of the drivers of the university's performance. In this way, it is possible to have more detailed information about the performance of departments, usefully complementing the existing teaching assessment exercises that are based on self-reported measures of student satisfaction, whose reliability is notoriously fraught with serious problems. As a result, some important factors behind the position of the university in the current league tables are revealed, and their relative importance can be assessed. More broadly, our analysis contributes to the field of learning analytics, by using data routinely produced and stored by HEIs in order to produce information of a relatively novel kind (the decomposition of students' efficiency in within-faculty and faculty-dependent components) and to relate it to some basic students' and faculty characteristics.

The use of this technique opens up several possibilities to university administrators. Typically, when faced with financial constraints, universities tend to react by limiting the turnover of academics, but no evidence exists on the impact of these measures on the performance of the students. On the contrary, the use of these DEA-based procedures allows understanding of whether the improvement in efficiency associated with the reduction in the academics' turnover has been achieved without affecting the performance of the students. Equally, these procedures allow an assessment of the extent to which student support activities can improve the performance of the students and to what extent they can adversely impact the efficiency of the department.

It should also be noticed that the evidence given in Section 5.5 heavily relied, for ease of presentation, on the use of mean and median values. Administrators may want to examine in detail the relevance of preenrollment and other characteristics of students within each faculty. Different patterns of performance (e.g., vis-à-vis gender, income) may thus emerge, with important consequences on the decision-making process.

5.7 Concluding Remarks

In this chapter, we have provided an example of how data routinely produced and stored by HEIs can be used to monitor the performance of students at the end of their first year and identify the component of the students' under performance that can be attributed to the universities' activities and therefore can be addressed with corrective measures. The empirical approach is based on DEA, which is used to decompose the academic performance of first-year students into a student-dependent (within-faculty) effect and a faculty-dependent effect. In order to understand the sources of variation in performance among the students, we correlate student and faculty characteristics with both types of efficiency scores. Our results suggest that faculty-dependent efficiency is higher for females, and for students with a low household income. Increasing the professor to student ratio has a small beneficial effect on this efficiency, but not on the efficiency component directly linked to the student's own effort. The latter is highly related to the student's characteristics, the contribution of preenrollment information being particularly strong in this ambit. The type of school attended before university is also important, both for faculty-dependent and student-dependent efficiency.

In future work, we plan to extend our empirical set-up, examining in greater detail the different patterns of performance within faculties as well as their sources. It may also be important to examine in greater detail performance over time, to assess the impact of eventual institutional reforms (this also applies to the study of the professor to student ratio, and can extended to other measures of resources). Another interesting extension relates to the connection of the methodology we used with the available measures of students' and professors' satisfaction.

References

Abbot, M., and Doucouliagos, C. 2003. The efficiency of Australian universities: A data envelopment analysis. *Economics of Education Review*, 22, 89–97.

Agasisti, T. 2011. Performances and spending efficiency in higher education: A European comparison through non-parametric approaches. *Education Economics*, 19(2), 199–224.

Agasisti, T., and Dal Bianco, A. 2009. Reforming the university sector: effects on teaching efficiency. Evidence from Italy. *Higher Education*, 57(4), 477–498.

Agasisti, T., and Johnes, G. 2010. Heterogeneity and the evaluation of efficiency: The case of Italian universities. *Applied Economics*, 42(11), 1365–1375.

Arnold, K. E. 2010. Signals: Applying academic analytics. *EDUCAUSE Quarterly*, 33, 1.

Arnold, K. E., and Pistilli, M. D. 2012. Course signals at Purdue: Using learning analytics to increase student success. *Proceedings of the 2nd International Conference on Learning Analytics and Knowledge*, 267–270, New York: ACM.

Arulampalam, W., Naylor, R., Robin, A., and Smith, J. P. 2004. Hazard model of the probability of medical school drop-out in the UK. *Journal of the Royal Statistical Society*, 167(1), 157–178.

Baker, R. S. J., Corbett, A. T., Koedinger, K. R., Evenson, S., Roll, I., Wagner, A. Z., and Beck, J. 2006. Adapting to when students game an intelligent tutoring system. In M. Ikeda . (Eds.), *Proceedings of the 8th International Conference on Intelligent Tutoring Systems,* 392–401, Berlin: Springer.

Banker, R. D., Charnes, A., and Cooper, W. W. 1984. Some models for estimating technical and scale inefficiencies in DEA. *Management Science*, 32, 1613–1627.

Barra, C., and Zotti, R. 2016. Managerial efficiency in higher education using individual versus aggregate level data. Does the choice of decision making unit count? *Managerial and Decision Economics*, 37, 106–126.

Bernardino, P., and Marques, R. C. 2010. Academic rankings: An approach to rank Portuguese universities. *Ensaio: aval. pol. públ. Educ., Rio de Janeiro*, 18(66), 29–48.

Boero, G., McNight, A., Naylor, R., and Smith, J. 2001. Graduates and graduate labour markets in the UK and Italy. *Lavoro e Relazioni industriali*, 2, 131–172.

Bowden, R. 2000. Fantasy higher education: University and college league tables. *Quality in Higher Education*, 6(1), 41–60.

Bratti, M., Broccolini, C., and Staffolani, S. 2010. Higher education reform, student time allocation and academic performance in Italy: Evidence from a faculty of economics. *Rivista Italiana degli Economisti*, 15(2), 275–304.

Charnes, A., Cooper, W. W., and Rhodes, E. 1978. Measuring the efficiency of decision making units. *European Journal of Operational Research*, 2, 429–444.

Charnes, A., Cooper, W. W., and Rhodes, E. 1981. Evaluating program and managerial efficiency: An application of data envelopment analysis to program follow through. *Management Science*, 27, 668–697.

Clarke, M. 2007. The impact of higher education rankings on student access, choice, and opportunity. *Higher Education in Europe*, 32 (1), 59–70.

CNVSU (DOC 07/2009). Comitato Nazionale per la Valutazione del Sistema Universitario, Indicatori per la ripartizione del Fondo di cui all'art. 2 della Legge 1/2009, Miur, Rome.

CNVSU 2011. Undicesimo Rapporto sullo Stato del Sistema Universitario. Rome, Italy.

Coelli, T., Prasada Rao, D. S., and Battese, G. E. 1998. *An Introduction to Efficiency and Productivity Analysis*. Boston, MA: Kluwer Academic.

Cooper, W. W., Seiford, L. M., and Zhu, J. 2004. *Handbook on Data Envelopment Analysis*. Dordrecht: Springer Kluwer Academic.

Dawson, S. 2011. *Analytics to Literacies: Emergent Learning Analytics to Evaluate New Literacies*. Workshop on New Media, New Literacies, and New Forms of Learning. London.

Dekker, G. W., Pechenizkiy, M., and Vleeshouwers, J. M. 2009. Predicting students drop out: A case study. In T. Barnes, M. Desmarais, C. Romero, and S. Ventura. (Eds.), *Proceedings of the 2nd International Conference on Educational Data Mining,*

41–50, New York: ACM. Retrieved from http://www.educationaldatamining.org/EDM2009/uploads/proceedings/dekker.pdf

De Witte, K., and Hudrlikova, L. 2013. What about excellence in teaching? A benevolent ranking of universities. *Scientometrics*, 96, 337–364.

Di Pietro, G. 2004. The determinants of university dropout in Italy: A bivariate probability model with sample selection. *Applied Economics Letters*, 11(3), 187–191.

Di Pietro, G., and Cutillo, A. 2008. Degree flexibility and university drop-out: The Italian experience. *Economics of Education Review*, 27(5), 546–555.

Essa, A., and Hanan, A. 2012. Student success system: Risk analytics and data visualization using ensembles of predictive models. *Proceedings of the 2nd International Conference on Learning Analytics and Knowledge*, 158–161, New York: ACM.

Ferguson, R. 2012. The state of learning analytics in 2012: A review and future challenges. Technical Report KMI-12-01. Milton Keynes: Knowledge Media Institute, The Open University. http://kmi.open.ac.uk/publications/techreport/kmi-12–01

Flegg, A. T., Allen, D. O., Field, K., and Thurlow, T. W. 2004. Measuring the efficiency of British universities: A multi-period data envelopment analysis. *Education Economics*, 12, 231–249.

Greller, W., and Drachslrer, H. 2012. Translating learning into numbers: A generic framework for learning analytics. *Educational Technology & Society*, 15(3), 42–57.

Guruler, H., Istanbullu, A., and Karahasan, M. 2010. A new student performance analysing system using knowledge discovery in higher educational databases. *Computers & Education*, 55(1), 247–254.

Halkos, G., Tzeremes, N. G., and Kourtzidis, S. A. 2012. Measuring public owned university departments' efficiency: A bootstrapped DEA approach. *Journal of Economics and Econometrics*, 55(2), 1–24.

Harvey, L. 2008a. Rankings of higher education institutions: A critical review, editorial. *Quality in Higher Education*, 14(3), 187–207.

Harvey, L. 2008b. Assaying Improvement. Paper presented at the 30th EAIR Forum, Copenhagen, Denmark, 24–27 August.

Hazelkorn, E. 2007. The impact of league tables and ranking systems on higher education decision making. *Higher Education Management and Policy*, 19, 2.

Hrabowski, F. A., Suess, J., and Fritz, J. 2011. Assessment and analytics in institutional transformation. 46, 5.

Huang, S. and Fang, N. 2013. Predicting student academic performance in an engineering dynamics course: A comparison of four types of predictive mathematical models. *Computers & Education*, 61, 133–145.

International Ranking Expert Group (IREG). (2006). Berlin Principles on Ranking of Higher Education Institutions. Retrieved from www.che.de/downloads/Berlin_Principles_IREG_534.pdf.

Johnes, G., and Johnes, J. 1995. Research funding and performance in UK university departments of economics: A frontier analysis. *Economics of Education Review*, 14(3), 301–314.

Johnes, J. 2006a. Measuring efficiency: A comparison of multilevel modelling and data envelopment analysis in the context of higher education. *Bulletin of Economic Research*, 58(2), 75–104.

Johnes, J. 2006b. Measuring teaching efficiency in higher education: An application of data development analysis to economics graduates from UK Universities 1993. *European Journal of Operational research*, 174(1), 443–456.

Jones, S. J. 2012. Technology review: The possibilities of learning analytics to improve learner centered decision making. *The Community College Enterprise*, 18(1), 89–92.

Kao, C., and Hung, H. T., 2008. Efficiency analysis of university departments: An empirical study. *Omega*, 36, 653–664.

Kovacic, Z. J. 2012. Predicting student success by mining enrollment data. *Research in Higher Education Journal*, 15, 1–20. Retrieved from http://www.aabri.com/manuscripts/11939.pdf

Lárusson, J. A., and White, B. 2012. Monitoring student progress through their written "point of originality." *Proceedings of the 2nd International Conference on Learning Analytics and Knowledge*, 212–221, New York: ACM.

Lassibille, G. 2011. Student progress in higher education: What we have learned from large-scale studies. *The Open Education Journal*, 4, 1–8.

Long, P., Siemens, G., Conole, G., and Gašević, D. 2011. *Proceedings of the 1st International Conference on Learning Analytics and Knowledge (LAK11)*, Banff, AB, Canada, February 27–March 1, 2011. New York: ACM.

Marginson, S. 2007. Global university rankings: Implications in general and for Australia. *Journal of Higher Education Policy and Management*, 29(2), 131–142.

Mattingly, K. D., Rice, M. C., and Berge, Z. L. 2012. Learning analytics as a tool for closing the assessment loop in higher education. *Knowledge Management & E-Learning: An International Journal*, 4(3), 236–247.

McNabb, R., Pal, S., and Sloane, P. 2002. Gender differences in educational attainment: The case of university students in England and Wales. *Economica*, 69, 481–503.

Montmarquette, C., Mahseredjian, S., and Houle, R. 2000. The determinants of university dropouts: A bivariate probability model with sample selection. *Economics of Education Review*, 20, 475–484.

Moreno, A. A., and Tadepalli, R. 2002. Assessing academic department efficiency at a public university. *Managerial and Decision Economics*, 23, 385–397.

Moridis, C. N., and Economides, A. A. 2009. Prediction of student's mood during an online test using formula-based and neural network-based method. *Computers & Education*, 53(3), 644–652.

Olmos, M., and Corrin, L. 2012. Learning analytics: A case study of the process of design of visualizations. *Journal of Asynchronous Learning Networks*, 16(3), 39–49.

Papke, L. E., and Wooldridge, J. M. 1996, Econometric methods for fractional response variables with an application to 401(k) plan participation rates. *Journal of Applied Econometrics*, 11(6), 619–632.

Pardos, Z. A., Baker, R. S. J. D., San Pedro, M. O. C. Z., Gowda, S. M., and Gowda, S. M. 2013. Affective states and state tests: Investigating how affect throughout the school year predicts end of year learning outcomes. In D. Suthers, K. Verbert, E. Duval, and X. Ochoa (Eds.), *Proceedings of the 3rd International Conference on Learning Analytics and Knowledge*, 117–124. New York: ACM.

Portela, M. C. S., and Thanassoulis, E. 2001. Decomposing school and school-type efficiency. *European Journal of Operational Research*, 132, 357–373.

Romero, C., and Ventura, S. (2007). Educational data mining: A survey from 1995 to 2005. *Expert Systems with Applications*, 33(1), 135–146.

Romero-Zaldivar, V. A., Pardo, A., Burgos, D., and Kloos, C. D. 2012. Monitoring student progress using virtual appliances: A case study. *Computers & Education*, 58(4), 1058–1067.

Salmi, J., and Saroyan, A. 2006. League tables as policy instruments: Uses and misuses. *Higher Education Management and Policy*, 19(2), 24–62.

Sarrico, C. S., and Dyson, R. G. 2000. Using DEA for planning in UK universities. "An institutional perspective." *Journal of the Operational Research Society*, 51, 789–800.

Sclater, N. 2014. Learning analytics: The current state of play in UK higher and further education. JISC. Retrieved from repository.jisc.ac.uk/5657/1/Learning_analytics_report.pdf

Sclater, N., Peasgood, A., and Mullan, J. 2016. Learning analytics in higher education: A review of UK and international practice. Retrieved from https://www.jisc.ac.uk/sites/default/files/learning-analytics-in-he-v3.pdf

Siemens, G. 2010. What are learning analytics. ELEARNSPACE. Retrieved from http://www.elearnspace.org/blog/2010/08/25/what-are-learning-analytics/

Smart Data Collective, 2005. http://www.smartdatacollective.com/ (last access date 20/06/2016).

Smith, J., and Naylor, R. 2001. Determinants of degree performance in UK universities: A statistical analysis of the 1990s student cohort. *Oxford Bulletin of Economics and Statistics* 63, 29–60.

Smith, V. C., Lange, A., and Huston, D. R. 2012. Predictive modeling to forecast student outcomes and drive effective interventions in online community college courses. *Journal of Asynchronous Learning Networks*, 16(3), 51–61.

Stella, A., and Woodhouse, D. 2006. Ranking of higher education institutions. Occasional Publications Series No: 6, Melbourne, AUQA.

Taylor, P., and Braddock, R. 2007. International university ranking systems and the idea of university excellence. *Journal of Higher Education Policy and Management*, 29(3), 245–260.

Thanassoulis, E. 1999. Setting achievement targets for school children. *Education Economics* 7(2), 101–119.

Thanassoulis, E., and Portela, M. C. S. 2002. School outcomes: Sharing the responsibility between pupil and school. *Education Economics*, 10(2), 183–207.

Thursby, J. G. 2000. What do we say about ourselves and what does it mean? Yet another look at Economics department research. *Journal of Economic Literature*, 38, 383–404.

Tofallis, C. 2012. A different approach to university rankings. *Higher Education*, 63(1), 1–18.

Tomkins, C., and Green, R. 1988. An experiment in the use of data envelopment analysis for evaluating the efficiency of UK university departments of accounting. *Financial Accountability & Management*, 4, 147–164.

Tyagi, P., Yadav, S. P., and Singh, S. P. 2009. Relative performance of academic departments using DEA with sensitivity analysis. *Evaluation and Program Planning*, 32, 168–177.

Van der Wende, M. 2008. Rankings and classifications in higher education: A European perspective. *Higher Education*, 23, 49–71.

Verbert, K., Manouselis, N., Drachsler, H., and Duval, E. 2012. Dataset-driven research to support learning and knowledge analytics. *Educational Technology & Society*, 15 (3), 133–148.

Wolff, A. and Zdrahal, Z. 2012. Improving retention by identifying and supporting "at-risk" students. *Educause Review Online*, http://www.educause.edu/ero/article/improving-retention-identifying-andsupporting-risk-students.

Chapter 6

Using Data Analytics to Benchmark Schools: The Case of Portugal

Maria C. Andrade e Silva and Ana S. Camanho

Contents

6.1 Introduction

In the majority of European countries, the evaluation of schools is at the heart of the educational system as a means to guarantee the quality of education. Every year, in most countries around the world, students perform national exams. Their results are analyzed by several stakeholders, including governmental agencies, the media, and researchers on educational issues. At present, advances in information and communication technology (ICT) and data analysis techniques allow schools to make use of massive amounts of data in their daily management. This chapter focuses in particular on the use of students' data to benchmark schools. It illustrates the potential contribution of the information gathered and analyzed through data analytics to promote the continuous improvement of schools' educational processes.

Benchmarking can be defined as a continuous process of performance comparison among different organizations, with the purpose of sharing best practices and improving performance (Beckford, 1998). Benchmarking is a recurrent and daily activity in the life of most individuals and organizations. Measuring performance in absolute terms is often less valuable than making comparisons with peers, since in general the assessment of the potential for improvement requires comparisons among units performing similar tasks. In a context where it is important for organizations to engage in improvements and gain competitiveness, benchmarking emerges as a useful tool to achieve this goal.

Key performance indicators (KPIs) are commonly used in quantitative benchmarking processes. However, benchmarking based on KPIs presents some problems. The first is the assumption of independence among KPIs, which often does not apply in practice. Trade-offs between different performance dimensions are usually in place, and it is difficult to identify the best performers, as the firms that excel in some aspects may underperform in other dimensions. The second problem is the assumption of constant returns to scale (since KPIs are generally scale independent). However, in practice, performance often needs to be assessed in light of the scale of operations. To overcome these problems and to be able to identify the best performers in a simple way, without dropping relevant information, it is common to use aggregate performance indicators or composite indicators, which enable the obtaining of a single summary measure of performance. Several techniques can be used to construct aggregate indicators (OECD, 2008a). This chapter reviews some of the approaches that have been applied to the educational context, focusing on the use of data analytics to evaluate schools (Section 6.2).

Section 6.3 explores in detail the case of secondary education in Portugal, where attempts to evaluate schools have gained momentum in recent years. New perspectives on school evaluation, as well as ideas on how the information can be used to improve the educational process at the school level are presented in this section.

6.2 Data Analytics in Education: Theory and Practice

6.2.1 Theory

The education field is rich in analytics including benchmarking studies. The idea of comparing schools' performance is quite old and dates back to the 1960s, when the U.S. Department of Education commissioned a group of social scientists to analyze educational equality at a national level. Coleman was the leader of the group that surveyed more than 150,000 students. The report, known as the Coleman Report (Coleman, 1966), concluded that schools do not matter and that the results of students are mainly determined by their socio-economic background. Jencks et al. (1972) followed up with further studies of American high schools, reinforcing the belief that schools make little difference to the life chances of pupils.

These results were disappointing for those with responsibilities for public education. A closer examination of the methods employed by the American studies revealed that their conclusions were based on macro-variables, such as the size of the school site, the nature of the facilities available, and the resources given to institutions. Other researchers started to collect information on micro-variables, such as staff behavior, pupils' attitudes, or the social climate of individual schools, and a second wave of research studies emerged. This trend, called *school effectiveness research*, started in England with the *Fifteen Thousand Hours* study (Rutter et al., 1979). This study used a new methodology to identify a set of student outcomes (involving aspects beyond learning the formal curriculum, such as the acquisition of social skills, self-control, or self-esteem) and to measure the range of effectiveness in a sample of schools by taking into account the different backgrounds and attributes of pupils when entering these schools. This study was praised for its pioneering approach that challenged the Coleman/Jencks thesis on the impotence of schooling, advocating that schools can make a difference. This resulted in the subsequent production of a large number of academic studies performing school comparisons and benchmarking.

Within the vast literature produced on the topic of school effectiveness, comparative studies of schools attempted to address the following issues: (1) to prove that schools could make a difference, (2) to identify the factors that increase the effectiveness of schools, (3) to analyze the efficiency of schools under a perspective of cost minimization, or simply (4) to identify benchmarking schools that could serve as best practices for other schools. These different types of analysis can be grouped within two strands. The first is the analysis of *school effectiveness*, where the most effective schools are identified and the factors underlying their effectiveness are studied. School effectiveness is mostly used in the literature as synonymous with value added (VA), since the most effective schools are usually those that are able to add more value to their students. The second strand is the analysis of *school efficiency*, where schools are regarded as consuming a set of inputs that are transformed into a set of outputs (outcomes). In this process, efficient schools are those that consume the least inputs (e.g., money and teacher's time) to produce the most outputs (e.g., graduates, high grades, and success rates). In the words of Mayston (2003), school efficiency studies measure the value for money, while school effectiveness studies measure VA.

These two strands often consider different units of analysis and employ different methodologies. Generally, pupil-level data are used to assess the VA or the effectiveness of schools, and students' results are observed over time such that scores on entry and on exit are matched. The most employed methodology for this type of study is multilevel statistical models (see e.g., OECD, 2008b). The use of these models is advocated for dealing with pupil-level data because they allow a simultaneous quantification of school effects (or the variance between schools) and an analysis of the drivers of student success. Some examples of multilevel studies applying pupil-level data include Ladd and Walsh (2002), Hanushek and Taylor (1990), Gray et al. (1996), and O'Donoghue et al. (1997).

Despite the methodological predominance of multilevel studies for pupil data analyses, frontier models have also been applied to pupil-level data (e.g., Portela and Thanassoulis, 2001; De Witte et al., 2010; Portela and Camanho, 2010; Thieme et al., 2013). Similarly, multilevel models have also been applied to school-level data to infer conclusions on school districts or countries, despite the prevalence of frontier models for studies involving the specification of schools as the unit of assessment (for recent reviews, see De Witte and López-Torres, 2017 and Johnes, 2015).

Recently, with the advent of business intelligence and Big Data methodologies, new methods are emerging to analyze pupil-level data and investigate patterns of student profiles and determinants of their success. Data mining in education is growing, although it remains a field where few publications reach international journals. In the review of Baker and Yacef (2009), the most cited articles are published in conference proceedings. The emphasis of this literature remains on the comparison of methodologies rather than on the implications of the analysis for decision making. The computer science community, dominating business intelligence techniques, has traditionally regarded conference proceedings as privileged publication outlets due to the speed of publication in a scientific field where technological evolution is extremely fast. Multidisciplinary research connecting state-of-the-art business intelligence with education services research is still emerging. We expect, in the near future, to see publications intertwining these topics available in top-ranked journals.

Regarding the use of frontier techniques in educational efficiency studies, according to the literature review by De Witte and López-Torres (2017), data envelopment analysis (DEA) is more prevalent than stochastic frontier analysis (SFA). Grosskopf et al. (2009) noted that the results of the studies are sensitive to the methodological approach followed, so researchers were advised not to rely exclusively on a specific method, but instead to use a mixed model approach to guide educational policy decisions.

Frontier methods allow the identification of benchmark schools, optimal cost levels, or optimal input and output levels. Some examples of DEA models applied to the measurement of school efficiency can be seen in the pioneering work by Bessent and Bessent (1980), Mancebón and Bandrés (1999), Kirjavainen and Loikkanen (1998), Grosskopf et al. (1999), and Haelermans and De Witte (2012). Examples of recent SFA models applied to schools can be seen in Cordero-Ferrera et al. (2011), Perelman and Santín (2011), Kirjavainen (2012), and Crespo-Cebada et al. (2014).

Few studies combine efficiency and effectiveness analysis despite their clear complementarity. As mentioned in De Witte and López-Torres (2017), the "efficiency and effectiveness literatures are currently rather distinct literatures." Three studies are exceptions that have attempted to bring together these fields of study. Two of these focus on higher education institutions (which are out of the scope of this chapter). As a result, only the study of Cherchye et al. (2015) simultaneously addresses the efficiency and effectiveness of schools. In particular, the authors compute a measure of school productivity and a measure of school performance (where inputs considered in the productivity analysis are disregarded). Clearly, the words *productivity* and *performance* (used in Cherchye et al., 2015) are related to the concepts that we use here of efficiency and effectiveness, respectively. According to this approach, schools can show a profile where performance is lower than productivity (suggesting that higher resources could foster even higher outputs) or a profile where performance is higher than productivity (suggesting that resource capacity is not being fully utilized).

Most efficiency and effectiveness studies on education are conducted at a national level, but cross-country analyses are increasing in number due to the availability of international datasets, such as Programme for International Student Assessment (PISA), Trends in International Mathematics and Science Study (TIMSS), and Progress in International Reading Literacy Study (PIRLS). Cross-country analyses are important for policy making since they allow the benchmarking of educational policies. In addition, these international datasets allow a better assessment of human capital (traditionally measured in terms of quantity of education that can now be supplemented with measures of its quality). These datasets have been used in studies where the impact of human capital on the economic growth of nations is analyzed (see e.g., Hanushek and Kimko, 2000; Hanushek and Woessmann, 2010). Most notably, the Organization for Economic Co-operation and Development (OECD) also produces very comprehensive reports with student results and benchmarking exercises across schools internationally. All results are publicly available at http://www.oecd.org/pisa/, where there is also the possibility of exploring the PISA data and accessing a set of indicators for several countries using the Education GPS, available within the PISA website. The TIMSS and PIRLS website (http://timssandpirls.bc.edu/) also has available reports describing the assessment framework and results obtained.

A recent application of frontier methodologies to European countries can be found in Cordero et al. (2017), where the efficiency of primary schools was assessed based on PIRLS test results. An interesting finding from this paper is that country variables seem to have a higher impact on student results than school variables, meaning that national educational policies do have an impact on student results. Along the same lines, but using a different methodology and database, Woessmann (2003) estimated, among other things, the percentage of variation in student results (in math and science TIMSS tests) that is due to the class, school, and country effects. Results suggested that the highest percentage of total variation is due to classes, followed by schools, and finally by the country. Schools and countries therefore play a considerable role in explaining differences in the achievement of students, but classes are usually more heterogeneous than schools themselves. Regardless of the impact of the country or school on test results, the fact is that the use of the international datasets provides an important means to assess national educational policies, enabling the benchmarking of schools within or between countries.

Note that cross-country data are frequently used for within-country analysis, given the richness of the datasets available. National databases on educational achievements are often not accessible to researchers. This is the case in Portugal, where, despite recent efforts to improve the accountability of schools and to disclose data on school performance (see next section), data on the socio-economic background of students remain unavailable for research purposes (see e.g., Faria and Portela, 2016 for a recent application of PISA data relating to Portuguese students).

6.2.2 Practice

In recent years, there has been an increase in public awareness of education in most countries worldwide. This means that research results need to be made available not only to policy makers and researchers, but also to the general public, such that informed choices of schools can be made. This movement has been called *accountability*, and has, among other impacts, increased the transparency and general knowledge of public institutions (including schools).

In this context, in the majority of European countries, the evaluation of schools is used as a means to guarantee the quality of education. This is both an aim of educational authorities, and an important topic for families. School performance indicators have been published by the media since the 1980s. England and France are the best-known examples, which disclose data on the percentage of successful students in the final exams. The debate in the scientific community regarding the viability and usefulness of these initiatives was intense, and several studies were conducted (e.g., Karsten et al., 2001) to explore the positive and negative sides of these initiatives.

In England, the publication of these indicators was intended to allow families to choose the best school for their children. This was expected to create a competitive system that would promote the attainment of efficiency in schools' administration and the increased decentralization of schools management. Conversely, in

France, the main driver was to create a culture of accountability with respect to the provision of public services.

The presentation of schools' performance indicators has evolved considerably over time, and different approaches have been followed in different countries. Since 1991, the Department of National Education in France publishes a report describing the "state of education," corresponding to an evaluation of the impact of the policies implemented. In 1992, league tables were introduced in the United Kingdom Shortly after, in 1993, the Tennessee Value-Added Assessment System (TVAAS) was introduced in Tennessee, in the United States. These tools are still available today, despite having been subject to several enhancements over the years. Most of these relate to the methodologies adopted to estimate the contextualized VA by schools, seen as the most appropriate way to benchmark schools, as well as the availability of more comprehensive datasets to describe schools and pupils.

In Portugal, the disclosure of data on schools' performance started in 2001, almost two decades after several other countries. The results started to be made available by the media, and focused exclusively on the results of national exams at the end of secondary education. The Ministry of Education provided raw exam data to the newspapers that presented the data as arithmetic averages of exam results per school. In 2002, the Ministry of Education followed a different approach and made available a study, named "Proposal for the Ranking of Secondary Schools," which followed a methodology designed by the Ministry, rather than relying only on media initiatives for the treatment of data. This approach was discontinued due to severe criticisms of the study, and since then, the Ministry of Education has continued to provide the media with raw exam results. At the same time, it improved the process of collecting student data, such that socio-economic information was also available. However, the Ministry did not provide contextual variables, in addition to raw exam results, to allow a more informative ranking of schools by the media until 2013. The socio-economic information is, however, collected at a more aggregate level than the school, is not available for private schools, and the Ministry can only provide it after a one-year lag. These are limitations that prevent a more informative and contextualized analysis of school rankings in Portugal.

With the development of ICT, several Internet-based tools have become available to publish information regarding schools' performance. The publication of results on school performance is normally the responsibility of national governments through their agencies. Some examples of the information made available online by these agencies are shown in Table 6.1.

In the United Kingdom, the Department for Education publishes performance tables. The user can select any particular school and gain access to details on the school demographics, as well as its performance on a number of indicators, including a measure of VA. Also in the United Kingdom, there is a web-based application called *RAISE* "report and analysis for improvement through school self-evaluation" (www.raiseonline.org), which enables schools to look at performance data in greater depth as part of their self-evaluation process. This application is, however,

Table 6.1 Some Internet-Based Tools Available in Some Countries

Country	Instrument	Website	Responsibility	Indicators Available
Portugal	Infoescolas	www.infoescolas.mec.pt	Ministry of Education	Users can select a school and have access to demographic indicators, progression rates, students' rates of retention, contextualized indicators of results, and an indicator comparing schools' internal grades with exam grades.
United Kingdom	Performance tables	www.compare-school-performance.service.gov.uk	Department for Education	Users can select a school and learn about its demographics and performance indicators, such as key stage achievements, progress of students, performance at A-levels, value-added scores and absence indicators.
France	Les indicateurs de resultats des lycees	www.education.gouv.fr/cid3014/les-indicateurs-de-resultats-des-lycees.html	Ministry of Education	Users can select a school and have access to indicators of the rate of success in the baccalauréat and the probability of success in the baccalauréat for students whose education took place entirely within that school.
Norway	Skoleporten	skoleporten.udir.no	Ministry of Education	Users can select a school and access key indicators of results, resource use and learning environment. Assessment grades from classroom work, grades from exams and results from national tests are also available.
United States (Tennessee)	Tennessee VA Assessment System	tn.gov/education/topic/tvaas	Private system of SAS statistical software company	School VA measures are available for each course and school. All measures of VA are defined in terms of student educational progress. District value-added reports are also available. Teacher reports are also prepared, but are confidential (only available to teachers and administrators).

not available to the general public, but just to schools (for details, see Ray, 2006; Ray et al., 2009).

France, like most countries in Europe, has an institutional website where the government publishes schools' performance indicators per academic year, enabling their comparison. The criteria used are mainly based on the grades of the *baccalauréat*, the national exam taken at the end of secondary education.

In Norway, Skoleporten is a national school accountability system, which contains publicly available data on indicators for results, resource use, and learning environment (details in Haegeland, 2006). The Swedish National Agency for Education also publishes data on all levels of the education system. Apart from data on several different indicators, the agency also publishes expected results for each individual school, estimated using linear regression.

In the United States, the TVAAS, developed by Sanders et al. (1997), has a public website where the general public can access reports on VA. This system is owned by SAS Educational Value-Added Assessment System (SAS® EVAAS®) and has been adopted by several other states in the United States.

In Portugal, the Ministry of Education developed the public website Infoescolas that enables the analysis of several indicators of schools' performance. The criteria considered include the progression rates (based on student's results on national exams at two points in time: the beginning and the end of the cycle), students' rates of retention, contextualized indicators of results, and an indicator comparing schools' internal grades with exam grades.

Note that the trend toward Internet-benchmarking platforms that allow online and immediate comparisons between production units can also be found in sectors beyond education. For example, the construction industry has a benchmarking platform icBench (icbench.net) (Costa et al., 2007) available in Portugal, whereas in the United States there is Benchmarking and Metrics (construction-institute.org), and in the United Kingdom there is KPIzone (kpizone.com). None of these examples, however, use DEA to carry out performance assessments. An example of a platform that allowed aggregate assessments through DEA was iDEAs-W (see Johnson and McGinnis, 2011). This platform was targeted at warehouses or other industrial systems and combined benchmarking and DEA to allow managers to benchmark their performance against others (apparently the platform is no longer available). Bogetoft and Nielsen (2005) report an Internet-based benchmarking system applied to Danish commercial and savings banks that incorporates a DEA model. The developed platform is currently being commercialized and applied to other industries (Ibensoft Aps, 2013).

6.2.3 BESP Platform: A Practical Example of Data Analytics in Education

As we have seen in the previous section, there are many alternatives for visualizing schools' performance on the Internet. Most of these alternatives rely on a number of indicators that are typically displayed on a comparative basis. The BESP platform (Benchmarking of Portuguese Secondary Schools) is an example of a benchmarking site for Portuguese secondary schools, with the distinctive feature (not available in any of the systems shown in Table 6.1) of incorporating frontier models and reporting aggregate performance indicators for schools. The indicators shown take into account not only students' outcomes on exit, but also the inputs used to produce such outcomes. In that sense, the aggregate indicators can be seen as a measure of the school-VA.

BESP was created in 2010 and is available at http://www.catolicabs.porto.ucp.pt/besp/. It can be used by both the general public and school managers, although the available information differs according to the type of user registration. The private area, designed for school managers, is only accessible with a username and password. The general public have access to a set of indicators computed using data from national exam databases. School managers can consult the same indicators, but they also have access to a private area with other indicators and an interface for uploading additional data (see also Portela et al., 2011). BESP is mainly a visual tool that is able to show performance on individual indicators and an aggregate indicator for a selected school. In both cases, schools can be compared with the set of all schools in the country or with any other comparative set (e.g., schools of the same type [private/public] or schools in the same district). The comparison between a school and its peers is done using percentiles.

The information displayed in BESP for an individual indicator is illustrated in Figure 6.1. Graph (a) shows the distribution of the indicator "average results on national exam," with the percentile for the selected school highlighted. In this case, the school chosen lies at the 73.39 percentile, meaning that 73.39% of the schools included in the comparator set obtained the same or a worse result, on average, in the national exams at the end of secondary education.

In the radar graph of Figure 6.1b, details are shown for the percentiles in which the school lies on each exam included in the overall average for the school. The radar shows the subjects where the school has a good percentile position (e.g., subjects 1 and 7) and those where the school has a bad percentile position (e.g., subject 6). These radars are shown for individual indicators, as well as for two indicators simultaneously, where direct comparisons of schools' results can bring important insights. For example, the radars can show the results obtained internally at the school and those obtained in national exams, allowing one to draw quick conclusions regarding the internal undervaluation or overvaluation of student performance by comparison with national standards.

BESP also allows the exploration of the evolution of performance over time for each indicator, through bar charts. This functionality is only available within the private area for school managers.

Figure 6.2 shows an illustrative example concerning the evolution of average results on national exams of secondary education. The left panel shows the evolution

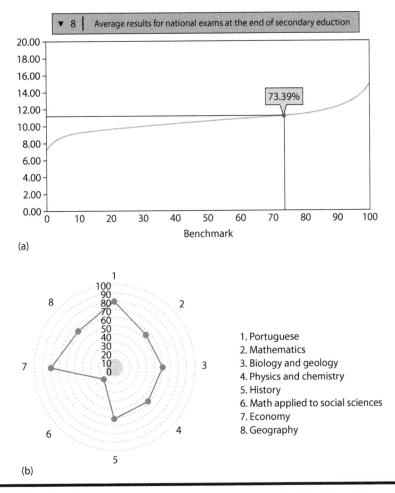

Figure 6.1 BESP—Results for the indicator average classification of the school in final exams. (Picture taken from Portela, M.C.A.S. et al., *Benchmarking: And International Journal*, **18(2), 240–260, 2011.)**

of average exam grades and the right panel shows the evolution of the same indicator presented in relative terms (divided by the average of national grades).

In the private area, there is also a customized tool that allows schools to choose the set of indicators that they want to aggregate to construct a composite performance indicator. This indicator is intended to enable schools to conduct robust quantitative self-assessments of performance. This tool is based on DEA; therefore, schools can know not only what their aggregate performance score is, but also which benchmark schools this score was based upon. DEA is a linear programing-based benchmarking tool that has been widely applied in the school context since the seminal work of Charnes et al. (1978). It looks at schools as a production process

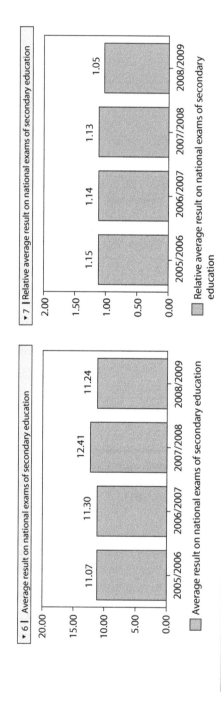

Figure 6.2   BESP—evolution of results over time for the indicator average classification in final exams, defined in absolute and relative terms. (From Portela, M.C.A.S. et al., *Benchmarking: An International Journal,* **18(2), 240–260, 2011.)**

Table 6.2   Set of Inputs and Outputs Available within BESP

Inputs	Outputs
Average grades in Portuguese in years t-2 and t-3	Average grades in the kth national exam in year t
Average grades in mathematics in years t-2 and t-3	Percentage of school students that took exam k
Parents' average years of schooling	Percentage of students concluding secondary education in the "normal" three years
Economic context of the school (computed based on the number of pupils in the school who receive subsidies from the state)	Percentage of students who proceeded to university
	Percentage of students who did not abandon the school

Note: k = Portuguese, mathematics, biology and geology, physics and chemistry, history, economy, geography, mathematics for social sciences.

using a set of inputs that are transformed into a set of outputs. For details on the methodology, see, for example, Thanassoulis et al. (2008).

Regarding the customized DEA assessment, it starts with the choice of inputs and outputs by the school, from the list shown in Table 6.2.

Outputs relate mainly to the grades of students in a number of subjects (whose choice is customized), but the platform is designed to include additional outputs such as the percentage of students in the school taking the exam, the percentage of students finishing secondary education in three years, or the percentage of students proceeding on to university. These additional outputs are only available if schools upload this information. Some of the registered schools have done so, but the set is still small for comparative purposes, and as a result these outputs cannot effectively be chosen. On the input side, a similar situation exists, where only the first two inputs are available for benchmarking purposes, corresponding to the grades on entry for a similar cohort of students (the cohort is not the same due to transfers of students between schools). Ideally, other inputs should also be taken into account, such as the indicator of the education level of students' parents and the economic context of the school (both present in Table 6.2 but not used in the BESP assessments due to the unavailability of the data).

After the selection of inputs and outputs, BESP enables solving online, in real time, DEA models with the inputs and outputs selected (see also Portela et al., 2011; 2012). After that, the results displayed by BESP are (1) the overall efficiency score of the school; (2) a radar showing how the observed inputs and outputs of

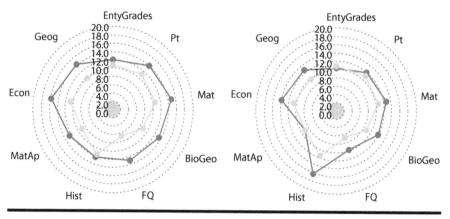

Figure 6.3 A school being compared with its peers in BESP. (From Portela, M.C.A.S. et al., *Benchmarking: An International Journal,* **18(2), 240–260, 2011.)**

the school compare to its potential attainments (targets); and (3) radars showing how the school compares with its peers, such that the school can identify the factors where other schools are doing better than itself. An example of such radars is shown in Figure 6.3 for a school with an efficiency score of 79.2%. Its inputs and outputs are represented by the inner line in Figure 6.3, and the indicators of its two peers (represented in the graph on the left and on the right) are identified by the outer line.

The peers have similar or slightly higher inputs (taken as aggregate grades on entry in this case—"EntryGrades") than the school assessed. Despite that, they both achieve clearly higher average scores in most of the subjects. The assessment shows the evaluation of the selected school against all schools in the country (but an alternative comparative set could have been used). Note that in BESP, the names of the peer schools are actually shown to the registered school such that best practices can be shared and emulated.

According to Google Analytics, the BESP website had over 5000 users and almost 8000 sessions over the last two years. Of the users, 76% were Portuguese, 6% were Brazilian, and 5% were from the United States. Clearly, the fact that the website is written in Portuguese is a handicap for foreign users (whose interest is mainly on the framework and not actually on the use of the results presented). The website is valued by the schools and the general public, but the use of the private area by schools and the availability of updated information are below the original expectation at the time of the site development. One possible reason for this is the fact that schools still have some resistance to analytic frameworks and tend to find quantitative/graphical analysis hard to interpret. We believe that by the time millennials (the generation that has grown up with computers) reach school boards, this reality will have changed drastically and this type of website, with enhanced analytical capabilities, will be used in the day-to-day management of schools.

Overall, we can state that BESP has helped schools to use data (publicly available or private) in a different and interactive way. Some schools are intense users of BESP and base their internal evaluation reports on this framework, as its visual interface and the imbedded possibility of constructing customized pdf reports is a handy and useful tool. Feedback from these schools, and also from other users, has been positive. The aggregate indicator constructed in BESP through DEA could work as a good basis for undertaking fairer rankings of schools. However, the ranking methodology of the media in Portugal, using the data made available by the Ministry of Education, is a very simple procedure, mostly based on exam results. Given the vast audience with interest in school rankings, this is understandable, as procedures that are more complex may be difficult for the general public to interpret. However, for policy-making purposes it is clear that tools like those presented in BESP are necessary. It is expected that the proliferation of analytic tools and analytic literacy will increase the importance of initiatives such as BESP.

6.3 Innovative Approaches for School Evaluation Taking Advantage of Data Analytics

Schools' benchmarking can be done from several perspectives. The BESP example presented here showed a comparison between schools adopting a value-added perspective, where schools are compared based on their students' results on their exit from secondary education contextualized by their grades on entry. Another interesting perspective from which to evaluate secondary schools could be to predict students' achievements at the next educational stage (university studies). Despite its relevance, this issue is often disregarded, due to the unavailability of data linking students' results in secondary schools to university results. The grades obtained by university students and/or the results of satisfaction questionnaires of students in higher education have been used for several other purposes, including comparisons of performance of university professors (Johnes, 2006) or faculty/department benchmarking (Halkos et al., 2012). However, few authors have analyzed the grades obtained in higher education and compared those with the grades of students on entry for the purpose of benchmarking the secondary schools of origin. The study by Cabral and Pechincha (2014) is an example of this type of study, which intended to explore the progression of students from the University of Porto, Portugal, during their higher education degrees. One of the explanatory variables considered was the school of origin, which had a significant impact on the performance of university students. In particular, it was concluded that students originating from public schools were more likely to be in the top 10% of their degrees in terms of the average classification than those originating from private schools.

Note that we can also include this topic within the vast literature on the analysis of determinants of university students' success, which is relevant to inform decision makers at various levels. For example, secondary school managers should rethink their pedagogical approaches given the results obtained by students in the next educational stage, national authorities can reflect on the adequacy of university entry requirements and criteria, and university managers can design efficient methods to follow up and promote enhanced academic achievements based on students' expected results given their paths in secondary education. As shown in Smith and Naylor (2005), the type of school attended prior to entrance to university may have a significant impact on university performance. In the same research vein, initial work on the subject by Sear (1983) analyzed the relationship in the United Kingdom, between attainment in secondary and university education. Conclusions point to weak correlations due to changing motivations and attitudes toward schooling in university students, and because the course chosen in university may be unrelated to the knowledge acquired in secondary education. The author concludes that exams at secondary education are poor measures of achievement as they can vary by board, by year, by subject of entry, and by university.

Next, we describe an exploratory study following the research line initiated by Cabral and Pechincha (2014), where we examine the performance of secondary schools based on their ability to promote student achievement during higher education. In particular, we focus only on the first-year achievements at university and we compare secondary schools based on two outcomes of students at the university. Note that this type of study is now possible due to the existence of databases that store more complete and richer datasets, as the storage capacity of servers increases, and enhanced data analytic tools become available.

6.3.1 Data Used and Indicators

In order to compare secondary schools on the basis of the achievement of their students in their first year of higher education, we used two years of data for students entering Católica Porto Business School (CPBS, a private university in the city of Porto) and the Faculty of Engineering of the University of Porto (FEUP, a public university in the city of Porto). We considered only the results at the end of the first year in higher education, because after that the university may have a stronger effect on determining students' achievements than the secondary school of origin. The students from CPBS attended economics and business degree programs (whose first year and entry requirements are the same) and the students from FEUP attended several different engineering degree programs (10 in total). Given the heterogeneity in entry requirements, degrees, and academic years considered, we used a measure of students' achievement that could be used for comparisons in these circumstances. The measure adopted in this study was the classification percentile of students on entry and exit, both within the degree attended and within the cohort of students enrolled in the same academic year. Using such a measure, it is possible to directly compare the percentile on entry with the percentile on exit for each student, irrespective of the degree attended or the year of analysis. As a result, if a given student in a given year entered a university degree in the 60th percentile, and if after one year of university studies that student was in the 40th percentile, this would imply that the entry grade may have been over-evaluated. This can be interpreted as a sign that the secondary school attended may have been less effective in the preparation of the student for higher education than another school from which a student entered in the same achievement percentile and ended the first year in the 90th percentile. Clearly, other student-related effects may be present and affect the progression of students, but in this section, we will restrict ourselves to a descriptive analysis of some indicators, and report only average values of indicators for schools with a significant number of students analyzed.

The indicators considered are listed next. Note that the classification on entry depends on the entry requirement defined for each degree at each faculty. For example, in Católica Porto Business School, the classification on entry is the average of internal school grades and the national maths exam; however, for the Faculty of Engineering the classification on entry is a weighted average of the internal school grades (with a weight of 50%) and two different national exams (each with a weight of 25%), but these exams differ between degrees (one of the exams is mathematics, but the other can be physics and chemistry, biology and geology, or Portuguese, depending on the course that the student is applying for).

1. Number of European Credit Transfer and Accumulation System (ECTS) credits completed at the end of first year (ECTSdone)
2. Percentile of average grade at the end of the first year in university (PUnivG)
3. Percentile of classification on entry (PEntryG)
4. Difference between (2) and (3) (PUnivG–PEntryG)

Indicators (1) and (2) reflect students' achievements at university. Indicator (1) is important for complementing indicator (2), as it is a measure of the quantity of ECTS completed with success, while indicator (2) is a measure of quality in the completion of courses. Indicator (4) measures the difference between the percentile of average grades at the end of the first year and the percentile of classification on entry (indicator [3] is based on students' rankings on entry to the university). This allows one to have an idea of whether the student improved or lost ranking positions during university studies. If students from a specific school tend to show negative differences in terms of this indicator, this suggests that the school did not prepare students adequately for university studies (despite having prepared them well for national exams ensuring their admission to the university).

6.3.2 Discussion of Results

6.3.2.1 Descriptive Statistics

We studied the grades for a population of 2075 students, from two different academic years, 2013/2014 and 2014/2015, in the two faculties previously mentioned (CPBS and FEUP). Table 6.3 reports the number of students per university and per year.

Students attended 10 different degrees in FEUP and 2 in CPBS, but the students in CPBS were aggregated, as their curricula were the same during the first year. The percentage of students analyzed belonging to each degree is shown in Figure 6.4.

In this analysis, we will focus essentially on two outcomes: the number of ECTS completed at the end of the first year of a university course and the difference between the percentile at the university and the percentile on entry. Irrespective of that, in Table 6.4 we present some descriptive statistics for all our variables per course.

Table 6.4 shows that average entry grades (EntryG) differ between degrees, with the degree in mining and geo-environmental engineering receiving students with the lowest average entry grades and the degree in bioengineering receiving students with the highest average entry grades. Despite these differences, the scores at the end of the first year (UnivG) are not as different as the grades on entry. As the percentiles are computed within each degree, the averages of the indicators associated with the percentiles on entry (PEntryG) and at the end of the first year (PUnivG) are very close to 0.5 (deviations from the value of 0.5 are due to ties). Using the same logic, the indicator of the difference between the university grade and entry grade percentiles (PUnivG–PEntryG) is, on average, very close to zero for all degrees. When this indicator assumes a positive value for a particular student, it means that the student increased his or her rank in university when compared with his or her rank on entry, both computed within the cohort of students enrolled in the same degree in the same academic year. Negative differences mean a deterioration in the rank position of the student. Under normal conditions, we expect that students will keep their rank position. If they do not, we expect that the number increasing their rank position will

Table 6.3   Distribution of Students

	Year	
	2013	*2014*
FEUP	889	795
UCP	200	191

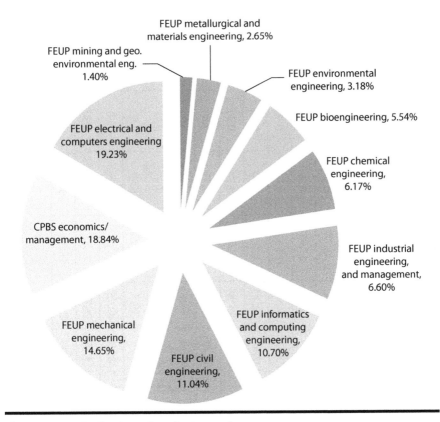

Figure 6.4 Distribution of students per degree.

be about the same as the number decreasing their rank position. As a result, we expect the distribution of this variable to be about normal. This result was confirmed for all degrees through a Kolmogorov-Smirnov test, except for two of the engineering degrees.

When computing correlations between grades on entry and grades at the end of the first year and ECTS, we found that the correlation between EntryG and UnivG varied between 0.209 (non-significant) for the degree in metallurgical and materials engineering, and 0.616 (statistically significant) for the degree in mining and geo-environmental engineering. This shows that for some degrees, entry grades may be a good predictor of performance, but for others they are poor predictors. When performance is measured in terms of the ECTS completed, the conclusion is similar, as the correlation between grades on entry and ECTS varies between −0.069 (non-significant) for the degree in metallurgical and materials engineering, and 0.54 (statistically significant) for the degree in civil engineering (see Table 6.5).

Table 6.4 Average Values of Indicators per Course

	No. Students	EntryG	ECTS	UnivG	PEntryG	PUnivG	PUnivG − PEntryG
CPBS Economics/management	391	152.86	44.3	12.77	0.52	0.51	−0.01
FEUP Electrical and computer engineering	399	157.89	35.16	13.55	0.51	0.50	0
FEUP Mechanical engineering	304	172.42	41.96	13.42	0.51	0.50	−0.01
FEUP Civil engineering	229	137.57	32.49	12.72	0.50	0.50	0
FEUP Informatics and computing engineering	222	167.83	46.98	13.63	0.51	0.50	0
FEUP Industrial engineering and management	137	180.28	50.57	14.21	0.51	0.50	−0.01
FEUP Chemical engineering	128	164.23	43.1	13.23	0.50	0.50	0
FEUP Bioengineering	115	181.10	44.45	14.58	0.51	0.51	0
FEUP Environmental engineering	66	143.78	39.7	13.32	0.50	0.50	0
FEUP Metallurgical and materials engineering	55	148.40	40.25	13.04	0.51	0.50	0
FEUP Mining and geo-environmental eng.	29	129.16	26.83	12.82	0.51	0.50	−0.01
Average		**159.95**	**41.03**	**13.35**	**0.51**	**0.50**	**0.00**

Table 6.5 Correlation with Entry Grades per Course

	University Grade	ECTS Done
CPBS Economics/management	.561[a]	.412 [a]
FEUP Mining and geo-environmental eng.	.616 [a]	.445[b]
FEUP Bioengineering	.539[a]	.430[a]
FEUP Civil engineering	.441[a]	.540[a]
FEUP Environmental engineering	0.216	0.12
FEUP Electrical and computer engineering	.327[a]	.316[a]
FEUP Industrial engineering and management	.487[a]	.352[a]
FEUP Informatics and computing engineering	.514 [a]	.349[a]
FEUP Mechanical engineering	.422[a]	.322[a]
FEUP Metallurgical and materials engineering	0.209	−0.069
FEUP Chemical engineering	.551[a]	.319[a]

[a] Correlation is significant at the 0.01 level (2-tailed).
[b] Correlation is significant at the 0.05 level (2-tailed).

6.3.2.2 *Influence of School Type*

An analysis of our two indicators of students' achievements (ECTS completed and classification percentile at the end of the first year) per secondary school type reveals that public school students, on average, perform better than private school students. The distribution of these two outcome indicators is presented in Figure 6.5a and b by the secondary school type (private/public) of university students. Public school students complete a higher number of ECTS at the end of the first year (average of 42.61 ECTS for public school students against 38.69 ECTS for private school students), and the classification percentile at the end of the first year is also higher (average of 0.54 for public school students against 0.44 for private school students). The difference between the percentile of the grades at the end of the first year of university and on entry (see Figure 6.5c) also reveal better performance by public school students (a value of 0.06 for public school students against a value of −0.08 for private). These differences are statistically significant. However, regarding the students' percentile on entry, the students from public and private schools are equivalent (see Figure 6.5d), meaning that differences in students' potential are only revealed during the first year of higher education.

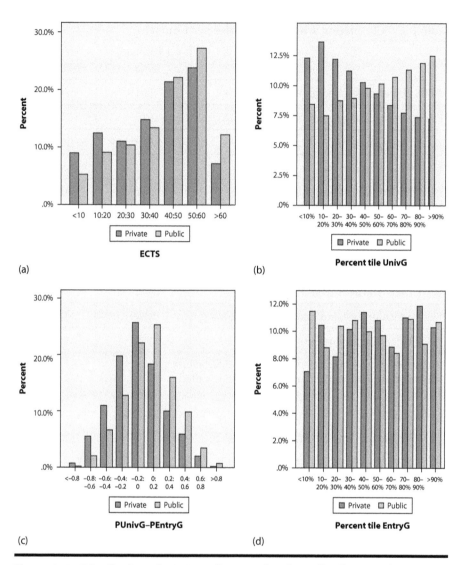

Figure 6.5 **Distribution of ECTS credits completed (a), distribution of percentile grades at the end of first year at university (PUnivG) (b), difference between the rank at the end of first year and on entry (PUnivG–PEntryG) (c), distribution of percentile grades on entry (PEntryG) (d), per type of secondary school previously attended by university students.**

Figure 6.5a shows clearly that for students completing a lower number of ECTS (up to 40 ECTS), the percentage from private schools is higher than the percentage from public schools. Conversely, for students completing a higher number of ECTS (above 40 ECTS), the percentage of students from public schools is larger

Table 6.6   Descriptive Statistics per Type of School

	Private	Public
N	835	1240
EntryG	160.83	159.35
ECTS	38.69	4261
UnivG	1296	13.62
PEntryG	0.53	0.5
PUnivG	0.44	0.54
PUnivG–PentryG	–0.09	0.05

than from private schools. Figure 6.5d shows that a higher percentage of private school students have negative values for the difference between the percentile at the end of the first year in university and on entry (meaning deterioration in the rank position), while the students having positive values (improvement in rank position) mostly come from public secondary schools.

Some descriptive statistics of our variables per type of school are shown in Table 6.6 (without distinguishing the degrees). These values show that private school students have, on average, a higher entry grade and a higher rank on the entry classification in relation to the cohort of students in the same degree and academic year. However, at the end of the first year in university, their rank is, on average, lower than that of colleagues from public schools. This suggests that private schools over-evaluated student grades, which puts students from these schools at an advantage for university entrance (this advantage is not, however, sustained after one year at university).

6.3.2.3 Influence of the School

Regarding the influence of the school, we analyzed for each school the average number of ECTS completed, the average percentile of the grades at the end of the first year at university, and the average difference in the percentile at the end of the first year in higher education and on entry. Table 6.7 reports results only for those schools that had more than 20 students entering one of the universities analyzed. Clearly, a larger sample of students (or additional years) would be required to confirm the preliminary results that we show here.

The three schools at the bottom of the list in Table 6.7 are private, and their students show, on average, the lowest number of ECTS completed in the first year at university, as well as low average percentiles for university grades. On average,

Table 6.7 Average of the Outcome Indicators per School

	N	ECTS	PUnivG	PUnivG – entryG	p-Value
Colégio Liceal de Santa Maria de Lamas	21	**48.07**	0.55	0	0.951
Escola Secundária Filipa de Vilhena	32	**47.09**	**0.6**	**0.12**	**0.009**
Escola Secundária Eça de Queirós—Póvoa de	31	**47.03**	**0.6**	0.09	**0.078**
Colégio Luso-Francês	42	46	0.55	–0.02	0.664
Escola Secundária Aurélia de Sousa	33	44.83	0.59	**0.13**	**0.019**
Escola Secundária de Santa Maria da Feira	21	44.55	0.57	0.01	0.947
Escola Básica e Secundária Clara de Resende	29	44.24	0.56	0.06	0.205
Escola Secundária da Maia	28	43.84	0.55	0.07	0.2
Colégio Internato dos Carvalhos	45	43.69	0.56	0.04	0.381
Colégio Nossa Senhora do Rosário	91	42.55	0.46	–0.1	**0.001**
Escola Secundária Garcia de Orta	54	42.06	**0.61**	0.05	0.284
Escola Secundária Alves Martins	29	41.78	0.54	–0.07	0.216
Externato Paulo VI	36	40.57	0.4	**–0.13**	**0.013**
Escola Secundária de Penafiel	25	39.38	0.49	0.01	0.842
Escola Secundária de Monserrate	23	39.11	0.52	0.05	0.592

(Continued)

Table 6.7 (Continued) Average of the Outcome Indicators per School

	N	ECTS	PUnivG	PUnivG – entryG	p-Value
Escola Secundária de Almeida Garrett	25	39.02	0.57	0.06	0.309
Escola Secundária Dr. Manuel Gomes de Almeida	26	38.73	0.51	0.02	0.672
Colégio INED Nevogilde	22	38.73	0.46	-0.07	0.241
Externato Camões	23	38.57	0.49	-0.01	0.865
Escola Secundária Santa Maria Maior	24	36.71	0.51	0.02	0.778
Centro de Estudos Básico e Secundário-CEBES	26	36.35	0.37	-0.09	0.163
Colégio da Trofa	41	35.49	0.43	-0.07	0.176
Externato Ribadouro	229	**33.69**	0.42	**-0.12**	**0**

they reduced their rank position at the university by comparison with their rank on entry. Regarding the schools at the top, two are public and one is a private school run with an association contract (Colégio Liceal de Santa Maria de Lamas), meaning that it has some features that are common to public school. They show, on average, students with the highest number of ECTS completed and a considerable increase in rank position at the end of the first year in university and on entry. Note that we also performed statistical tests for each school to verify the hypothesis that the mean of the variable PUnivG–PEntryG is zero. Table 6.7 shows the p-value (last column) for this test, and not many schools show a statistically significant value for the difference between grades at the end of the first year in university and on entry.

In Table 6.8, we look at the school of origin of the best students in each degree—those that ranked in the 85th percentile or above and completed more than 50 ECTS. Only schools with more than 20 students are reported.

The school that originates more students in the top percentile is Colégio do Rosário (12). Note that Externato Ribadouro has more students in the degrees considered in our sample (229 students in total), but only 3% of its students are in the top rank. This contrasts, for example, with Escola Secundária de Monseratte and Escola Secundária Almeida Garrett, which placed 21.74% and 20% of their students, respectively, in the top percentiles within their degrees.

A similar analysis was done for the worst performing students at the end of the first year in university (those in the 15th percentile or below and with less than 50 ECTS done). The schools of origin of these students are shown in Table 6.9, where only schools with more than 20 students are shown.

In percentage terms, CEBES is the school with the greatest proportion of students with poor performance in the first year in higher education (26.92%). Externato Ribadouro is the school that places most students in the lowest position for university grade rankings (50 students), representing about 22% of the students from this school. Note that, interestingly, the average percentile on entry of the cohort of weaker students is quite similar to the average percentile on entry of the remaining students from this school (0.49 vs. 0.55). In contrast, we see Escola Secundária Aurélia de Sousa, where the students with the worst performance in the first year of higher education also have a low percentile on entry (0.16). Escola Secundária Clara de Resende has the lowest proportion of weak students at the end of the first year in higher education (3.45%). These students also entered university with a low percentile in terms of their classifications on entry (0.26), so it could be expected that their performance would be poor.

Note that, in order to make more sound conclusions regarding the comparison of schools, we need to extend the dataset to other degrees/universities and/or other years. This is something we hope to do in the future. For now, the analysis just presented can be considered a simple exercise crossing data from secondary education and higher education and showing the potential of this type of analysis.

Table 6.8 Origin of Top Students

Secondary School	Total Number of Students in the Sample	Number of Top Students in the Sample	Percentage of Students in the Top at the End of the First Year in University	Percentile on Entry of the Other Students	Percentile on Entry of Top Students at the End of the First Year in University
Escola Secundária de Monserrate	23	5	**21.74**	0.45	0.56
Escola Secundária de Almeida Garrett	25	5	20.00	0.44	0.81
Escola Sec. Eça de Queirós Póvoa Varzim	31	6	19.35	0.41	0.87
Colégio Liceal de Santa Maria de Lamas	21	4	19.05	0.47	0.85
Escola Secundária Aurélia de Sousa	33	6	18.18	0.4	0.75
Externato Camões	23	4	17.39	0.44	0.8
Escola Básica e Sec. Clara de Resende	29	5	17.24	0.46	0.66
Colégio Luso-Francês	42	6	14.29	0.53	0.81
Escola Sec. de Santa Maria da Feira	21	3	14.29	0.58	0.47
Escola Secundária Alves Martins	29	4	13.79	0.56	0.89
Colégio Nossa Senhora do Rosário	91	**12**	13.19	0.52	0.89
Escola Secundária Filipa de Vilhena	32	4	12.50	0.45	0.65

(Continued)

Table 6.8 (Continued)   Origin of Top Students

Secondary School	Total Number of Students in the Sample	Number of Top Students in the Sample	Percentage of Students in the Top at the End of the First Year in University	Percentile on Entry of the Other Students	Percentile on Entry of Top Students at the End of the First Year in University
Escola Secundária de Penafiel	25	3	12.00	0.44	0.79
Colégio Internato dos Carvalhos	45	5	11.11	0.49	0.79
Escola Secundária da Maia	28	3	10.71	0.43	0.91
Colégio da Trofa	41	4	9.76	0.46	0.97
Escola Secundária Garcia de Orta	54	5	9.26	0.54	0.85
Colégio INED Nevogilde	22	2	9.09	0.48	0.97
Escola Secundária Santa Maria Maior	24	2	8.33	0.46	0.84
Centro de Estudos Básico e Sec. CEBES	26	2	7.69	0.43	0.82
Escola Sec. Dr. Manuel Gomes de Almeida	26	2	7.69	0.48	0.56
Externato Ribadouro	229	8	3.49	0.52	0.88
Externato Paulo VI	36	0	0.00	0.53	.

Table 6.9 Origin of Weak Students

Secondary School	Total Number of Students in the Sample	Number of Weak Students in the Sample	Percentage of Weak Students at the End of the First Year in University	Percentile on Entry of the Other Students	Percentile on Entry of Weak Students at the End of the First Year in University
Centro de Estudos Básico e Sec.—CEBES	26	7	**26.92**	0.47	0.43
Colégio da Trofa	41	11	**26.83**	0.52	0.46
Externato Ribadouro	229	**50**	21.83	0.55	0.49
Escola Sec. de Monserrate	23	5	21.74	0.49	0.41
Externato Camões	23	5	21.74	0.55	0.35
Escola Sec. Santa Maria Maior	24	5	20.83	0.53	0.35
Escola Sec. de Penafiel	25	5	20.00	0.51	0.36
Colégio INED Nevogilde	22	4	18.18	0.57	0.33
Escola Sec. Dr. Manuel Gomes de Almeida	26	4	15.38	0.52	0.33
Colégio Luso-Francês	42	6	14.29	0.59	0.45
Escola Sec. Alves Martins	29	4	13.79	0.64	0.39
Colégio Nossa Senhora do Rosário	91	10	10.99	0.58	0.43

(Continued)

Table 6.9 (Continued)   Origin of Weak Students

Secondary school	Total Number of Students in the Sample	Number of Weak Students in the Sample	Percentage of Weak Students at the End of the First Year in University	Percentile on Entry of the Other Students	Percentile on Entry of Weak Students at the End of the First Year in University
Escola Secundária Filipa de Vilhena	32	3	9.38	0.5	0.27
Escola Secundária Aurélia de Sousa	33	3	9.09	0.49	**0.16**
Escola Secundária de Almeida Garrett	25	2	8.00	0.53	0.26
Escola Secundária da Maia	28	2	7.14	0.49	0.35
Escola Sec. Eça de Queirós Póvoa de Varzim	31	2	6.45	0.51	0.32
Externato Paulo VI	36	2	5.56	0.53	0.58
Colégio Liceal de Santa Maria de Lamas	21	1	4.76	0.55	0.35
Escola Sec. de Santa Maria da Feira	21	1	4.76	0.55	0.77
Colégio Internato dos Carvalhos	45	2	4.44	0.53	0.23
Escola Secundária Garcia de Orta	54	2	3.70	0.57	0.48
Escola Básica e Sec. Clara de Resende	29	1	3.45	0.5	0.26

6.4 Conclusion

Educational research has travelled a long path, with drastic perception changes from its beginning to the present day. The first educational articles advocated that schools did not matter (or did not matter much), while recent literature shows that schools can indeed make a difference. Recent developments in analytic methodologies and the enhancement of data collection and storage capabilities are opening the door to a new set of possibilities for research in the education field (either through the use of new methods to analyze existing data, such as data mining techniques, or through the use of old methods on expanded datasets).

This chapter described two experiences involving comparisons between secondary schools. One is an analytic visual platform (BESP) where individual indicators and aggregate indicators based on national exams are made available to the general public and also to school managers. The other is a comparison of secondary schools on the basis of an innovative indicator of secondary school's outcome: the preparation of their students for university studies. This second analysis provided interesting results, as well as new insights into aspects of secondary schools' educational efforts that are often disregarded. In Portugal, annual school rankings place schools with average exams results that outperform their peers at the top. Private schools are often those at the top of these rankings, so it is indisputable that private schools prepare students very well for national exams and for entering university. However, university success depends on other factors (e.g., autonomy, maturity, and engagement) that public schools seem to be providing in a higher dose than private schools. The ranking of our secondary schools based on these new indicators is an interesting topic for future research.

Acknowledgments

The authors would like to acknowledge the assistance of Mara Carvalho from CEGE, Católica Porto Business School, in cleaning and preparing the database for analysis.

References

Baker, R. S. J. D. and Yacef, K. (2009). The state of educational data mining in 2009: A review and future visions. *Journal of Educational Data Mining*, 1(1), 3–16.

Beckford, J. (1998). *Quality: A Critical Introduction*. London: Routledge.

Bessent, A. M. and Bessent, E. W. (1980). Determining the comparative efficiency of schools through data envelopment analysis. *Educational Administration Quarterly*, 16(2), 57–75.

Bogetoft, P. and Nielsen, K. (2005). Internet based benchmarking. *Group Decision and Negotiation*, 14(3) (May), 195–215.

Cabral, J. A. S. and Pechincha, P. (2014). *Análise do percurso dos estudantes admitidos pelo regime geral em licenciatura—1º ciclo e mestrado integrado na Universidade do Porto em 2008/09, 2009/10 e 2010/11*. Reitoria da Universidade do Porto. Serviço de Melhoria Contínua (in Portuguese).

Charnes, A., Cooper, W. W. and Rhodes, E. (1978). Measuring the efficiency of decision making units. *European Journal of Operational Research*, 2(4), 429–444.

Cherchye, L., Perelman, S. and De Witte, K. (2015). A unified productivity-performance approach applied to secondary schools in the Netherlands. Leuven Economics of Education Research, KU Leuven, Mimeo.

Coleman, J. S. (1966). *Equality of Educational Opportunities*. U.S. Office of Education, Washington, DC.

Cordero, J. M., Santín, D. and Simancas, R. (2017). Assessing European primary school performance through a conditional nonparametric model. *Journal of the Operational Research Society*, 68(4), 364–376.

Cordero-Ferrera, J. M., Crespo-Cebada, E., Pedraja-Chaparro, F. and Santín-González, D. (2011). Exploring educational efficiency divergences across Spanish regions in PISA 2006. *Revista de Economía Aplicada*, 57(XIX), 117–145.

Costa, J. M., Horta, I. M., Guimarães, N., Nóvoa, M. H., e Cunha, J. F. and Sousa, R. (2007). icBench: A benchmarking tool for Portuguese construction industry companies. *International Journal for Housing Science and Its Applications*, 31(1), 33–41.

Crespo-Cebada, E., Pedraja-Chaparro, F. and Santín, D. (2014). Does school ownership matter? An unbiased efficiency comparison for regions of Spain. *Journal of Productivity Analysis*, 41, 153–172.

De Witte, K., Thanassoulis, E., Simpson, G., Battisti, G. and Charlesworth-May, A. (2010). Assessing pupil and school performance by non-parametric and parametric techniques. *Journal of the Operational Research Society*, 61, 1224–1237.

De Witte, K. and López-Torres, L. (2017). Efficiency in education: A review of literature and a way forward. *Journal of the Operational Research Society*, 68(4), 339–363.

Faria, S. and Portela, M. C. S. (2016). Student performance in mathematics using PISA-2009 data for Portugal. *Working Paper Management, 1-2016*, Católica Porto Business School.

Gray, J., Goldstein, H. and Jesson, D. (1996). Changes and improvements in schools' effectiveness: Trends over five years. *Research Papers in Education*, 11(1), 35–51.

Grosskopf, S., Hayes, K. and Taylor, L. L. (2009). The relative efficiency of charter schools. *Annals of Public and Cooperative Economics*, 80(1), 67–87.

Grosskopf, S., Hayes, K. J., Taylor, L. L. and Weber, W. L. (1999). Anticipating the consequences of school reform: A new use of DEA. *Management Science*, 45(4), 608–620.

Haegeland, T. (2006). *School Performance Indicators in Norway: A Background Report for the OECD Project on the Development of Value-Added Models in Education Systems*. Paris: OECD.

Haelermans, C. and De Witte, K. (2012). The role of innovations in secondary school performance: Evidence from a conditional efficiency model. *European Journal of Operational Research*, 223(2), 541–549.

Halkos, G., Tzeremes, N. G., Kourtzidis, S. A. (2012). Measuring public owned university departments' efficiency: A bootstrapped DEA approach. *Journal of Economics and Econometrics*, 55(2), 1–24.

Hanushek, E. A. and Kimko, D. D. (2000). Schooling, labor-force quality, and the growth of nations. *American Economic Review*, 90(5), 1184–1208.

Hanushek, E. and Taylor, L. (1990). Alternative assessments of performance of schools: Measurement of state variation in achievement. *The Journal of Human Resources*, 25(2), 179–201.

Hanushek, E. A. and Woessmann. L. (2010). The economics of international differences in educational achievement, No. w15949. National Bureau of Economic Research.

Ibensoft ApS. (2013). Interactive benchmarking: State-of-the-art in performance evaluation. http://www.ibensoft.com/.

Jencks, C., Smith, M., Ackland, H., Bane, M., Cohen, D., Gintis, H., Heyns, B. and Micholson, S. (1972). *Inequality: A Reassessment of the Effect of Family and Schooling in America*. New York: Basic Books.

Johnes, J. (2006). Measuring teaching efficiency in higher education: An application of data envelopment analysis to economics graduates from UK universities 1993. *European Journal of Operational Research*, 174, 443–456.

Johnes, J. (2015). Operational research in education. *European Journal of Operational Research*, 243, 683–696.

Johnson, A. L. and McGinnis, L. (2011). Performance measurement in the warehousing industry. *IIE Transactions*, 43(3), 220–230.

Karsten, S., Visscher, A. and Jong, T. (2001). Another side of the coin: The unintended effects of the publication of school performance data in England and France. *Comparative Education*, 37(2), 231–242.

Kirjavainen, T. (2012). Efficiency of Finnish general upper secondary schools: An application of Stochastic Frontier Analysis with panel data. *Education Economics*, 20(4), 343–364.

Kirjavainen, T. and Loikkanen, H. A. (1998). Efficiency differences of Finnish senior secondary schools: An application of DEA and Tobit analysis. *Economics of Education Review*, 17(4), 377–394.

Ladd, H. F. and Walsh, R. P. (2002). Implementing value-added measures of school effectiveness: Getting the incentives right. *Economics of Education Review*, 21(1), 1–17.

Mancebón, M. and Bandrés, E. (1999). Efficiency evaluation in secondary schools: The key role of model specification and of ex post analysis of results. *Education Economics*, 7(2), 131–152.

Mayston, D. J. (2003). Measuring and managing educational performance. *Journal of the Operational Research Society*, 54(7), 679–691.

O'Donoghue, C., Thomas, S., Goldstein, H. and Knight, T. (1997). 1996 DfEE study of value added for 16–18 year olds in England. *DfEE Research Series March*. London: HMSO.

OECD (2008a). *Handbook on Constructing Composite Indicators: Methodology and User Guide*. Paris: OECD (http://composite-indicators.jrc.ec.europa.eu/).

OECD (2008b). *Measuring Improvements in Learning Outcomes: Best Practices to Assess the Value Added of Schools*. Paris: OECD.

Perelman, S. and Santín, D. (2011). Measuring educational efficiency at student level with parametric stochastic distance functions: An application to Spanish PISA results. *Education Economics*, 19(1), 29–49.

Portela, M. C. A. S. and Camanho, A. S. (2010). Analysis of complementary methodologies for the estimation of school value-added. *Journal of the Operational Research Society*, 61, 1122–1132.

Portela, M. C. A. S., Camanho, A. S. and Borges, D. (2011). BESP: Benchmarking of Portuguese secondary schools. *Benchmarking: An International Journal*, 18(2), 240–260.

Portela, M. C. A. S., Camanho, A. S. and Borges, D. (2012). Performance assessment of secondary schools: The snapshot of a country taken by DEA. *Journal of the Operational Research Society*, 63, 1098–1115.

Portela, M. C. A. S. and Thanassoulis, E. (2001). Decomposing school and school type efficiency. *European Journal of Operational Research*, 132(2), 114–130.

Ray, A. (2006). School value added measures in England: A paper for the OECD project on the development of value-added models in education systems. London: Department for Education and Skills.

Ray, A., Evans, H. and McCormack, T. (2009). The use of national value-added models for school improvement in English schools. *Revista de Educación*, 348, 47–66.

Rutter, M., Maughan, B., Mortimore, P. and Ouston, J. (1979). *Fifteen Thousand Hours: Secondary Schools and Their Effects on Children*. London: Open Books. Reprinted 1995, Paul Chapman Publishing.

Sanders, W. L., Saxton, A. M. and Horn, S. P. (1997). The Tennessee value-added assessment system: A quantitative, outcomes-based approach to educational assessment. In J. Millman (Ed.), *Grading Teachers, Grading Schools: Is Student Achievement a Valid Evaluation Measure*, Thousand Oaks, CA: Corwin Press (Sage Publications), 137–162.

Sear, K. (1983). The correlation between A level grades and degree results in England and Wales. *Higher Education*, 12(5), 609–619.

Smith, J. and Naylor, R. (2005). Schooling effects on subsequent university performance: Evidence for the UK university population. *Economics of Education Review*, 24, 549–562.

Thanassoulis, E., Portela, M. C. A. S. and Despic, O. (2008). Data envelopment analysis: The mathematical programming approach to efficiency analysis. In H. O. Fried, C. A. K. Lovell and S. S. Schmidt, SS. (Eds.), *The Measurement of Productive Efficiency and Productivity Growth*, Oxford: Oxford University Press, 251–420.

Thieme, C., Prior, D. and Tortosa-Ausina, E. (2013). A multilevel decomposition of school performance using robust nonparametric frontier techniques. *Economics of Education Review*, 32, 104–121.

Woessmann, L. (2003). Schooling resources, educational institutions and student performance: The international evidence. *Oxford Bulletin of Economics and Statistics*, 65(2), 117–170.

Chapter 7

The Use of Educational Data Mining Procedures to Assess Students' Performance in a Bayesian Framework

Kristof De Witte, Grazia Graziosi, and Joris Hindryckx

Contents

7.1 Introduction

Understanding what factors influence students' achievement is crucial to increase the effectiveness and efficiency of higher educational systems. From a statistical perspective, it is challenging to model the correlation between the outcome variable (e.g., enrollment, retention, high school grades) and several students, teacher, learning, and educational characteristics (e.g., personal and educational background of students, course size and its composition, teacher, and curriculum). In addition, in large datasets it is unclear what variables should be included in the analysis. Several studies have sought to identify the factors that impact students' performance using different model specifications. Nevertheless, the question of which specification should be used has not been thoroughly addressed in the literature (Tobias and Li, 2004).

Recently, there has been a considerable expansion in the collection and use of educational data, which provides the opportunity to model potentially useful information, especially over large datasets; that is, those composed of huge numbers of observations and/or variables. One emerging field specifically addressing the use of "big data" in education is known as *educational data mining* (EDM) (Romero and Ventura, 2010). As the methodology is relatively new, it is not clear which data mining techniques are preferable (Mohamad and Tasir, 2013). Romero and Ventura (2007) have emphasized the need for more specialized and oriented work on educational settings for successful applications. The history and current trends in EDM have been reviewed and discussed in Baker and Yacef (2009), while examples of how to apply EDM techniques to the specific case of higher education are provided in Kotsiantis (2009).

Dealing with large datasets often leads to the use of techniques aimed at synthesizing variables or selecting variables that are associated with the outcome of interest. Variable selection has been extensively studied in the statistical literature (see e.g., Tibshirani, 1996; Fan and Li, 2001; Zou and Hastie, 2005). Of several applicable methods, the Lasso technique (Tibshirani, 1996) is one of the most popular.

As pointed out by Romero et al. (2014), variable selection is a crucial step in EDM, because there could be a large number of attributes for learning schemes to handle in many situations, and this number of attributes can result in a lower accuracy of statistical models. Several variable selection techniques have been used in education studies. Beikzadeh et al. (2008) applied a decision tree technique to identify the most important variables in the context of higher educational systems to enhance managerial decision-making processes. Marquez-Vera et al. (2013), in the presence of high dimensional and imbalanced data, proposed a genetic algorithm to select which features or attributes have the largest effect for predicting student failure at school. Dupuis and Victoria-Feser (2013) adopted a streamwise regression approach based on the variance inflation factor (VIF) to deal with variable selection problems in several large datasets, including college data on factors impacting an individual's educational attainment. Zimmermann et al. (2015) applied regression models in combination with variable selection and variable aggregation embedded in a double-layered cross-validation loop to predict graduate-level performance using indicators of undergraduate-level performance.

One of the most recent advances in the variable selection literature is the Bayesian approach, by which, rather than searching for the single optimal model, one can estimate the posterior probability of all models within the considered class of models (or in practice, of all models with non-negligible probability) (O'Hara et al., 2009). While Bayesian methods have become somewhat more popular in the scientific literature in recent years, there is still significant resistance to their use as a means of making statistical decisions in the social sciences and, in particular, in the field of educational studies (see, among others, Rubin, 1983 and Subbiah et al., 2011). In particular, the use of Bayesian models has become popular in the item response theory literature in order to estimate item parameters (Fox, 2010) and to predict individual test scores (Ishii and Watanabe, 2001).

To the best of our knowledge, few educational studies have adopted a Bayesian approach to variable selection. An exception is Rubin (1980), who applied model selection techniques on validity coefficients to find a more suitable model with respect to the classical least squares regression. In Zwick (1993), four empirical Bayesian regression models were investigated to analyze the factors for predicting the first-year average and final grade point average in business and management doctoral programs. An example of a variable selection procedure with the random Lasso technique is provided in Chies et al. (2014) to estimate the dropout probability in higher education.

The Bayesian approach to the problem of variable selection is conceptually straightforward. Any feature of interest is a deterministic function of the posterior distribution over the model space. Examples of such features are the highest posterior probability model and the inclusion probabilities of covariates (Garcia-Donato and Martinez-Beneito, 2013). In addition, a key feature of Bayesian model selection is that results are typically highly sensitive to the choice of priors (Bayarri et al., 2012), since the conclusion of the analysis is the posterior distribution, a compromise between both the prior and the data information (Weiss, 2010).

The choice of a prior distribution is a sensitive issue in general and in the context of Bayesian variable selection in particular. Usually, in performing Bayesian analyses, many examples and uses of prior distributions are provided (see Kass and Wasserman, 1996 for full discussions on the theoretical principles for distributions and many references on the topic). Among them, Zellner's (1986) g-prior remains a common conventional prior for use in the linear regression model due to its computational efficiency in evaluating marginal likelihoods and model search (Feng et al., 2008).

In the present chapter, we propose a two-step procedure for variable selection exploiting the potential information embedded in large datasets, thus suggesting an alternative approach to specify prior distributions, especially suitable in the presence of large sample sizes and/or with a high number of possible covariates. Our procedure aims to capture the potential information in the data by first computing an importance measure of the variables in explaining the outcome of interest. In order to obtain this measure, we repeatedly perform the Lasso variable selection technique on bootstrap subsamples of a portion of the original dataset. In particular, we use this approach on a rich and large dataset—having $n = 9807$ observations and $p = 46$ variables—from a large university college, VIVES, which is part of the KU Leuven Association in Flanders, and offers vocational study programs oriented to professional training. Our aim is to select, in a linear regression framework, which student, teacher, learning, and didactic characteristics can explain differences in students' performance, measured by their final grade.

This chapter contributes to the literature by bridging the EDM approaches with the Bayesian framework, and is innovative for several reasons. First, it provides a flexible methodology to select the variables of interest in the presence of a huge number of explanatory variables, a situation that is common in educational-related datasets. Second, it supplies an innovative way to choose a prior probability distribution for Bayesian analysis, from which we obtain a suitable final model with a smaller set of the original variables.

The chapter is organized as follows: In Section 7.2, we discuss the proposed two-step variable selection procedure. Section 7.3, describes the principal characteristics of the dataset and the group of possible explanatory variables. Section 7.4 is devoted to the empirical application of our approach. Section 7.5 concludes with some final remarks. We also provide in the Appendix the Bayesian factor inclusion probabilities obtained by using conventional prior, likewise Zellner's g-prior.

7.2 Methodology

We propose a two-step procedure for variable selection exploiting the potential information embedded in large educational datasets. The procedure consists of applying the Lasso variable selection techniques on a bootstrap subsample of the original dataset. The latter will be used as prior information in a Bayesian analysis in order to compute a posterior distribution of different models for predicting a given outcome. Without loss of generality, in our application we consider the specification of a simple linear regression model, but it would be easy to use different kinds of models (e.g., logit models and hierarchical models).

In the linear regression model, it is typically the case that only an unknown subset of the coefficients β_j are non-zero, so in the context of variable selection each candidate model is indexed with one binary vector $\delta = \left(\delta_1, \ldots, \delta_p \right)'$ where each element δ_j takes the value 1 or 0 depending on whether it is included or excluded from the model (Krishna et al., 2009).

In the following, we explain in detail the two-step procedure: BL (first step) and BF (second step), which is a Bayesian alternative to classical hypothesis testing.

7.2.1 Bootstrap Lasso

The Lasso technique (Tibshirani, 1996) is one of the most popular methods for variable selection. It consists of selecting which variables should enter in a given model by maximizing the penalized likelihood:

$$\sum_{i=1}^{n}(y_i - X'\beta)^2 + n\lambda \sum_{j=1}^{p}|\beta_j|, \; \lambda > 0 \qquad (7.1)$$

In the linear regression model, Lasso allows the shrinking of some coefficients and sets others to 0. As in the maximalization of Equation 7.1 many coefficients β_j are equal to zero, it retains the good features of both subset selection and ridge regression. However, it suffers from some limitations, as outlined by Zou and Hastie (2005). In particular, in the presence of the high dimensionality of correlated covariates, the Lasso will select one of them and set the other coefficients to zero. This may be an undesirable property if we aim to discover all the existing relationships between the response and the covariates.

In the context of very large datasets, in order to overcome this issue, we adopt a BL procedure by repeatedly performing the Lasso on bootstrap selected subsamples (similar to what was proposed by Bach, 2008) with the aim of obtaining a measure of relevance, that is, a probability of inclusion of each covariate, and to solve the optimization problem efficiently. Bach (2008) points out that if several datasets generated from the same distribution were available, all relevant variables would always be selected for all datasets. The logic underpinning the BL is to use resampling methods (i.e., bootstrap) in order to simulate the availability of several datasets by resampling B samples from the same unique dataset (for details on bootstrap and resampling method see Efron and Tibshirani, 1993).

Since our aim is to obtain prior information to be used in a Bayesian framework, we specifically employ the BL on a randomly selected subset of the original dataset (of size n_{BL}). We assume the frequency of selection of each variable in the model over the total number of B bootstrap repetitions to be the importance measure for each possible explanatory variable that can be used as *a priori* information on the remaining dataset.

7.2.2 Bayes Factor

In the Bayesian framework, a set of prior distributions is specified by the parameters $\theta_\delta = (\beta_\delta, \sigma^2)$ for each model, along with a meaningful set of prior model probabilities over the class of all models. Model selection is then done based on the posterior probabilities.

Therefore, our final goal is to estimate the posterior probability that a variable should have in the (linear regression) model. Under the Bayesian approach, it is commonly perceived that the optimal predictive model is the model with the highest posterior probability (O'Hara et al., 2009). To this end, we apply BF to calculate the posterior likelihood distribution of different models. In particular, we use a particular Monte Carlo Markov Chain (MCMC) method: the Gibbs sample (George and McCulloch, 1993; Garcia-Donato and Martinez-Beneito, 2013).

In its simplest form, the BF is the ratio of the posterior odds of one hypothesis (H_1) to its prior odds, regardless of the value of the prior odds (Kass and Raftery, 1995).

$$B_{12} = \frac{pr(\mathbf{D}\,|\,(H_1))}{pr(\mathbf{D}\,|\,(H_2))}$$

which means

Posteriors probability = Bayes factor × Prior probability

We do not assume that every possible model is equally likely, but we use the inclusion frequency of each predictor obtained by the BL procedure as *a priori* information on the importance of each variable in explaining our outcome.

7.3 Dataset

The analysis is based on a rich dataset from a large university college, VIVES, which is part of the KU Leuven Association in Flanders, and offers vocational study programs oriented to professional training. The VIVES administrative data (see Hindryckx and De Witte, 2015 for an explanation on the construction of the administrative dataset) covers academic years from 2006 to 2012—the academic year of reference, when the course took place—and it is organized at course level. A course is described as a defined set of educational, learning, and examination activities aimed at acquiring well-defined competences regarding knowledge, understanding, skills and attitudes. In total, we have $n = 9807$ observations, on which $p = 46$ variables are considered.

Table 7.1 reports descriptive statistics of the sample. The group of personal and educational background of students' variables includes age, gender, and pre-higher vocational education information. About 32% of the students were enrolled in general education, which prepares students for higher education at both universities and higher vocational institutions, while most students in the sample (62%) completed a technical education, which prepares students for higher education and the labor market.

According to the characteristics of the course, less than 50% of students took the exam in the first period and almost 95% of students were enrolled for the first time. Moreover, to enroll for a professional bachelor program, students are required to meet the admission requirements related to qualifications and languages. Of

Table 7.1   Descriptive Statistics for Groups of the Explanatory Variables

Number of Observations (courses)		9807	
Personal and Educational Background of Students: (in %)		**Characteristics of the Course: (in %)**	
Age of students (average)	21.4	No. of students in the first exam period (average)	47.7
Gender (female)	50.5	Students enrolled for the first time in the course	94.4
Previously in general education	31.6	Students retaking the course	4.9
Previously in technical education	62.0	Students retaking the course three times	0.5
Previously in vocational education	3.3	Students retaking the course four times	0.2
Previously in art education	0.7	Belgian students	98.5
Previously in combined education	2.4	Non-EU students	0.3
Working students	1.1	Non-EU students with Islamic background	0.2
Regular students	93	Students from the Netherlands, France, and Germany	0.5
		EU students not from the Netherland, France, and Germany	0.2
Learning Materials: (in %)		% of courses offered as distance learning	15.4
Own book	93.4	Students with scholarship	25.5
Traditional book	93.4	**Personal and Professional Characteristics of Teachers: (in %)**	
Other materials	43.8	Sex of teacher (female)	50.7

(Continued)

Table 7.1 (Continued) Descriptive Statistics for Groups of the Explanatory Variables

Number of Observations (courses)		9807	
Evaluation Procedures: (in %)		Teacher with pedagogical degree	63.5
Verbal examination	35.5	Teachers with professional training	76.1
Written examination	69.6	Teachers with PhD	7.3
Multi-choice examination	7.1	Teachers with Master's	63.7
Permanent examination	54.6	Teacher with Bachelor's	13.8
Internship	8.4	Teachers from industry	15.2
		Year of birth (mode)	1,969
Academic Year of Reference: (in %)			
2006	5.1	**Learning Approach: (%)**	
2007	10.1	Cognitive learning approach	83.2
2008	13.2	Behavioral learning approach	57.3
2009	15.6		
2010	17.6		
2011	18.8		
2012	19.6		

Note: If not specified in brackets, the percentage of students having that characteristic is reported.

students with a Belgian higher secondary degree, 98.5% satisfied the degree requirement. Students from abroad may also be admitted to a professional bachelor program after approval, and the language requirement is met if the student has at least one year of education in Dutch-speaking secondary or higher education. If not, a language certificate must be submitted or a language test has to be done. The data also provided a large set of teacher characteristics (e.g., highest diploma, education qualification, gender, and age) and characterized the examination process (i.e., written exam, verbal exam, multiple choice, continuous assessment, and internship). Furthermore, we have information on the learning approach (i.e., the cognitive approach, which is concerned with *learning to think*, and the behavioral approach, based on the response to stimuli from the environment) and the educational materials used in a course (own book, traditional book, and other materials).

In our model, we include all the variables described in Table 7.1.

7.4 Empirical Application

In this section, we present the results of our two-step procedure according to the variable inclusion probabilities based on both the bootstrap Lasso (P_{BL}) and Bayes factor (P_{BF}). We are interested in specifying a linear regression model where the outcome is the students' performance, measured by their final grade. By adopting our procedure, we will be able to select which student, teacher, learning, and didactic characteristics have a significant effect on the outcome, that is, which is the model with the largest posterior probability given the chosen prior probabilities. In the Appendix, we provide the Bayesian factor inclusion probabilities obtained by using Zellner's g-prior.

7.4.1 Bootstrap Lasso Results

We employ the BL on a randomly selected subset of $n_{BL} = 3000$ out of the $n = 9807$ total observations. We assume the frequency of selection of each variable in the model over the total number of $B = 1500$ bootstrap repetitions as the importance measure for each possible explanatory variable. Table 7.2 reports the relative frequency of selection of each covariate.

The BL allows us to deduce a measure of relevance (the probability of inclusion). P_{BL} indicates the number of times a given variable is included in the model over the B replications, according to the Lasso shrinkage. Covariates with higher probabilities of inclusion ($P_{BL} > 0.90$) are linked to the characteristics of the course (e.g., number of students in the first exam period, students enrolled for the first time, and course offered as distance learning), the evaluation procedures (written examination, multi-choice examination, permanent examination, and internship), and the 2012 academic year.

Table 7.2 Variable Inclusion Probabilities Based on the Bootstrap Lasso (P_{BL})

Covariates	P_{BL}
Personal and Educational Background of Students:	
Age	0.489
Gender (female)	0.392
Previously in general education	0.492
Previously in technical education	0.006
Previously in vocational education	0.545
Previously in art education	0.519
Previously in combined education	0.048
Working students	0.484
Regular students	0.130
Characteristics of the Course:	
No. of students in the first exam period	0.995
Students enrolled for the first time	1.000
Students retaking the course	0.068
Students retaking the course three times	0.871
Students retaking the course four times	0.545
Belgian students	0.145
Foreign students	0.304
Islamic students	0.434
Students from other European countries	0.658
Students from the Netherlands, France, and Germany	0.469
Students from other countries (non-EU)	0.508
Students with scholarship	0.211
Course offered as distance learning	0.995
Learning Materials:	
Own book	0.108
Traditional book	0.894

(Continued)

Table 7.2 (Continued)   Variable Inclusion Probabilities Based on the Bootstrap Lasso (P_{BL})

Covariates	P_{BL}
Other materials	0.110
Personal and Professional Characteristics of Teachers:	
Sex of teacher	0.024
Teacher with pedagogical degree	0.098
Teacher with professional training	0.409
Teacher with PhD	0.013
Teacher with Master's	0.284
Teacher with Bachelor's	0.077
Teacher from industry	0.107
Year of birth	0.017
Evaluation Procedures:	
Verbal examination	0.831
Written examination	1.00
Multi-choice examination	0.997
Permanent examination	0.997
Internship	0.931
Learning Approach:	
Cognitive learning	0.519
Behavioral learning	0.103
Academic Year of Reference:	
2006	0.326
2007	0.099
2008	0.927
2009	0.181
2010	0.399
2011	0.145
2012	0.998

7.4.2 Bayes Factor Results

The second step consists of the BF computation according to our prior information obtained by the BL procedure. In particular, the BF is applied to the remaining $n_{BF} = 6807$ observations of the original dataset. Table 7.3 shows the estimated posterior probabilities.

With respect to students' characteristics, we observe high posterior probability for both general and vocational education variables. Unexpectedly, neither the age nor the gender of students have been selected by the BF, despite these variables, in the literature, often being found useful in explaining differences in students' performance. Among several characteristics of the class composition, students in the first exam period, students enrolled for the first time, and both foreign students and students from other European countries have always been included in the model by the BF. Furthermore, the variable "course offered as distance learning" shows high probability of inclusion. The analysis also takes into account the material employed for learning, divided into own books, traditional books, and other general materials. We notice higher inclusion probability selected by the BF only for the traditional books. Variables linked to the characteristics of teachers selected by the BF show higher inclusion probability when pedagogical and master's degrees are considered. No other characteristics concerning the preparedness of teacher, age, or gender have high posterior probability to be selected by the BF. With respect to the evaluation procedures, all the variables show high inclusion probabilities, except for the variable "internship." According to the BF selection, both variables indicated that cognitive and behavioral approaches should not enter the final model. Finally, the results for the academic year indicate that only the year 2012 has a non-negligible effect on students' performance, since its inclusion probability is much higher than the other years.

7.5 Concluding Remarks

When dealing with very large datasets, variable selection is a crucial task. Nowadays, very large datasets are common in many fields, including educational studies. Learning providers, institutes, universities, schools, and colleges have always had the ability to generate huge amounts of educational data. In this case, the large sample size is accompanied by the presence of a huge number of possible explanatory variables because of the intrinsic hierarchical nature of educational data.

This chapter proposed a procedure for variable selection in higher education studies where there are a large number of possible contender variables that produce several possible models. The variable selection starts from Lasso variable selection techniques on bootstrap subsamples of the original dataset. From the Lasso model, we specify the prior distributions, which are used in a Bayesian analysis in order to compute posterior distribution of different models.

Table 7.3 Variable Inclusion Probabilities Based on the Bayesian Factor (P_{BF}) According to Our Prior Information Computed with Bootstrap Lasso

Covariates	P_{BF}
Personal and Educational Background of Students:	
Age	0.102
Gender (female)	0.075
Previously in general education	0.894*
Previously in technical education	0.711*
Previously in vocational education	0.149
Previously in art education	0.133
Previously in combined education	0.116
Working students	0.046
Regular students	0.075
Characteristics of the Course:	
No. of students in the first exam period	1.00*
Students enrolled for the first time	0.919*
Students retaking the course	0.089
Students retaking the course three times	0.093
Students retaking the course four times	0.099
Belgian students	0.021
Foreign students	1.00*
Islamic students	0.031
Students from other European countries	0.999*
Students from the Netherlands, France, and Germany	0.029
Students from other countries (non-EU)	0.008
Students with scholarship	0.018
Course offered as distance learning	1.00*
Learning Materials:	
Own book	0.018
Traditional book	1.00
Other materials	0.019

(Continued)

Table 7.3 (Continued) Variable Inclusion Probabilities Based on the Bayesian Factor (P_{BF}) According to Our Prior Information Computed with Bootstrap Lasso

Covariates	P_{BF}
Personal and Professional Characteristics of Teachers:	
Sex of teacher	0.02
Teacher with pedagogical degree	0.996
Teacher with professional training	0.113
Teacher with PhD	0.064
Teacher with Master's	0.602*
Teacher with Bachelor's	0.338
Teacher from industry	0.023
Year of birth	0.01
Evaluation Procedures:	
Verbal examination	1.00*
Written examination	1.00*
Multi-choice examination	0.942*
Permanent examination	0.979*
Internship	0.102
Learning Approach:	
Cognitive learning	0.009
Behavioral learning	0.013
Academic Year of Reference:	
2006	0.013
2007	0.019
2008	0.054
2009	0.042
2010	0.088
2011	0.078
2012	1.00*

* Included in the final model.

In our application, we obtained a parsimonious model formed by a small number of variables that have the highest impact on the explanation of student performance.

The proposed procedure provided a suitable approach to variable selection in higher education studies, where there are a large number of possible contender variables that produce several possible models. To facilitate further use of the technique, the R-codes are available upon request.

To demonstrate the features of our approach, we tested it on a multiple linear regression model; in principle, our methodology is quite flexible to allow for more complex models, likewise hierarchical models, which are useful when data are nested within a natural hierarchical structure.

Future work will be devoted to applying this approach to even larger datasets that are now common in the field of education at national and international level.

Acknowledgment

The authors would like to thank participants in the IV Efficiency in Education Workshop in Politecnico di Milano.

This work has been partially funded as part of the project "Structural Policies and Reforms. Analysis of indicators and evaluation of the effects," FRA 2015, University of Trieste.

References

Bach, F. R. (2008). Bolasso: Model consistent lasso estimation through the bootstrap. In *Proceedings of the 25th International Conference on Machine Learning*, 33–40. New York, NY: ACM.

Baker, R. S. J. D., and Yacef, K. (2009). The state of educational data mining in 2009: A review and future visions. *Journal of Educational Data Mining*, 1(1), 3–17.

Bayarri, M. J., Berger, J. O., Forte, A., and Garcia-Donato, G. (2012). Criteria for Bayesian model choice with application to variable selection. *Annals of Statistics*, 40(3), 1550–1577.

Beikzadeh, M. R., Phon-Amnuaisuk, S., and Delavari, N. (2008). Data mining application in higher learning institutions. *Informatics in Education: An International Journal*, 7(1), 31–54.

Chies, L., Graziosi, G., and Pauli, F. (2014). Job opportunities and academic dropout: The case of the University of Trieste. *Procedia Economics and Finance*, 17, 63–70.

Dupuis, D. J., and Victoria-Feser, M.-P. (2013). Robust vif regression with application to variable selection in large data sets. *Annals of Applied Statistics* 7(1), 319–341.

Efron, R., and Tibshirani, R. (1993). *An Introduction to the Bootstrap*. Dordrecht: Chapman & Hall/CRC Monographs on Statistics & Applied Probability.

Fan, J., and Li, R. (2001). Variable selection via nonconcave penalized likelihood and its oracle properties. *Journal of the American Statistical Association*, 96(456), 1348–1360.

Feng, L., Rui, P., German, M., Merlise, A. C., and Berger, J. O. (2008). Mixtures of g priors for bayesian variable selection. *Journal of the American Statistical Association*, 103(481), 410–423.

Fox, J.-P. (2010). *Bayesian Item Response Modeling: Theory and Applications*. Berlin: Springer Science & Business Media.

Garcia-Donato, G., and Martinez-Beneito, M. (2013). On sampling strategies in bayesian variable selection problems with large model spaces. *Journal of the American Statistical Association*, 108(501), 340–352.

George, E. I., and McCulloch, R. E. (1993). Variable selection via Gibbs sampling. *Journal of the American Statistical Association*, 88(423), 881–889.

Hindryckx, J., and De Witte, K. (2015). The influence of the learning environment on course efficiency. Evidence from Flanders. *TIER Working Paper Series*, 15/04.

Ishii, H., and Watanabe, H. (2001). A Bayesian predictive analysis of test scores. *Japanese Psychological Research*, 43(1), 25–36.

Kass, R. E., and Raftery, A. E. (1995). Bayes factors. *Journal of the American Statistical Association*, 90(430), 773–795.

Kass, R. E., and Wasserman, L. (1996). The selection of prior distributions by formal rules. *Journal of the American Statistical Association*, 91(435), 1343–1370.

Kotsiantis, S. (2009). Educational data mining: A case study for predicting dropout-prone students. *International Journal of Knowledge Engineering and Soft Data Paradigm*, 1(2), 101–111.

Krishna, A., Bondell, H. D., and Ghosh, S. K. (2009). Bayesian variable selection using an adaptive powered correlation prior. *Journal of Statistical Planning and Inference*, 139(8), 2665–2674.

Marquez-Vera, C., Cano, A., Romero, C., and Ventura, S. (2013). Predicting student' failure at school using genetic programming and different data mining approaches with high dimensional and imbalanced data. *Applied Intelligence*, 38(3), 315–330.

Mohamad, S. K., and Tasir, Z. (2013). Educational data mining: A review. *Procedia: Social and Behavioral Sciences*, 97, 320–324.

O'Hara, R. B., and Sillanpää, M. J. (2009). A review of Bayesian variable selection methods: What, how and which. *Bayesian Analysis*, 4(1), 85–117.

Romero, C., Romero, J. R., and Ventura, S. (2014). A survey on pre-processing educational data. In A. Peña-Ayala (Ed.), *Educational Data Mining: Applications and Trends. Studies in Computational Intelligence*, 29–64. Cham: Springer International Publishing.

Romero, C., and Ventura, S. (2007). Educational data mining: A survey from 1995 to 2005. *Expert System with Applications*, 33(1), 135–146.

Romero, C., and Ventura, S. (2010). Educational data mining: A review of the state of the art. *Transactions on Systems, Man, and Cybernetics Part C*, 40(6), 601–618.

Rubin, D. B. (1980). Using empirical Bayes techniques in the law school validity studies. *Journal of the American Statistical Association*, 75(372), 801–816.

Rubin, D. B. (1983). Some applications of Bayesian statistics to educational data. *Journal of the Royal Statistical Society. Series D (The Statistician)*, 32(1/2), 55–68.

Subbiah, M., Srinivasan, M., and Shanthi, S. (2011). Revisiting higher education data analysis: A Bayesian perspective. *International Journal of Science and Technology Education Research*, 2(2), 32–38.

Tibshirani, R. (1996). Regression shrinkage and selection via the lasso. *Journal of the Royal Statistical Society. Series B (Methodological)*, 58(1), 267–288.

Tobias, J. L., and Li, M. (2004). Returns to schooling and bayesian model averaging: A union of two literatures. *Journal of Economic Surveys*, 18(2), 153–180.

Weiss, R. E. (2010). Bayesian methods for data analysis. *American Journal of Ophthalmology*, 149(2), 187.

Zellner, A. (1986). On assessing prior distributions and Bayesian regression analysis with g-prior distributions. In P. K. Goel and A. Zellner (Eds.), *Bayesian Inference and Decision Techniques: Essays in Honor of Bruno De Finetti*, Vol. 6, 233–243, North-Holland, Amsterdam.

Zimmermann, J., Brodersen, K. H., Heinimann, H. R., and Buhmann, J. M. (2015). A model-based approach to predicting graduate-level performance using indicators of undergraduate-level performance. *Journal of Educational Data Mining*, 7(3), 151–176.

Zou, H., and Hastie, T. (2005). Regularization and variable selection via the elastic net. *Journal of the Royal Statistical Society: Series B (Statistical Methodology)*, 67(2), 301–320.

Zwick, R. (1993). The validity of the GMAT for the prediction of grades in doctoral study in business and management: An empirical Bayes approach. *Journal of Educational Statistics*, 18(1), 91–107.

Appendix

In Table 7.4, we report the posterior probabilities of inclusion of each covariate of the BF when the conventional Zellner's g-prior is used. The results show that all the previous variables with our prior are included, plus three other variables (students retaking the course four times, vocational education, and combined education), leading to a less parsimonious model compared to our approach.

Table 7.4 Variable Inclusion Probabilities Based on the Bayesian Factor (P_{BF}) According to the Zellner's g-prior

Covariates	P_{BF}
Personal and Educational Background of Students:	
Age	0.03
Gender (female)	0.107
General education	0.998*
Technical education	0.972*
Vocational education	0.524*
Art education	0.606
Combined education	0.015
Working students	0.022
Regular students	0.022
Characteristics of the Course:	
# of Students in the First Exam Period	1.00*
Students enrolled for the first time	0.722*
Students retaking the course	0.297
Students retaking the course three times	0.297
Students retaking the course four times	0.563*
Belgian students	0.069
Foreign students	1.00*
Islamic students	0.141
Students from other European countries	0.566
Students from the Netherlands, France, and Germany	0.019
Students from other countries (non-EU)	0.018

(Continued)

Table 7.4 (Continued) Variable Inclusion Probabilities Based on the Bayesian Factor (P_{BF}) According to the Zellner's g-prior

Covariates	P_{BF}
Students with scholarship	0.019
Course offered as distance learning	1.00*
Learning Materials:	
Own book	0.019
Traditional book	1.00*
Other materials	0.015
Personal and Professional Characteristics of Teachers:	
Sex of teacher	0.012
Teacher with pedagogical degree	0.994*
Teacher with professional training	0.056
Teacher with PhD	0.035
Teacher with Master's	0.928*
Teacher with Bachelor's	0.06
Teacher from industry	0.018
Year of birth	0.011
Evaluation Procedures:	
Verbal examination	1.00*
Written examination	1.00*
Multi-choice examination	0.586*
Permanent examination	0.983*
Internship	0.268
Learning Approach:	
Cognitive learning	0.014
Behavioral learning	0.012
Academic Year of Reference:	
2006	0.015
2007	0.029

(Continued)

Table 7.4 (Continued)   Variable Inclusion Probabilities Based on the Bayesian Factor (P_{BF}) According to the Zellner's g-prior

Covariates	P_{BF}
2008	0.072
2009	0.095
2010	0.218
2011	0.195
2012	1.00*

Note: The asterisk denotes that the variable is included in the final model.

Chapter 8

Using Statistical Analytics to Study School Performance through Administrative Datasets

Tommaso Agasisti, Francesca Ieva, Chiara Masci, Anna Maria Paganoni, and Mara Soncin

Contents

8.1 Introduction

In the majority of European countries, the evaluation of schools is at the heart of the educational system as a means to guarantee the quality of education. Every year, in most countries around the world, students perform national examinations. Their results are stored in (administrative) datasets and analyzed by several stakeholders, including governmental agencies, media, and researchers on educational issues. These are not the only data that can be considered useful for evaluative purposes, however. Indeed, quantitative indicators also cover wider areas of school characteristics: inputs (financial and human resources), processes (hours of lessons, types of materials that are used, classroom schedules, etc.), and outputs other than tests (i.e., grades on several subjects, scores assigned to disciplinary behaviors, etc.). Overall, this amount of data constitutes a patrimony that schools could use to improve the quality of the educational processes that happen within them. At present, advances in information and communication technology (ICT) and data analysis techniques allow schools to make use of massive amounts of data in their daily management. This chapter focuses in particular on the use of students' data to benchmark schools and to assess their performances. It illustrates the potential contribution of information gathered through data analytics to promote the continuous improvement of schools' educational processes. Overall, we show that such objectives can be pursued by leveraging the information that is contained in administrative datasets. Such databases are collected for different purposes—especially for purely administrative duties—and can instead be really fruitful in assisting analysts in school assessment. For this purpose, techniques of data analysis are a crucial standpoint for making the most out of school evaluations. Once the data are available, the analytical problem lies in having the right instruments for using them and correctly interpreting the results. The use of data depends on two critical resources: (1) political commitment (the decision makers must be convinced of the importance of informing policies through evidence and quantitative information) and (2) the involvement of skilled workforce that can apply innovative and advanced methodologies to work in data analytics.

For correctly interpreting the results, policy makers must be open to collaborate with these technical personnel. The hope is that the interaction between analysts, academics, and policy makers could improve the understanding of educational processes and the evidence around the determinants of achievement—and can suggest potential for interventions. The main point that we would raise in this chapter is how techniques for data analyses can help analysts to estimate the so-called *school effect,* in other words, the very specific contribution that each institution is able to provide to students enrolled in it, and—how it contributes to higher/lower achievement of students, net of other personal and contextual factors. The search for estimating the *school effect* in a quantitative fashion is a very topical argument since early studies in the educational field (in one sense, the Coleman Report can be interpreted as the first attempt in this direction—see Coleman et al., 1966).

Since then, not only has the theory advanced substantively, but also the available techniques for methodological and empirical analyses have reached a high level of sophistication. The modern analytical techniques, if properly employed, hold the promise of contributing substantially to the identification of the school effect. This way, they would help data analysts and school managers in defining better practices to be introduced for the improvement of schools. The specific aim of this chapter is thus threefold: (1) to discuss the desirable characteristics of administrative datasets for allowing the estimation of school effects; (2) to present one viable use of an advanced statistical group of techniques to analyze school effects; (3) to assess how these techniques have been applied in literature, and their relative utility and drawbacks.

Accordingly, the remainder of this chapter is organized as follows. In Section 8.2, we discuss how an administrative dataset is structured, as well as it should be organized. We refer specifically to the theoretical framework introduced by the Organisation for Economic Co-operation and Development (OECD) and the International Association for the Evaluation of Educational Achievement (IEA) in their international-level surveys, as they represent examples and standards for data collection that are being increasingly adopted worldwide. In Section 8.3 we introduce some methodological topics, with special reference to the use of statistical modeling and analyses for studying school performances. Within the broad group of methods that can serve the score, we focused on multilevel models, and explain why we consider them superior in many circumstances for assessing schools' results specifically. Section 8.4 critically presents a number of studies, already published in academic journals, that contain empirical applications of multilevel models for assessing schools' results. We use these studies as a reference point for showing strengths and weaknesses of the proposed methods, as well as recent advancements. Lastly, Section 8.5 concludes the chapter, also discussing briefly the possible role of policy makers (and school managers) in using data analyses.

8.2 How Administrative Datasets Are Structured

In this section, the aim is to outline the desirable characteristics of an administrative dataset that could be analyzed by applying suitable statistical tools with assessment purposes. In particular, two main administrative databases are illustrated: the OECD's Programme for International Student Assessment (PISA) and the data collected by the Italian Institute for the Evaluation of Educational System (INVALSI).

8.2.1 The Main Features of Administrative Datasets

In the general framework of economics of education, finalized to explore the determinants of students' and schools' results, different sources of data have been used at country and international level. In addition to survey data specifically designed to serve this purpose (see, for instance, the IEA's Trends in International Mathematics and Science Study [TIMSS] and Progress in International Reading Literacy Study [PIRLS]), the high potential of administrative dataset has increased. This source of data, with a high number of observations collected by government departments and other organizations for administrative and bureaucratic purposes, has specific advantages that make it particularly attractive for stakeholders and analysts in the field of educational policies. Such advantages are mainly related to (1) the high number of observations collected (usually covering a universe of students, not samples), (2) the regularity of collection, (3) the consistency of data collected by a governmental organization, and (4) the possibility to link data to external datasets, enriching the original information. On the other hand, dealing with administrative datasets implies some drawbacks, such as (1) the cost of data extraction and cleaning, (2) the increasing data protection issue, (3) the usually high amount of missing data, and (4) the lack of a specific research design (since data are collected for administrative purposes and not for answering well-defined research questions, see Table 8.1).

In general, the particular characteristic of the administrative databases poses a broader issue of theory and methods' needs in their application to social science research (see Wallgren and Wallgren, 2007). However, education is an application context of particular interest thanks to the existence of administrative datasets built on specific theoretical frameworks, results of a long tradition of educational science. Decades of empirical research on economics of education have outlined a theoretical framework in which student achievement is influenced by a specific set of characteristics bearing to four main classes. Specifically, they can be classified according to (1) the student's socio-economic background and innate ability, (2) his/her peers' characteristics, (3) specific educational and managerial practices implemented at the school (called, in a technical sense, *school effect*), and (4) the broader context in which the school operates (Figure 8.1).

8.2.2 Examples of International and National Surveys: OECD, PISA, and INVALSI Data

Before structuring administrative datasets in this setting, it is useful to review the main features of well-designed international surveys that inform the evolution of

Table 8.1 Advantages and Disadvantages of Administrative Datasets

Advantages	Disadvantages
High number of observations	Need of data cleaning
Regularity of collection	Data protection and privacy
Data consistency (governmental source)	High amount of missing data
Data link across datasets	Lack of a research design

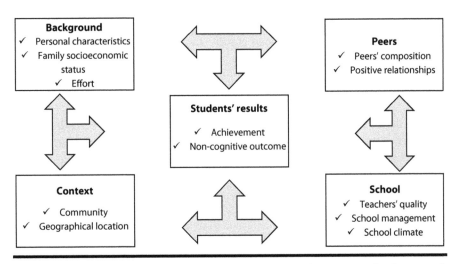

Figure 8.1 Studying the determinants of students' performances: the framework proposed by the economics of education.

the data warehouses (DWH) that develop the practical tree of information (informative system) behind recent administrative databases. Among so-structured datasets developed in a survey-specific context, the most used is the OECD Programme for International Student Assessment (PISA). The test has taken place every three years since 2000, in OECD countries all over the world. The target population is 15-year-old students, whose competencies are tested in three different subjects: reading, mathematics, and science.

Moreover, every wave has a focus on a specific subject: reading literacy was the focus of PISA in 2000 and 2009, and will be again in 2018; mathematics was the focus of PISA in 2003 and 2012, and will be again 2021; science was the focus of PISA in 2006 and 2015, and will be again in 2024. In the last wave whose data are available (PISA, 2015), more than 540,000 students of 72 economies took part at the assessment. In each country,* schools are randomly selected to be statistically representative of the target population. The broad goals of the data collection are clearly stated by the OECD Secretary-General Ángel Gurria in the introduction to PISA 2012:

> Over the past decade, the OECD Programme for International Student Assessment (PISA), has become the world's premier yardstick for evaluating the quality, equity and efficiency of school systems [...]. But the evidence base that PISA has produced goes well beyond statistical

---

* PISA assesses students in almost 70 countries in the world. Appendix A contains a list of these countries.

benchmarking. By identifying the characteristics of high-performing education systems, PISA allows governments and educators to identify effective policies that they can then adapt to their local contexts.

(OECD, 2012)

In order to meet these goals, a large amount of data need to be collected. In particular, along with the cognitive tests, students are asked to fill a questionnaire with background information about their families and learning experiences; school principals are provided with a questionnaire about the school system and educational activities; and in some countries, parents are asked to fill a questionnaire about their involvement in and support for their children's school activities. The educational outcomes that PISA test wants to observe are related to both cognitive and non-cognitive skills. Cognitive skills are the core part of the assessment, led through a two-hour test with both open-ended and multiple-choice questions. Non-cognitive skills are investigated mainly through the student questionnaire, and partially through the school questionnaire. Given the importance that non-cognitive skills have demonstrated in the development of personal success and labor market outcomes (see Heckman et al., 2006), this aspect is investigated through general questions on students' motivation and cognitive aspects, such as reading engagement, interest in mathematics, and enjoyment of science. Among the determinants of students' achievement, the student questionnaire also aims to collect information about students' socio-economic status and ethnic background, the two background aspects most correlated with school outcomes (see Corak, 2013 and Schnepf, 2007). With reference to students' socio-economic status, OECD computes an aggregate index able to predict the family condition with a high level of accuracy. The so-called "Economic, Social, and Cultural Status" (ESCS) index is computed considering (1) parents' occupational status, (2) parents' education, and (3) household possessions. This final aspect ranges from the availability of a place to study to the number of books owned at home. Finally, given the importance of early childhood education in determining school success and adult outcomes (Heckman and Masterov, 2007), the PISA questionnaire also collects information about pre-primary and primary education of students. At a higher level, school-level information deals with two major groups of variables: school processes and school background. With reference to school processes, the school questionnaire gathers information about (types of) programs offered, extracurricular activities, school climate, leadership, managerial practices, and parental involvement in school activities. Moreover, in light of the crucial role that teacher quality plays in influencing student achievement (see Rivkin et al., 2005 and Rockoff, 2004), the dataset reports information about teachers' qualifications and teaching practices, as well as information about disciplinary climate in the classroom. Regarding school background, aggregated student data are available with reference to social/ethnic/academic composition, allowing to control for the existence of an influence of these factors on peers' achievement (the so-called

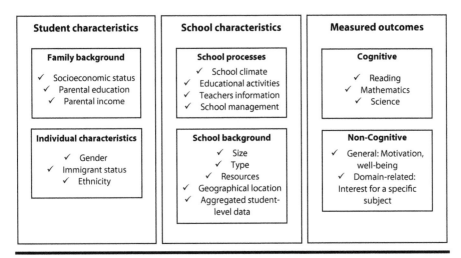

Student characteristics	School characteristics	Measured outcomes
Family background	**School processes**	**Cognitive**
✓ Socioeconomic status ✓ Parental education ✓ Parental income	✓ School climate ✓ Educational activities ✓ Teachers information ✓ School management	✓ Reading ✓ Mathematics ✓ Science
Individual characteristics	**School background**	**Non-Cognitive**
✓ Gender ✓ Immigrant status ✓ Ethnicity	✓ Size ✓ Type ✓ Resources ✓ Geographical location ✓ Aggregated student-level data	✓ General: Motivation, well-being ✓ Domain-related: Interest for a specific subject

Figure 8.2 An example of dataset structure: the OECD Programme for International Student Assessment (PISA).

"peer-effect," see Van Ewijk and Sleegers, 2010) for a dedicated analysis of this topic). Other information about school location, type and size of school/classrooms, and amount and source of resources gives the possibility to control for the school's context and general characteristics. In addition to these domain-general topics, part of the questionnaire deals with domain-specific topics related to the subject on which each wave is focused (e.g., science-teaching practices and school environment for science in the 2015 survey). Keeping the core set of questions constant over time, the dataset allows for trend analysis, giving analysts the ability to test the stability or variability of processes, practices, and educational activities at school. In Figure 8.2, an overview of the main groups of variables that are available in the PISA dataset (edition: 2012) is provided. They are classified by macro-categories, giving an outline of the kind of information that can be extracted from the survey.

National governments and organizations are realizing the high potential and usefulness of the information provided by administrative data for education if properly designed following a theoretical framework, like the one presented above. Therefore, they have started to collect systematically country-specific datasets. In Italy, the organization in charge of collecting data about student achievement is the National Evaluation Committee for Education (hereafter INVALSI). Students' competencies have been assessed on a yearly basis in both reading and mathematics since the 2004/2005 school year. Tests are given at grades two and five during the primary school, at grade eight, which corresponds to the last year of lower secondary school, and at grade 10, the second year of upper secondary school.* Every year, more than 500,000 students for each grade mentioned take

---

* Until recently, information was also available for the first year of lower secondary school. However, the test at grade six has been discontinued since the 2013/14 school year.

the test at the national level. The dataset is structured similarly to that of the OECD PISA, with information collected at student, school, and territorial level. At student level, the data available concern test achievement, gender, immigrant status (divided into first- and second-generation immigrants), age of schooling (students who enrolled one year before the standard age of six are defined as "early-enrolled"; students who enrolled after the age of six or repeated one or more years are defined as "late-enrolled"), socio-economic status of the family (calculated through the same ESCS index computed by OECD), and family size (number of siblings for each child). All of this information is collected by a student questionnaire that also aims at understanding the students' attitudes toward the INVALSI test, their motivations, and their home possessions (used in the ESCS index computation). This questionnaire is provided at all grades assessed except for grade eight, when the test is taken during the national exam for the certification of transition from lower to upper secondary school. As a bureaucratic consequence, no questionnaire is administered to students. At class and school level, it is possible to aggregate student-level data in order to obtain information about class and school composition. Moreover, available data concern the class and school size as well as the school's status as public or private. Finally, territorial and contextual information deals with the geographic localization of the school (with a regional detail) and the dimension and population of the municipality in which the school is located (whose name is instead anonymous). In addition to "traditional" data, two questionnaires have been introduced to be filled by a representative sample of schools. The first is the teacher questionnaire (since the 2011/2012 school year), which aims at collecting information about teachers' attitudes toward standardized tests and teaching practices. The second is the school questionnaire (since the 2013/2014 school year), which is filled out by school principals with the aim of gathering information about their attitudes toward INVALSI tests, parental engagement, and managerial practices implemented in the school. Both of these questionnaires are only provided to schools randomly selected to be part of the national sample, the reference sample of schools where tests are monitored by external evaluators. These additional questionnaires provide information about two fundamental determinants of student achievement that were missing in the first waves of the test: teaching and managerial practices. The test is assessed yearly, so it enables the constitution of panel data where a single student is followed over time, from primary to upper secondary school. This requires the creation of an anonymous student code to be maintained over time, a fact that still encounters technical problems. This procedure, which allows the school to trace a student through the years, started in Italy in 2010 (the name of the project is Informative System of Education [SIDI]). Originally, the collection of students' codes did not happen systematically, so the loss of information is still very high. After having reviewed the main features of administrative datasets, it must be clarified that some problems in the way such data are collected, maintained, and developed still remain. In Italy, as in other national and international contexts, the main challenges to be faced for exploiting the most potential from administrative databases are the following (and they must be considered in an interdisciplinary approach):

- *Missing data.* In these kinds of administrative datasets, the amount of missing data deriving from answers not given by respondents adds up to data lost because of technical problems in data entry and linkage, making this a central point of the discussion. Methods for inputting missing data do exist (see, among others, Enders, 2010 and reference therein), but none of them is robust enough to be considered as a golden standard.
- *Person-specific code.* Another point to be developed is the availability of an anonymous code that univocally identifies the student, allowing not only the construction of a panel dataset (following different cohorts of students over time), but also the possibility of matching different sources of administrative data, taking full advantage of the potential offered by these sources of data. Such perspective could even be strengthened by the opportunities offered by big data; however, the growing issue of protecting individual data and other primary issues also challenge the use of such codes.

8.3 Applying Data Analytics to Study School Performance

As indicated in the previous section, the educational process is a very complex system and there are several variables that play a role within it. The main aim of this section is to analyze what are the statistical tools that best fit the nature of the educational data and are able to extract significant information from them.

Educational data have a hierarchical structure, the three main levels in which students are nested being (1) classes, (2) schools, and (3) geographical areas (which, in turn, may be stratified into districts, regions, macroareas, etc.). The characteristics of each of these levels influence the educational performances of the students, leading to intraschool/intraclass correlations in pupils' responses. Often, much of what is referred to as "pupil-level characteristics" may instead be attributable to the environment, such as the family, the school, or the geographical area. Indeed, the need to control for grouping in the analysis of hierarchically structured data is well known (see, for example, Goldstein, 2011). The advent of statistical techniques that deal with nested data structures has made it possible to differentiate between elements of this complex social environment (Rasbash et al., 2010). To this purpose, multilevel models are the most suitable statistical methods to catch the stratification effects. Sections 8.3.1 and 8.3.2 explain why multilevel models well serve the purpose and how to interpret the random part of multilevel models.

8.3.1 Why Multilevel Models Well Serve the Purpose

First of all, consider a traditional three-level model in which pupils (level 1) are nested in classes (level 2), which are in turn nested in schools (level 3).* This model can be written as:

$$y_{ilj} = \beta_0 + \sum_{k=1}^{K} \beta_k x_{kilj} + b_j + u_{lj} + \epsilon_{ilj}$$

$$b_j \sim N\left(0, \sigma_b^2\right), \quad u_{lj} \sim N\left(0, \sigma_u^2\right), \quad \epsilon_{ilj} \sim N\left(0, \sigma_\epsilon^2\right), \tag{8.1}$$

$$i = 1, \ldots, n_{lj}, \qquad l = 1, \ldots, m_j, \quad j = 1, \ldots, J.$$

where y_{ilj} is the scholastic performance of the ith pupil within the lth class within the jth school, and x_{kilj} is the corresponding value of the kth predictor variable at student level. The typical predictor variables at student level are students' prior achievements, gender, age, ethnicity, socio-economic index and other specific features. b_j and u_{lj} are school and class effects respectively. They are assumed to be independent of one another and of the covariates, normally distributed with mean 0 and variance σ_b^2 and σ_u^2 respectively. The model is able to estimate the effect given by the school (b_j) and by the class (u_{lj}) after adjusting for pupils' characteristics. σ_b^2 represents the between-school variance component, σ_u^2 the between-class (and within-school) variance component, and σ_ϵ^2 the between-student (and within-school, within-class) variance component. Therefore, the model is able to decompose the total variability of pupils' scores in parts that vary between schools, classes, and students. In particular, it is possible to compute the Percentage of Variation captured by each Random Effect (PVRE) that is obtained by the proportion of a random-effect variance over the total variation. This is key quantitative information, as it gives a first assessment about the relative weights of various elements (class, school, etc.) in affecting students' academic results, so it is possible to understand their relative importance in the educational process. The proportions of variance explained at school, class, and pupil level are:

$$PVRE_{school} = \frac{\sigma_b^2}{\sigma_b^2 + \sigma_u^2 + \sigma_\epsilon^2},$$

$$PVRE_{class} = \frac{\sigma_u^2}{\sigma_b^2 + \sigma_u^2 + \sigma_\epsilon^2}, \tag{8.2}$$

$$PVRE_{student} = \frac{\sigma_\epsilon^2}{\sigma_b^2 + \sigma_u^2 + \sigma_\epsilon^2}.$$

---

* The levels of grouping may be less or more numerous, depending on the effects that are investigated and on the available data.

Each of these three PVREs can be interpreted as the proportion of the total variance that is due to differences between schools, classes, and pupils respectively.

In this specific linear model, covariates at pupils' levels are taken into account, while random intercepts for class and school effects are added. However, the model can be easily extended to the case in which there are covariates also at school or class level. Consider, for example, a two-level model in which pupils (level 1) are nested in schools (level 2) and covariates both in the fixed and random parts are included (for ease of notation and without loss of generality, just two levels and one school-level covariate in the random part are considered). The model can be written as follows:

$$y_{ij} = \beta_0 + \sum_{k=1}^{K} \beta_k x_{kij} + b_{1j} \tilde{z}_{1j} + \epsilon_{ij}$$

$$b_j = \left(b_{0j}, b_{1j} \right)^T \sim N_2 \left(0, \Sigma_b \right),$$

$$\Sigma_b = \begin{pmatrix} \sigma_{b_0}^2 & Cov\left(b_0, b_1 \right) \\ - & \sigma_{b_1}^2 \end{pmatrix} \tag{8.3}$$

$$\epsilon_{ilj} \sim N\left(0, \sigma_\epsilon^2 \right),$$

$$i = 1, \dots, n_j, \qquad j = 1, \dots, J.$$

where b_{0j} is the random intercept and $\tilde{z}_{1j}$ is the corresponding value of the predictor variable at school level. School managerial practices, average socio-economic index, percentages of disadvantaged students, and the private/public index are examples of influential variables at school level. In this case, the between-school variance is not only σ_b^2, but it depends also on the predictor variables at school level according to the variance equation (see Snijders and Bosker, 1999):

$$Var_{school} = \sigma_{b_0}^2 + 2Cov\left(b_0, b_1 \right) \tilde{z}_1 + \sigma_{b_1}^2 \tilde{z}_1^2 \tag{8.4}$$

In the context of multilevel models, it is worth taking into account that there are two different ways to interpret them. The first way is to consider the multilevel model as "structural model," in the sense that the regression coefficients are causal parameters and the error terms represent the effect of omitted covariates; in contrast, the second way is to interpret the multilevel model as a "statistical model," in which the regression coefficients represent associations or linear projections and the error terms are uncorrelated with all covariates by definition (see Castellano et al., 2014). From this perspective, we interpret multilevel models in the second way, since we are interested in the associations between variables and in estimating how much of the variance of students' test scores is attributable to structural differences between schools and classes. We refer to this as "school/class effect," in other words, how attending a specific school/class statistically influences students' test scores, and, after accounting for their individual characteristics, what is the primary piece of descriptive information that can help school managers understand how their action is affecting students' results. We do not investigate mechanisms through which such school/class effect can be considered as causal. Under the "structural model" assumptions, b_j and u_{ly} can be considered independent of one another and independent of the predictor variables that are included in the model. Moreover, considering multilevel models in the first way leads to endogeneity problems, because if there are omitted confounders in the model that are correlated with included covariates, then the error terms are correlated with the included covariates, leading to bias for standard estimators. From this point of view, the literature on the effect of schools on the achievements of pupils deals with the difficulties given by the endogeneity at the school-variables level and the intraschool (and intraclass) correlations in pupils' responses, as described in Castellano et al. (2014) and Steele et al. (2007).

Therefore, the statistical multilevel model is perfectly suitable for analyzing hierarchical educational data under certain assumptions for several reasons: it disentangles the effects at different levels, it estimates them, and it points out how much of the total variability is explained at each level. Moreover, beyond the random effect at each level, multilevel models also allow the estimation of associations between the outcome (such as pupils' test scores) and covariates at all the different levels present in the model.

8.3.2 How to Interpret the Random Effects in a Multilevel Setting

In the application of multilevel models on educational hierarchical data, it is important to understand how to interpret random effects. On this depends the ability to understand the role that schools play in influencing students' performances, all else equal. The literature shows how studies about school/class effects actually embody two different concepts of *school effect,* named *type A* and *type B* effects (see Castellano et al., 2014). Both types of effect involve the difference between the performance of a pupil in a particular school/class and the performance that might have been expected if that pupil had been in some other setting. However, *type A* effect is defined as the impact individual schools have on student achievements, both considering school practices and school context. In contrast, *type B* effect is designed to isolate the effect of school practices from school context, measuring only the impact of school practice that is the only part schools can control. From a practical point of view, *type A* effect is appropriate for parents choosing schools for their pupils, while *type B* for agencies evaluating school practice. In order to analyze both types of effects, spatial data and appropriate statistical methods are necessary. To this purpose, further investigations confirm that the technical requirements for producing unbiased estimators of *type A* effects are much more modest than the ones for producing unbiased estimators of *type B* effects (see Raudenbush and Willms, 1995). As said before, when computing b_j and u_{lj} in Equation 8.1, we are interested in estimating the impact of attending school j/class l on students' test scores, and we refer to this as "school/class effect," that is, *type A* effect. Multilevel models evaluate how much of the variance of students' test scores is attributable to structural differences between schools and classes. This is exactly what is done by estimating the random effects and computing the PVREs; this looks at the impact that attending certain schools or classes has on students' achievements. Certainly, the positive or negative impact that schools have on pupils' achievements may depend both on school practices (such as the school principal's decisions, school board, roles of teachers, etc.) and on school context (such as average socio-economic index, percentages of disadvantaged students, location, etc.). But the baseline multilevel approach that we are proposing here cannot separate the two hypotheses.

8.4 Examples: Empirical Applications from the Literature

In this section, five examples of multilevel models applied to educational administrative dataset taken by previous literature are selected and discussed. The main objective is to show different ways in which multilevel models can be applied to understand and describe the determinants of students' performance, with the aim of isolating the specific "school effect." The criteria used in selecting these five papers and their order of presentation are the following: the first paper reports a traditional example of a univariate two-level linear model in which students are nested within schools, where, among the fixed effects, only a random intercept is considered; the second paper consists of a three-level (students, classes, and schools) model, similar to the previous one, but where the outcome is bivariate; the third paper is an extension of the first one that allows for random slopes, meaning that the variance of random effect is allowed to differ across groups; the fourth paper adopts a multilevel simultaneous equation model, in which the authors face the frequent problem of endogeneity; and the last example considers a logistic multilevel model.

Table 8.2 contains a summary of the five examples, described in details later on.

The first example that we present is by Agasisti et al. (2017). The authors apply a multilevel linear model to the INVALSI dataset, containing detailed information for more than 200,000 students at grade six in the year 2011/2012. The aim of their work is to find out what are the variables at pupil and school levels that are associated with student achievements. In particular, they develop a two-stage analysis: at the first stage they fit a two-level linear model in which students are nested within schools, where the outcome variable is the INVALSI math score of students; at the second stage, they regress the estimated school effects against a series of school-level

Table 8.2 Summary of the Five Papers, Taken from the Literature, Described in This Section

Paper	Variables Used	Statistical Model Employed	Key Results
Agasisti et al. (2017). *Heterogeneity*, school effects and achievement gaps across Italian regions: further evidence from statistical modeling.	Students' test scores (grade six) and prior achievements (grade five), individual characteristics, school-level variables.	Two stage analysis: (1) univariate multilevel linear model and (2) LASSO regression model.	Big differences elapse across the three geographical areas; school effect explains a significant part of student achievements variability, and it is stronger in Southern than in Northern Italy.
Masci et al. (2016). Bivariate multilevel models for the analysis of mathematics and reading pupils achievements.	Students' test scores (grade six) and prior achievements (grade five), individual characteristics.	Bivariate multilevel linear models	Different associations between student characteristics and math and reading scores; class matters more than school.
Plewis (2011). Contextual variations in ethnic group differences in educational attainments.	Students' test scores (age 11) and prior achievement (age seven), individual characteristics (among which ethnic group), family characteristics and school features.	Univariate multilevel linear model (with random slopes)	Ethnic group does have a role in influencing students' attainment. The highest variance is at student level, and the between-school variance is diversified according to the ethnic group composition.
Steele et al. (2007). The effect of school resources on pupil attainment: a multilevel simultaneous equation modeling approach.	Students' test scores (age 14), individual characteristics, school and LEA-levels variables.	Simultaneous equation model involving multilevel models	School effects are strong, especially in reading, while LEA ones are very weak. Some variables at school level are endogenous to attainments.
Rumberger (1995). Dropping out of middle school: a multilevel analysis of students and schools.	School dropout status, student level, family characteristics, and school-level variables	Nonlinear HLM analysis with students nested in schools	Students' background characteristics explain the most of variation in dropout rates at student level. School composition plays an important role.

variables, in order to describe the characteristics of schools that are associated with their higher/lower performances.

First, they introduce a traditional two-level school effectiveness model, which provides value-added estimates of secondary school performance. So, consider the multilevel model with only the random intercept for pupils' Corrected Math Scores (CMSs), where they treat pupils (level one) as nested within schools (level two). The model can be written as:

$$y_{ij} = \beta_0 + \sum_{k=1}^{K} \beta_k x_{kij} + b_j + \epsilon_{ij}$$

(8.5)

$$b_j \sim N\left(0, \sigma_b^2\right), \quad \epsilon_{ij} \sim N\left(0, \sigma_\epsilon^2\right),$$

where y_{ij} is the CMS for the i-th pupil within the j-th school, x_{kij} is the corresponding value of the k-th predictor variable at student level, $\beta = (\beta_0, ..., \beta_k)$ is the $(K + 1)$-dimensional vector of parameters to be estimated. The random effect b_j for the j-th school is assumed to be Gaussian distributed and independent of any predictor variables that are included in the model. Considering only statistical units with no missing information at any level, the database consists of 259,757 Italian students in 4119 schools. The authors fit the model in each geographical macroarea: North, Center and South of Italy.

The analysis employs six student-level variables: gender, immigration status, whether or not the student is in the model grade, whether or not the student is not living with both parents, prior achievement, and a composite indicator for socio-economic status (ESCS). Results are shown in Table 8.3.

By means of this model, the paper shows the associations between student-level variables and student achievements. Furthermore, the portions of total variance explained at school level are computed. The authors find that the PVREs are different across the geographical areas: the variance between schools in the North explain the 7.91% of the total variability, the one in the Center 10% and the one in the South 20%. This means that the differences across sample schools in the South represent a more relevant part of the total variability across student achievements than in the North. In other words, the impact of the school on achievements is stronger in the South than in the North.

When considering the second-stage analysis, the authors regress the estimated school effects of each macroarea against the school-level variables, by means of LASSO regression model (see Tibshirani, 1996):

$$\hat{b}_j = \gamma_0 + \sum_{l=1}^{L} \gamma_l z_{l_j} + \eta_j$$

(8.6)

$$\eta_j \sim N\left(0, \sigma_b^2\right)$$

Table 8.3   Table Shows the ML Estimates (with Standard Errors) of Model (5), Fitted in North, Center, and South of Italy

Fixed Effects			
	North	Center	South
Intercept	1.157∗∗∗	7.914∗∗∗	16.833∗∗∗
	(0.196)	(0.357)	(0.311)
Female	−1.695∗∗∗	−2.659∗∗∗	−2.141∗∗∗
	(0.069)	(0.126)	(0.102)
First-Generation Immigrant	−0.623∗∗∗	−0.590	0.436
	(0.169)	(0.323)	(0.485)
Late-Enrolled Student	−2.566∗∗∗	−1.794∗∗∗	−3.933∗∗∗
	(0.215)	(0.394)	(0.413)
ESCS	1.943∗∗∗	2.428∗∗∗	3.181∗∗∗
	(0.038)	(0.071)	(0.054)
Student Not Living with Both Parents	−1.216∗∗∗	−1.335∗∗∗	−1.485∗∗∗
	(0.100)	(0.182)	(0.175)
CMS Fifth Year Primary School Corrected Mathematics Score	0.700∗∗∗	0.571∗∗∗	0.387∗∗∗
	(0.002)	(0.004)	(0.003)
Random Effects			
σ_b	3.645	4.510	7.354
$\sigma_\in$	12.434	13.527	14.622
PVRE	7.91%	10%	20.18%
Size			
Number of Observations	130,256	46,529	82,972
Number of Groups (Schools)	1,843	712	1,564

Note: Asterisks Denote Different Levels of Significance: . $0.01 < p$-val < 0.1; * $0.001 < p$-value < 0.01; ** $0.0001 < p$-value < 0.001; *** p-value < 0.0001.

where

$$\gamma = \operatorname{argmin} \left(\hat{b}_j - \gamma_0 - \sum_{l=1}^{L} \gamma_l z_{l_j} \right)^2$$

(8.7)

$$\sum_l |\gamma_l| \leq \lambda$$

where $\hat{b}_j$ is the j-school effect estimated by Equation 8.5 and z_{l_j} is the value of the l-th predictor at school level. In this way, they can point out which are the variables at school level that are associated with positive or negative school effects. Table 8.4 shows the results of Equation 8.6 in each macroarea.

Therefore, in this kind of analysis, by means of multilevel linear models it is possible to estimate school effects on pupil achievements after adjusting for pupils' characteristics and, by means of a second-stage regression model, to determine the variables at school level associated with the estimated school effects.

Multilevel models can also handle multiple outcomes. In this vein, the second example that we present is by Masci et al. (2016), from which we show an application of multilevel model with a multivariate output. This work is a further

Table 8.4 ML Estimates (with *p*-values) for Model 6, Fitted to Data of Northern, Central, and Southern Area Schools

LASSO Model Coefficients			
	North	Center	South
Intercept	−0.6996	−3.5284***	−2.2368.
Mean School ESCS		0.9171.	1.9452***
% Female	0.0312*	0.0627**	0.0686**
% First-Generation Immigrants	−0.0601**	0.0547.	0.1383**
% Early-Enrolled		−0.1958*	−0.1585**
% Late-Enrolled	−0.0713**		−0.2474***
Number of Students	0.0027*	0.0050*	0.0118***
Instituto Comprensivo			0.0085***
Private	−0.7481**	−2.570**	

Note: Asterisks Denote Different Levels of Significance: . 0.01 < *p*-value < 0.1; * 0.001 < *p*-value < 0.01; ** 0.0001 < *p*-value < 0.001; * * * *p*-value < 0.0001.

development of the paper previously presented, in which the authors fit a bivariate three-level linear model in which the outcome is bivariate, that is, mathematics and reading pupil achievements (INVALSI test scores). Such a study departs from the tradition of literature on the economics of education that considers one subject at a time as an output; instead, the model proposed here explicitly takes interactions and dependencies between subjects into account. The three levels of grouping are students (level one), classes (level two) and schools (level three). The administrative dataset contains information about 221,529 students from 16,246 classes, within 3920 schools, provided by INVALSI.

The bivariate three-level linear model is the following:

$$y_{ilj} = \beta_0 + \sum_{k=1}^{K} \beta_k x_{kilj} + b_j + u_{l_j} + \epsilon_{ilj} \tag{8.8}$$

with pupil i, in class l, in school j and

$y = \begin{pmatrix} y_{\text{math}} \\ y_{\text{read}} \end{pmatrix}$ = mathematics and reading INVALSI test scores

$\beta = \begin{pmatrix} \beta_{\text{math}} \\ \beta_{\text{read}} \end{pmatrix}$ = matrix of parameters

$x = (x_0, \ldots, x_K)$ = covariates at student's level

$u = \begin{pmatrix} u_{\text{math}} \\ u_{\text{read}} \end{pmatrix} \sim N_2(0, W)$ = bivariate class effect

$b = \begin{pmatrix} b_{\text{math}} \\ b_{\text{read}} \end{pmatrix} \sim N_2(0, \Sigma)$ = bivariate school effect

This model disentangles the effects given by the class and by the school on student achievements, after adjusting for pupils' characteristics. Furthermore, these effects are estimated both for reading and mathematics, and it is therefore possible to analyze both the individual reading and math effects as well as the way in which they are related. Again, the authors fit the model in each geographical macroarea: North, Center, and South of Italy. We report in Table 8.5 the estimates of random effects, that is, the variance/covariance matrices W and Σ of class and school effect respectively. The key information is that such kinds of models could and should advise the set of variables that policy makers and school managers actually consider.

By means of this method, it is possible to compare the variance of school and class effects and make a different kind of consideration. First of all, a comment on the comparison between class and school effect: in all three macroareas, it is clear that the variances of class effect are higher than variances of school effect. This

Table 8.5 Variance/Covariance Matrices of the Two Random Effects Across Macroareas Estimated by Equation 8.8 and Correlation Coefficients of Random (School or Class) Effects between Mathematics and Reading

	North	Center	South
School	$\begin{pmatrix} 4.99 & 1.82 \\ 1.82 & 1.65 \end{pmatrix}$ corr = 0.63	$\begin{pmatrix} 5.89 & 3.49 \\ 3.49 & 3.56 \end{pmatrix}$ corr = 0.76	$\begin{pmatrix} 15.9 & 5.74 \\ 5.74 & 4.54 \end{pmatrix}$ corr = 0.67
Class	$\begin{pmatrix} 6.20 & -1.13 \\ -1.13 & 17.5 \end{pmatrix}$ corr = −0.10	$\begin{pmatrix} 13.9 & -0.88 \\ -0.88 & 18.1 \end{pmatrix}$ corr = −0.05	$\begin{pmatrix} 40.9 & 0.07 \\ 0.07 & 20 \end{pmatrix}$ corr = −0.002

means that the effect that classes have on student achievements are, on average, stronger than that of schools. Moreover, looking at the correlation coefficients, it is possible to observe that while the correlation between reading and math school effects is positive (0.63, 0.76, and 0.67 in the North, Center, and South respectively), the correlation between reading and math class effects is not statistically significant (−0.10, −0.05, and −0.002 in the North, Center, and South respectively). This means that the effects that a school has in math and reading are quite coherent, while the ones given by the class are totally independent, one of the other. One final observation deals with the comparison across geographical areas: both school and class effects have higher variances in the South than in the North, suggesting that the effects of schools and classes on student achievements are stronger in the South than in the North.

Multilevel models have been used also to approach specific educational issues, such as the gender or immigrant gap, allowing to control for the variability of these characteristics at different levels of investigation. An example in this direction is provided by Plewis (2011), who uses UK administrative data to study (1) how ethnic groups differ in a national standardized test and (2) which contextual factors have a higher influence on attainment. Data refer to the National Pupil Database (NPD), that records students' yearly achievement in English (reading) and mathematics at given grades, and to the Pupil Level Annual School Census (PLASC), which provides contextual information. In particular, data refer to more than 500,000 11-year-old students attending state schools in England. In addition to test scores, the dataset is provided with students' individual characteristics and prior achievements (at age seven), family background characteristics, and school characteristics about the context and composition. The nested structure of data is described at three levels: pupil, school and Local Education Authority (LEA). The model is univariate, with the two test scores considered separately, while the ethnic classification is based on the 12 groups identified in the PLASC dataset.

Two alternative models are presented: the first is a three-level model with random intercepts, specified as

$$y_{ijk} = b_{0jk} + b_1 x_{1ijk} + \sum_{p=2}^{P} b_p x_{pijk} + \sum_{p=2}^{P} C_p x_{1ijk} x_{pijk} + e_{ijk},$$

$$b_{0jk} = b_{00k} + u_{0jk}, \qquad (8.9)$$

$$b_{00k} = b_{000} + v_k$$

where the output is the test score obtained by student i, in school j, and LEA k. x_1 is a vector of contextual variable at individual and family level, x_p are dummies for the ethnic groups, and $x_1 x_p$ is the interaction between the two terms. The terms e_{ijk}, u_{0jk}, v_k refer to random effects respectively at student, school, and LEA level. The extension of this model allows for random slopes, which in turn means that the between-school variance is allowed to differ by ethnic group. This study is of particular interest because it suggests a method for employing multilevel models in the issue of analyzing the heterogeneity of school effect and describe how it can depend upon students' background characteristics (in this case, ethnicity). The model is

$$y_{ijk} = b_{0jk} + b_{1j} x_{1ijk} + \sum_{p=2}^{P} b_{pj} x_{pijk} + \sum_{p=2}^{P} C_p x_{1ijk} x_{pijk} + e_{ijk},$$

$$b_{0jk} = b_{00k} + \sum_{q=1}^{Q} b_q z_{qjk} + u_{0jk},$$

$$b_{1j} = b_{10} + u_{1jk}, \qquad (8.10)$$

$$b_{pj} = b_{p0} + \sum_{q=1}^{Q} d_q z_{qjk} + u_{pjk},$$

$$b_{00k} = b_{000} + v_k$$

where b_{pj} are the random slopes and z_q are school-level variables about school type and composition. In this context, random effects at level two (u_{pjk}) are allowed to covary.

Results report differences among ethnic groups, especially between Chinese (high performers) and Afro-Caribbean students, boys in particular (low performers). From estimates of model 8.9, evidences show that 85% of the variance is at individual level, 13% is between schools, and 1% between LEA, with pupil and family contexts playing a particularly important role. Finally, Equation 8.10 shows how the between-school variance is actually different between ethnic groups. Moreover, the attainment decreases when the proportion of an ethnic group increases, though the effect becomes smaller when the proportions get higher.

Another interesting example is taken by Steele et al. (2007). Their aim is to adopt a multilevel simultaneous equation modeling approach to assess the effect of school resources on pupil attainment at age 14. The authors focus on a traditional, crucial topic for the economics of education, namely, the correlation between resources employed on educational processes and their results. The paper faces one major methodological difficulty in the literature of school resources: endogeneity of school-level variables. The empirical strategy uses a multilevel model to allow for clustering of pupil outcomes by schools and local education authorities (LEAs), as well as clustering of school resources by LEAs.

A simultaneous equation model is used to adjust for endogeneity of school-resource allocation. The first model that they develop is a standard three-level linear model in which students (level one) are nested within schools (level two), that are in turn nested within LEAs (level three):

$$y_{ijk} = \alpha^T x_{ijk} + \beta z_{jk} + v_k^{(y)} + u_{jk}^{(y)} + \epsilon_{ijk}$$

$$v_k^{(y)} \sim N\left(0, \sigma_{v(y)}^2\right), u_{jk}^{(y)} \sim N\left(0, \sigma_{u(y)}^2\right), \epsilon_{ijk} \sim N\left(0, \sigma_\epsilon^2\right)$$

(8.11)

where student i is in school j that is in LEA k and x_{ijk} is a vector of explanatory variables defined at student level, z_{jk} is a measure of school resources, and $v_k^{(y)}$ and $u_{jk}^{(y)}$ are LEA and school effect respectively. At this point, a way to allow for the potential endogeneity of resources z_{jk} with respect to attainment y_{ijk} is to model the resource allocation process jointly with attainment. A two-level random-intercept model for school resources is:

$$z_{jk} = \gamma^T w_{jk} + v_k^{(z)} + u_{jk}^{(z)}$$

$$v_k^{(z)} \sim N\left(0, \sigma_{v(z)}^2\right)$$

(8.12)

where w_{jk} is a vector of explanatory variables at school level and $v_k^{(z)}$ is the LEA effect. Together, Equations 8.11 and 8.12 define a simultaneous equation model. The equations are linked via the school and LEA residuals and must therefore be estimated jointly. At each level, it is assumed that the random effects follow bivariate normal distributions, that is, $u_{jk} = \left(u_{jk}^{(y)}, u_{jk}^{(z)}\right)^T \sim N_2\left(0, \Sigma_u\right)$ and $v_k = \left(v_k^{(y)}, v_k^{(z)}\right)^T \sim N_2\left(0, \Sigma_v\right)$. The covariances at the school and LEA level are denoted by $\sigma_u^{(yz)}$ and $\sigma_v^{(yz)}$ respectively. Likelihood ratio tests may be used to test whether either $\sigma_u^{(yz)}$ or $\sigma_v^{(yz)}$ or both are equal to 0. A covariance that is significantly different from 0 implies that z_{jk} is endogenous, and the nature of the selection effect is given by the direction of the covariance estimate.

The data come from the federal agency of civic education (BPDB) and the PLASC. The model estimates the effect of school resources on pupils' achievement in English, mathematics, and science at age 14, that is, key stage three in 2002–2003. The results show estimates of the residual variance at each level, from which estimates of the intraschool and intra-LEA correlations have been calculated. The intraschool correlations for attainment show that there are moderate school effects on adjusted performance in all three subjects, with the strongest effect on English scores. 22% of the total variance in progress in English is due to differences between schools. After taking into account school effects on progress, LEA effects are very weak. Turning to the school resource measures, it is found that 16% of the total variance in expenditure per pupil can be explained by differences between LEAs. In this sense, the role of resources seems stronger on a wider territorial basis than at a specific school level. Moreover, the paper reports strong evidence that some variables at school level are endogenous to attainments. Indeed, comparing (1) the results of simultaneous multilevel models that take into account this endogeneity, and (2) simple multilevel models that consider all variables as exogenous, they observe significant differences, asserting that models that do not allow for this endogeneity have an important source of bias.

In a data-analytics framework, the choice of the best model to adopt not only depends on the structure of data, but also on the kind of output to be investigated. The last example presented from the literature is by Rumberger (1995) and aims at analyzing the determinants of dropping out of school at individual and school level through a Hierarchical Linear Model (HLM). The author uses data from the National Education Longitudinal Survey (NELS) of 1988, a survey held in the United States that involved grade-eight students, families, teachers, and school principals in a national probability sample of about 1,100 public and private middle schools, with an average of 25 students per school surveyed. Part of this sample was surveyed again in 1990 (two years later), in order to identify if they were still enrolled or if they dropped out, with a final sample of 981 schools. In detail, the aim of this research was to understand (1) what factors influence students' decision to drop out, (2) how these factors differ among ethnic groups, and (3) what factors have an impact on dropout rate both at student and institutional level.

As in the traditional multilevel structure, the problem is first investigated at student level (within schools) and then studied at the between-schools variation. The difference concerns the dependent variable, which is dichotomous and equal to 1 when the student drops out and 0 otherwise. Moreover, because NELS data are weighted both at student and school level, the author first applies a logistic regression with weighted estimates at student level, and then performs a nonlinear hierarchical analysis. This second part is the main point of attention in this chapter, and it requires two types of models: a level-one model to estimate the effects of student-level variables on student outcome, and a level-two model to estimate the effects of school-level variables on the coefficients from the level-one analysis. The level-one model is expressed as:

$$\text{logit}\left(p_{ij}\right) = \beta_{0j} + \beta_{1j}\text{Black}_{ij} + \beta_{2j}\text{Hispanic}_{ij} + \beta_{3j}\text{Second}_{ij}$$

$$+ \beta_{4j}\text{SES}_{ij} + \beta_{5j}\text{Supervision}_{ij} + \beta_{6j}\text{Expectations}_{ij} + \beta_{7j}\text{Heldback}_{ij} \quad (8.13)$$

$$\beta_{8j}\text{Change}_{ij} + \in_{ij},$$

$$\beta_{pj} = \gamma_{p0} + u_{pj}, \qquad\qquad p = 0,\dots,8. \qquad (8.14)$$

where p_{ij} is the probability that student i drops out from school j, expressed as a log of the odds (or logit) output and as a function of demographic variables, family, and academic background. Respectively, Black and Hispanic are dummies for the ethnicity, Second is a dummy for second-generation immigrants, SES refers to the socio-economic status of the family, Supervision and Expectations stand for parental attitude toward school activities, and Heldback and Change report respectively if the student was ever held back in school and how many times they changed school. Finally, $\in_{ij}$ is the error term. The coefficients from the student-level model, β_{pj}, are allowed to vary across schools according to Equation 8.14, in which u_{pj} is the random component at student level. From Equation 8.14 derives a second stage of the analysis, that is, the level-two model, specified as:

$$\beta_{pj} = \gamma_{p0} + \gamma_{p1}\text{STUCOMP}_j + \gamma_{p2}\text{STRUCHAR}_j + \gamma_{p1}\text{CLIMATE}_j + u_{pj} \quad (8.15)$$

where student-level models, β_p, are computed for each j-th school as a function of student composition variables (STUCOMP), structural characteristics of the school such as size and localization (STRUCHAR), and school climate and organization (CLIMATE). Moreover, HLM estimates are weighted using school weights to adjust for the non-random structure of NELS survey data. Results presented by the authors suggest that differences in the background characteristics of students account for 36% of the differences in dropout rates. Among individual-level variables, SES makes the difference and explains most of the difference in the odds of dropping out between ethnic groups. Adding school-level variables, the total amount variance explained raises to 41.5%, obtained through the sequential introduction of school-level vectors mentioned in Equation 8.15. Therefore, in other words school factors weigh less than 6% of variability in test scores. Student composition is particularly important in explaining between-schools variation, especially in terms of SES composition, although a restriction of the analysis to low-SES schools shows a high degree of variability in the dropout rates and composition among these schools. What we learn from these reviewed academic contributions is that multilevel models, in their different forms, are able to clarify one of the most important aspects of the educational system, that is, the understanding of the levels, on which it is possible to act, that play a role in influencing student outcome. Thus, it is possible to identify at which level and in what direction school managers should take action.

8.5 Concluding Remarks: Suggestions for the Use of Results from Data Analytics for Policy Makers

After having seen the potential of data analytics applications for estimating school effects, this final section highlights some important points in favor of a practical use of results by policy makers and school administrators. A potential risk, indeed, is that the various analyses that are provided through innovative and robust techniques will not actually provide any change in the real world if the relevant actors in schools do not turn their attitudes toward an extensive use of data-driven decision making (in this vein, see the contribution by Marsh et al., 2006). First, the way data and results are presented should be clear for decision makers. However, being the model statistically complex, non-technical people in charge of making decisions must trust the validity of estimates, and should understand the implications clearly. In other words, if the obtainment of results about school evaluations is based on sophisticated technical activity, the transmission of information and baseline interpretation must be understandable for a wider audience. Second, the discussion about data and results of quantitative analysis should engage a high number of stakeholders, including teachers, principals, middle management, and parents when necessary. The error of considering the reading and use of data only to be in the hands of a small group of experts must be avoided. Data information should circulate, and many actors should be stimulated to propose changes, innovations, and interventions based on evidence provided by data. Although not all suggestions would be accommodated, this wide involvement of people will help in growing critical thinking based on data, and can bring the use of quantitative information more into the day-to-day culture of educational institutions. Third, analyses of school processes, activities, and output should be sustained over time. The propensity to use quantitative data for assessing schools' performance must not be an interesting one-shot exercise. If decision making should be renewed, for accommodating more data in support of it, data collection and analyses should become somehow a routine. The collection of data can be facilitated by a more intensive use of information systems, and analyses can be made available periodically, also formulating new research questions to be answered during phases of intensive work on reports produced by schools during summer breaks. Lastly, the effort of changing the culture toward data should be accompanied by a strong investment on adequate skills. Data analysts should become a reference professional figure within the boundaries of schools. The data analyst we have in mind holds three distinctive features: (1) is able to read and run the statistical models that we presented in this chapter, (2) can "translate" the models and their results to decision makers within the school, supporting their process of making choices, and (3) can interact with academic scholars and government personnel to formulate new research questions and possible patterns for new empirical explorations of available datasets. In concluding this chapter, it is worth recalling the great potential that analysts, decision makers, and school principals have in their hands: by challenging the ability of working adequately on quantitative data, they would be able to equip schools with new, powerful information that can help decision makers toward interventions that can, day-to-day, improve the quality of educational experiences and students' results. It is in this vein, and with these specific aims, that data analytics will clarify its fundamental contribution to the economics and policy of educational outputs.

Acknowledgments

This work is conducted within FARB—Public Management Research: Health and Education Systems Assessment, funded by Politecnico di Milano. The authors are grateful to INVALSI for having provided the original dataset.

References

Agasisti, T., Ieva, F., and Paganoni, A. M. (2017). Heterogeneity, school-effects and the north/south achievement gap in Italian secondary education: evidence from a three-level mixed model. *Statistical Methods and Applications*, 26 (1), 157–180.

Castellano, K. E., Rabe-Hesketh, K. E., and Skrondal, A. (2014). Composition, context, and endogeneity in school and teacher comparisons. *Journal of Educational and Behavioral Statistics*, 39 (5), 333–367.

Coleman, J. S., Campbell, E., Hobson, C., McPartland, J., Mood, A., Weinfeld, F., and York, R. (1966). The Coleman report. *Equality of Educational Opportunity*. Washington, DC: Government Printing Office, pp. vi, 737.

Corak, M. (2013). Income inequality, equality of opportunity, and *intergenerational mobility*. *The Journal of Economic Perspectives*, 27 (3), 79–102.

Enders, C. K. (2010). *Applied Missing Data Analysis*. New York: Guilford Press.

Goldstein, H. (2011). *Multilevel Statistical Models*, Volume 922. Chichester: Wiley.

Heckman, J. J. and Masterov, D. V. (2007). The productivity argument for investing in young children. *Applied Economic Perspectives and Policy*, 29 (3), 446–493.

Heckman, J. J., Stixrud, J., and Urzua, S. (2006). The effects of cognitive and noncognitive abilities on labor market outcomes and social behavior. *Journal of Labor Economics*, 24 (3), 411–482.

Marsh, J. A., Pane, J. F., and Hamilton, L. S. (2006). Making Sense of Data-Driven Decision Making in Education: Evidence From Recent RAND Research. Santa Monica, CA: RAND Corporation. http://www.rand.org/pubs/occasional_papers/OP170.html.

Masci, C., Ieva, F., Agasisti, T., and Paganoni, A. M. (2016). Bivariate multilevel models for the analysis of mathematics and reading pupils' achievements. *Journal of Applied Statistics*. In press.

OECD. (2012). Results in focus: What 15-year-olds know and what they can do with what they know. https://www.oecd.org/pisa/keyfindings/pisa-2012-results-overview.pdf.

Plewis, I. (2011). Contextual variations in ethnic group differences in educational attainments. *Journal of the Royal Statistical Society: Series A (Statistics in Society)*, 174 (2), 419–437.

Rasbash, J., Leckie, G., Pillinger, R., and Jenkins, J. (2010). Children's educational progress: partitioning family, school and area effects. *Journal of the Royal Statistical Society: Series A (Statistics in Society)*, 173 (3), 657–682.

Raudenbush, S. W. and J. Willms. (1995). The estimation of school effects. *Journal of Educational and Behavioral Statistics*, 20 (4), 307–335.

Rivkin, S. G., Hanushek, E. A., and Kain, J. F. (2005). Teachers, schools, and academic achievement. *Econometrica*, 73 (2), 417–458.

Rockoff, J. E. (2004). The impact of individual teachers on student achievement: Evidence from panel data. *The American Economic Review*, 94 (2), 247–252.

Rumberger, R. W. (1995). Dropping out of middle school: A multilevel analysis of students and schools. *American Educational Research Journal*, 32 (3), 583–625.

Schnepf, S. V. (2007). Immigrants' educational disadvantage: An examination across ten countries and three surveys. *Journal of Population Economics*, 20 (3), 527–545.

Snijders, A. T. and Bosker, R. J. (1999). Multilevel Analysis: An Introduction to Basic and Advanced Multilevel Modeling. London: Sage.

Steele, F., Vignoles, A., and Jenkins, A. (2007). The effect of school resources on pupil attainment: A multilevel simultaneous equation modelling approach. *Journal of the Royal Statistical Society: Series A (Statistics in Society)*, 170 (3), 801–824.

Tibshirani, R. (1996). Regression shrinkage and selection via the lasso. *Journal of the Royal Statistical Society. Series B (Methodological)*, 58 (1), 267–288.

Van Ewijk, R. and Sleegers, P. (2010). The effect of peer socioeconomic status on student achievement: A meta-analysis. *Educational Research Review*, 5 (2), 134–150.

Wallgren, A. and Wallgren, B. (2007). *Register-based statistics: Administrative data for statistical purposes*, Volume 553. Chichester: Wiley.

Appendix: Countries and States Involved in OECD PISA Program

Albania	United Arab Emir.	Argentina	Australia
Austria	Belgium	Bulgaria	Brazil
Canada	Switzerland	Chile	Colombia
Costa Rica	Czech Republic	Germany	Denmark
Spain	Estonia	Finland	France
United Kingdom	Greece	Hong Kong	Croatia
Hungary	Indonesia	Ireland	Iceland
Israel	Italy	Jordan	Japan
Kazakhstan	Korea	Liechtenstein	Lithuania
Luxembourg	Latvia	Macao-China	Mexico
Montenegro	Malaysia	The Netherlands	Norway
New Zealand	Peru	Poland	Portugal
Qatar	Shanghai-China	Perm	Florida
Connecticut	Massachusetts	Romania	Russian Federation
Singapore	Serbia	Slovak Republic	Slovenia
Sweden	Chinese Taipei	Thailand	Tunisia
Turkey	Uruguay	United States	Viet Nam

POLICY
RELEVANCE AND
THE CHALLENGES
AHEAD

Chapter 9

The Governance of Big Data in Higher Education

Kurt De Wit and Bruno Broucker

Contents

9.1 Introduction

The higher education sector in many countries in Europe and elsewhere has been subject to major reforms in recent years, not least because of global and European financial crises and the perceived need to increase the efficiency of (public) investment in higher education as an economic good (Peters et al., 2015). On top of the economic rationale, the public value of higher education is now becoming an important issue in higher education reform (Broucker et al., 2016). At the same time, technological advances in data availability and data processing have made it increasingly possible to base decisions on and in higher education on quantitative evidence. For this possibility to become a meaningful reality, however, the complexity of the large amount of data available on different levels must be governed: how do you make sure that the data can be used optimally, on different levels, with a view to a coherent higher education policy? This chapter explains how such a Big Data governance structure can be designed for the higher education sector.

Let us start by stating the obvious: we now find ourselves in a world where the Internet, apps, social networking tools, and the like are almost unavoidable, and where data generated by these and other sources are ubiquitous. Web applications such as Google, YouTube, and Facebook have an unprecedented number of users, and the online actions of these users can be traced in nearly every detail. Not only private companies, but also governments increasingly collect and use large amounts of data regarding their citizens. For citizens, the current technological possibilities have had an empowering effect. They are now able to make their voices heard and can more easily participate in the political and public debate. In this way, technology has brought into question the governments' ability and willingness to address public concerns and requests (World Economic Forum, 2011). The increased connectivity of citizens and business, the possibility to distribute work regardless of distances and boundaries, as well as the availability of previously undisclosed or non-existent data and information mean that, fundamentally, government tasks could also be performed by citizens, companies, and others (Broucker and Crompvoets, 2014). The advent of social media, ubiquitous mobile connectivity, and Web 2.0 activities allow for other forms of action than mass production and collaboration (Linders, 2012). Consequently, the focus is no longer only on governments or only on the market. Old and new partnerships and groups are both feasible and needed (Millard and Wimmer, 2012).

For governments, this entails a shift toward another form of government. One of the terms used to describe this shift is *digital era governance* (Dunleavy et al., 2005; Höchtl et al., 2015). Not only is e-government expanding, e-governance is also on the rise (Greve, 2015), meaning that data analysis is not only being used as a tool, but is also transforming the governance process itself. This shift of perspective has also been termed *transformational government*: "the exploitation of eGovernment such that benefits can be realized" (Irani et al., 2007). In other words, transformational government aims to move beyond purely technical aspects of enhancing e-government processes, in order to address the cultural and organizational barriers which have hitherto hindered the realization of public service benefits. It also points to digitalization of the public sector, in the sense of putting electronic delivery at the core of the government business model.

The increased penetration of technology in all aspects of society has generated a trend of recording ever more data (McAfee and Brynjolfsson, 2012). In the 2010s, the buzzword to describe this trend is *Big Data* (Fosso Wamba et al., 2015). Big Data is the all-encompassing term for any collection of datasets so large and complex that it becomes difficult to process them using traditional data processing applications (Laney, 2013; Snijders et al., 2012). The term *Big Data* refers not only to the sheer amount of data that is becoming available, but also to the speed with which the data are produced, and to the variety of formats and structures of that data. Moreover, not just the availability of the data, but also the capability to transform these data into information, and in particular into information that was not available before, is part of what is called *Big Data analytics*. From these large datasets, additional information can be derived that would not be derivable from separate smaller sets of data with the same total amount of data, thus allowing correlations to be found to spot business trends, prevent diseases, combat crime, and so on (Cukier, 2010; Reichman et al., 2011). Big Data has only recently come to the fore, first in IT and consultancy circles, but not much later also in the area of government itself and in public sector domains, although it is still much less developed there (Eynon, 2013). It has also been termed the *data revolution*, pointing to the novel information that Big Data and Big Data analytics can provide (Data Revolution Group, 2014; Kitchin, 2014).

In the higher education (HE) sector, the Big Data theme seems to be less developed. In a literature review on Big Data, Fosso Wamba et al. (2015) found only two articles regarding the education sector. One strand of Big Data analytics that has gained ground since then is learning analytics; that is, using Big Data to improve the learning process (Savin-Baden, 2015). However, the use of Big Data to inform policy making, what can be termed *academic analytics*, is only in its infancy in higher education. It is this aspect of Big Data that we want to explore in this chapter. We contend that Big Data and academic analytics may have their place and value in decision making in higher education, but that there are a number of technical and non-technical issues that have to be addressed. For that reason, a governance structure is needed, as is leadership, to provide room to maneuver within the policy domain or organizations for Big Data and academic analytics, and to create the willingness to take the results of the analyses into account.

In the remainder of this chapter, we first define what Big Data is and what it can mean in higher education. Second, we go into the data-related issues that need to be addressed. Third, we specify what a governance structure for Big Data in higher education would entail. Next, we illustrate what this can actually mean in practice by going into recent developments in Belgium (Flanders), on the level of the Flemish higher education system, and on the level of a higher education institution. This case is interesting, because at both levels data-driven decision making, supported by interconnected databases and purpose-built analytical tools, has expanded in recent years. Our main conclusions will be presented in the final paragraph.

9.2 Big Data in Higher Education

9.2.1 Big Data

It is common practice to define Big Data by using the three Vs introduced by Laney (2001). The three Vs are the volume, velocity (or speed of production), and variety in formats and structure of the data. *Volume* refers to the sheer amount of data that is becoming available. The digitalization of information is of course not new. It is estimated that more than 98% of data is digital (Cukier and Mayer-Schoenberger, 2013). Furthermore, a process of "datafication" is under way (Cukier and Mayer-Schoenberger, 2013). More facts and particulars are being turned into digital data than was previously possible. Think, for instance, of sport tracking devices that monitor distances moved, heart rate, and speed; online tracking of number of clicks, time spent on websites, or watching film clips; and commercial tracking of online transactions, purchases, and payments. In other words, not only is more data digitally available, new kinds of data are also available. Moreover, many of these data are created in real time or in near-real time. The *velocity*, or the rate, at which data are created or renewed is therefore high. And as the examples already suggest, these data also come in a *variety* of formats, both structured and unstructured.

Several authors have added other Vs to this triad (e.g., Chen et al., 2013; Daniel, 2015; Fosso Wamba et al., 2015; Höchtl et al., 2015). For instance, *value* refers to the (economic) benefits that can be gained from insights generated by Big Data, which, according to Fosso Wamba et al. (2015), might be achieved by creating transparency, segmenting populations to customize actions, or innovating decision making and business models. Another V stands for *veracity* (Daniel, 2015). Big Data is "inherently unpredictable" (Fosso Wamba et al., 2015) and therefore the reliability of the data is an issue. The data must be of sufficient quality to make analyses meaningful, but at the same time, an amount of error and noise is always part of Big Data. In other words, Big Data allows for a certain amount of uncertainty, while nonetheless trusting the data, the analyses, and the resulting information. A final example of a V as a separate feature of Big Data is *visualization* (Kellen et al., 2013). If the data or the results of analyses are to be used in decision-making processes, the way of presenting the data is crucial, because they must be readable and interpretable by decision makers.

The discussion about which V to include in the definition of Big Data illustrates that there is no agreement on what actually constitutes Big Data. It is a catch-all phrase that can, in fact, refer to very different forms of data (Kitchin and McArdle, 2016). Some therefore state that the usefulness of the term is very limited (Power, 2014). We will nevertheless use the term *Big Data*, but we want to stress that the concept is not just about the "Big." A large volume of data is, in fact, just noise, if it does not lead to meaningful insights that can form the basis for actions and interventions. To quote Campbell et al. (2007, p. 42), "Analytics marries large datasets, statistical techniques, and predictive modeling. It could be thought of as the practice of mining institutional data to produce 'actionable intelligence." In other words, the key to Big Data in our view is that large, connected sets of data are the basis for analyses that can reveal insights, previously not within the reach of analytics, which make more and better data-driven or data-informed policy interventions possible.

9.2.2 Big Data in Higher Education: Learning Analytics and Academic Analytics

If we translate the definition discussed previously to higher education we see that Big Data is certainly available. From the very first information session a potential student attends or the first enrolment of a student in an institution; over the courses, study activities, and results during studies, to graduation or even later; to participation in activities as an alumnus of the institution, much of what a student does in relation to higher education studies is registered electronically. This is true for traditional administrative data such as application or enrolment data, as well as for "digital era" data such as data generated by using an electronic learning platform, data from online courses, entrance logging at libraries, blogs kept by students, mobile app-based measurements of activities and opinions, and so on (see the proceeding case study for some concrete examples).

These data of different types are also of different value. The administrative data an institution collects are necessary for internal processes and are checked for correctness. For instance, when a student has registered for a study program, the courses he takes have to be registered in a correct way because exams have to be planned, results have to be recorded, and eventually a degree has to be awarded. Other data (e.g., blog posts) are less—or not—structured, and are not subject to control by the institution. It is obvious, therefore, that higher education institutions will primarily use the first kind of data.

The use of this (Big) Data in higher education has two main purposes. First, the data are used to improve the learning process and the learning experience of the students. This way of applying data on the level of the student is termed *learning analytics* (Picciano, 2012; West, 2012; Siemens et al., 2013; Savin-Baden, 2015; Sin and Muthu, 2015). It is aimed at providing students with insight into their own learning process and at giving teachers and counselors information, about the students and patterns of success and failure, which allows them to improve the learning environment for the student. For this purpose, student dashboards are often created to visualize a number of key (measurable) components of the students' learning process.

Second, Big Data are the basis for "academic analytics," that is, applying Big Data analytics to aggregated levels (programs, departments/faculties, the institution, the national level) in order to provide input for policy making (Long and Siemens, 2011; Daniel, 2015; Savin-Baden, 2015). Academic analytics allows for evidence-based or evidence-informed decision making about, for instance, quality assurance, identifying students at risk, or defining targeted action for specific groups of students. With higher education increasingly under pressure to be transparent and accountable (OECD, 2015), and to be more efficient with the funding it receives, academic analytics are a means to achieve this.

In the remainder of this chapter, we focus on the use of Big Data in the context of policy making. Big Data can play a role throughout the policy circle (Höchtl et al., 2015). Given the increased role of social media, Big Data analytics can help in setting the agenda, by analyzing or even predicting issues that are trending or are beginning to trend. It can provide the evidence needed for evidence-informed policy discussion and the formation of policy, and with predictive analyses it can help in formulating scenarios to accept, to decide on the funding of, and to implement policies. Additionally, as Höchtl et al. (2015) contend, Big Data can provide evidence and feedback for continuous assessment throughout the entire policy cycle, including during its implementation.

In the following sections, we look at Big Data's internal use within higher education, external use (e.g., reporting to government), and the interaction between both (e.g., measuring quality of education and refining HE institutions' quality assurance policies, but also reporting to government with a view to combining these and other data to formulate other policies, e.g., labor market policy).

9.3 Big Data-Related Problems

For academic analytics to be achievable, efficient, and useful, a number of issues related to Big Data have to be resolved. These issues can be situated at three levels: the micro level of technical issues, the meso level concerning how to deal with data in an organization, and the macro level of (cross-organizational and cross-policy domain) processes and policy. Table 9.1 gives an overview of Big Data-related problems.

From the definition of Big Data, many of the technical issues on the micro level quickly become clear. For these technical problems, we would argue, technology can, or even should, provide solutions. The growth in data and the speed with which data are generated and renewed necessitates a technological infrastructure that is able to stock and process all these data. The variety in data asks for tools that can connect and integrate these data. To make sense of the data, data reduction techniques and data visualization tools have to be available. These are issues and solutions that go beyond the possibilities of traditional business intelligence tools (Sin and Muthu, 2015), but for which new tools are being created and implemented, including in higher education institutions. For instance, an early example of the use of SAP HANA for the in-memory handling of large datasets can be found in the University of Kentucky (see Kellen et al., 2013).

Table 9.1.   Problems Related to Big Data

	Principal Nature of Problems	*Problematic Issues*
Micro	Technical problems	• Technological infrastructure • Tools for data integration, data reduction, data visualization
Meso	Non-technical problems	• Provision to make (reliable) data available • HR policy; i.e., skilled professionals • Non-traditional leadership (adaptive, collaborative)
Macro	Non-technical problems	• Policy directed toward Big Data • Culture oriented toward Big Data

Besides technical issues, however, there are also a number of non-technical problems that, in our view, are crucial in the debate about Big Data in higher education, but are not yet well-developed. In general, evaluation studies focusing on the public sector are limited to technical issues (Lavertu, 2014). Although public sector leaders acknowledge the importance of Big Data, the policy, culture, and human resources in the public sector are not geared toward processing Big Data (Mullich, 2013). In other words, the leadership and management of public sector organizations does not sufficiently take into account the importance of Big Data and does not make provisions to incorporate working with Big Data into the organization. More generally, it is not self-evident for public sector organizations to leave more traditional ideas and methods behind in order to work within this innovative context. Moreover, the public sector often lacks the people with the appropriate skills to handle Big Data (database designers, warehousing experts, institutional researchers, etc.). In this sense, the public sector is sometimes found to be simply not ready to take full advantage of the potential of Big Data (Romijn, 2014).

Regarding the HE sector specifically, several reports by EDUCAUSE, a US-based non-profit association for the advancement of higher education through the use of IT (e.g., Long and Siemens, 2011; Bichsel, 2012; EDUCAUSE, 2013), point to a similar situation of slow take-up of, and lack of preparedness for, Big Data and academic analytics: "It appears that the majority of institutions are in the data-collection or data-monitoring stage in most areas and have not yet matured to the point where they are using data for prediction or decision-making" (Bichsel, 2012). The United Kingdom's Higher Education Commission arrives at a similar conclusion, stating that the higher education sector "has not yet capitalised on the enormous opportunities presented by the data revolution" (Higher Education Commission, 2016, p. 3). More in particular, problems can occur both at the meso level of the organization of the higher education institution, and at the macro or policy level.

At the meso level, three main problems can occur. First, there might be insufficient provision made, for example by establishing a dedicated data and/or analytics center, to make relevant data available for the higher education institution and to guarantee the reliability of the data. Data must be gathered from within the institution and from national and international sources, their coherence and trustworthiness must be evaluated, and an infrastructure must be put in place to deal with these Big Data.

Second, human resources within the organizational structure must be brought to a level that is able to deal with Big Data. This can be compared to the European e-competence framework (e-CF) that was established in 2014 in the context of the European Union with a view to describing the skills and knowledge requirements for IT professionals in the 21st century (European Committee for Standardization: European e-Competence Framework, http://bit.ly/1wJWqNt). Decisions on which competencies to hire can be based on this framework. Similarly, in higher education it is important to define the competencies needed in Big Data analytics, which would involve both technical and analytical skills, but also the competency to interpret the results of analysis in the context of an HE institution or on the level of the HE sector, and to present the results in meaningful ways. These competencies could be taken on by different profiles, or by people combining different skills, such as scholar-practitioners (Streitwieser and Ogden, 2016). In any case, in order to turn data into information, and information into action, there is a need for skilled analysts that can not only handle Big Data technically, but can apply data reduction, data visualization and so on, and that can interpret the outcomes of the analyses into the appropriate context.

The third problem at the meso level concerns leadership. In general, public organizations that need to be flexible, adaptable, and innovative can no longer rely on the same form of leadership as traditional bureaucracies (Nedović-Budić et al., 2011). E-government projects often fail because of a lack of top management support or the inadequacy of leadership (Janssen et al., 2013; Pérez-Mira, 2010; Rigg and O'Mahony, 2013; Sauer and Davis, 2012). In an e-governance context this is exacerbated, and a new form of leadership is crucial, which can be described in many ways, for instance collaborative, adaptive, network, integral, or complexity leadership (Silvia and McGuire, 2010; Van Wart, 2013; Uhl-Bien et al., 2007). This new form of leadership is about sharing leadership throughout the organization (Uhl-Bien et al., 2007).

On the macro level, across policy domains and across institutions, the issue is foremost that policy is not sufficiently oriented toward the challenges posed by technology in general, and Big Data in particular. For the public sector as a whole, economic and budgetary pressures to become more efficient are paramount (OECD, 2015). Although the effects of the financial crisis on most European public sectors are clear, and, according to some, might not be a passing phase but might become a systemic feature to be reckoned with (Peters et al., 2015), governments are not really preparing for similar events in the future, but are focusing instead on short-term issues (Pollitt, 2014).

With regard to higher education, it is also the case that there is a lack of preparation for future challenges and to seize the opportunities that could be brought about by Big Data. There is not (yet) an institutional policy, nor an institutional culture, that favors Big Data, let alone that there would be openness and willingness to cooperate in this respect on the cross-institutional level. HE institutions are, generally speaking, not yet ready to make use of Big Data and academic analytics. According to Long and Siemens (2011) "For many leaders in higher education, however, experience and 'gut instinct' have a stronger pull."

9.4 Big Data Governance

The problems described in the preceding section must be tackled, if Big Data is to fulfil its potential for higher education. We contend that this implies a governance structure in higher education in order to provide space for Big Data analytics and to create the willingness to take the results of the analyses into account. In this section, we specify what such a governance structure might entail. To this end, we schematically present three levels of Big Data Governance in Table 9.2 (adapted from Broucker, 2016).

In the preceding section, we described data-related problems on the micro, meso, and macro level. Table 9.2 indicates how three types of governance can be instrumental in tackling these issues.

Technical issues are situated on the micro level and require IT governance. Good quality data must be a key focal point. As mentioned in the introduction, one of the (additional) Vs defining Big Data is *veracity* (Daniel, 2015), that is, the quality and reliability of the data. From the nature of Big Data itself, which includes large, fine-grained and volatile datasets, and unstructured and fuzzy data, it follows that errors and noise are part and parcel of these data. Nevertheless, if the data and the academic analytics resulting from them are to be trusted, it is necessary to make the data as reliable as possible. The challenges in this respect concern the data infrastructure, the integration of data, and the regulation of data (Cook, 2014). A basic requirement is to be able to capture, store, and process the data. Furthermore, the data from different datasets and sources must be interconnected and integrated, thereby reducing redundancies and cleaning the data, but also taking care of the security of sensitive data. To this end, data warehouses, central data repositories containing "a living memory of data" (Daniel 2015, p. 907) must be built, and the tools to turn the data into meaningful information for decision making must be developed. This in turn requires the regulation, or standardization and streamlining, of data formats and data processes. Consistency in the data allows for better and more accurate analytics and visualization.

Table 9.2   Three Levels of Big Data Governance

	IT Governance		Internal Governance	External Governance
	Input	*Throughput*	*Output*	*Outcome*
Micro	• High-quality data • Data standards	• Optimal technical use of data		
Meso	• Big Data as input for one organization	• Optimizing organizational processes through data	• Data in function of organizational performance • Efficiency and effectiveness of organizational policy • Goal achievement	
Macro	• Big Data as input for several organizations	• Optimizing cross-organizational processes through data • Alignment of data input	• Data in function of governmental performance • Efficiency and effectiveness of cross-organizational policy	• Data in function of public policy outcomes • Cross-organizational • Several policy domains/policy layers • With involvement of stakeholders

In our view, IT issues are the first step in Big Data governance and are, in that sense, an important step. But at the same time, the biggest challenge in using Big Data is not, or no longer, technical, but non-technical aspects. Technology opens up the possibilities of Big Data, but more steps need to be taken to avail of these possibilities.

The next step, at the meso level, is to use data to optimize organizational processes. An important aspect involves human resources, that is, to hire the appropriate people, able to do complex analyses (e.g., predictive modeling). These personnel must be able to not only handle the complexity on the technical level, but also interpret the data in the relevant context and turn Big Data into actionable intelligence. Working in Big Data requires turning the mass of numbers into meaningful patterns and looking inside those patterns for actionable information. For higher education institutions, this means they need not only IT specialists but also analysts that can make use of data, interpret the data, and apply insights gained from the data to make proposals for the improvement of the functioning of the institution itself, and provide appropriate information as input for the policy process within the institution.

Hiring HR talent is therefore of concern for senior management. It is one of the ways in which support for Big Data and Big Data analytics can take shape. Another way to make adequate provision to use the potential of Big Data is to reorganize units within the HE institution in such a way that both the technical and the business sides of dealing with Big Data are adequately and logically integrated within the organization, with a view to gearing these units toward mutual networking and cooperation with regard to Big Data. After all, Big Data is about large and connected databases, about combining all relevant data available, and about making coherent, reliable, and relevant data available throughout the institution.

In other words, an organizational culture is needed that is supportive of data-driven or data-informed decision making. This involves the will to invest in both a data center (on the IT side) and in a data analytics center (on the business side). Moreover, there is a need for intra- and inter-organizational transparency and accountability. Otherwise, the danger is that data will be kept "hidden" by separate units, thus limiting the possibilities to combine available datasets. Establishing an open network is therefore necessary, because units have to cooperate, be open about the data they have, and agree on standards for the data that have to be exchanged and connected.

The internal governance of Big Data thus entails establishing an organizational culture that is supportive of Big Data and incorporates Big Data as a resource to enhance organizational performance (compare McAfee and Brynjolfsson, 2012). An essential element in this respect is support of the leadership. As mentioned in the preceding section, this involves a new form of leadership based on sharing leadership throughout the organization. This means, while networking or centralizing the analytics, decentralizing the intelligence gained from it. In other words, the intelligence should be pushed to various channels, toward as many different parts of the institution as necessary, so that decision making at any level can be informed by the data. In short, make the data meaningful and useful for every level. This will also help to let decision makers and administrators at all levels see why they have to feed data into a larger digital system; they get a return on their investment.

At the macro level, some similar issues are at stake. To begin with, a centralization of Big Data is under discussion. As Greve (2015, p. 54) points out, this is a complex and difficult issue "because local units and local managers are not always pleased to give up influence over data collection and data use because they (rightly) fear that it will remove considerable decision making power out of their hands." Nevertheless, openness between units and managers seems a necessary step for efficient data processing and cross-checking datasets against each other. That is why, similar to the situation in single institutions, at the governmental level decentralization of intelligence is also an issue. Here too, the challenge is to make information available where it is needed.

An important issue, which is raised by connecting and/or centralizing information and then dispersing it, is privacy. If and when more data become available, and if and when more datasets can be combined, more private information can be brought together. The technological possibilities seem to be ahead of laws and the administration of justice. For example, court cases brought by the EU against Google and Facebook illustrate that, currently, privacy problems cannot be prevented.

9.5 National Case

As an illustration of a working and evolving governance structure with regard to Big Data, we present a national case, that is, Flanders (Belgium), and more in particular the "higher education database" that was developed. We will describe the governance structure, the properties, and the uses of this database, both at the level of the government (Section 9.5.1) and at the level of a higher education institution, namely KU Leuven (Section 9.5.2). What makes the Flanders case interesting is that data-driven, or at least data-informed, decision making has clearly been on the rise in recent years, and that, to that end, interconnected databases have been set up and analytical tools have been purposefully built. The reforms in higher education in Flanders have thus been accompanied by an increasing significance of (Big) Data and have led to more explicit attention on the governance of these data.

9.5.1 The Higher Education Database

In Flanders, higher education went through a series of reforms in the early 2000s, introducing the bachelor-master structure and making the education structure more flexible for students. The final piece of the reforms was a new funding model, adopted in 2008. The new funding model entailed a shift from primarily input funding toward a system based mainly on output funding, and based on many parameters allowing targeted policies (e.g., toward students receiving financial aid, students with disabilities, working students, students from diverse ethnic backgrounds). These parameters included, among others, the number of credits earned, the number of degrees granted, weightings by discipline, weightings with regard to target groups, special provisions for students who reoriented, the number of PhDs awarded, and publications and citations.

In order for the funding mechanism to work, the government needed to have information regarding all parameters included in the mechanism. It decided therefore to build a "higher education database." The legislation that introduced the new funding mechanism (Decree on the funding and the operation of colleges and universities in Flanders, 2008) also introduced this new database, giving it a legal basis. It is operational since the academic year 2008–2009. The governance of this database (see Figure 9.1) is based on communal management between government and higher education institutions. In the legally defined steering committee there is equal representation of the government on the one hand, and the higher education institutions (through their associations, i.e., cooperation structures between a university and one or more colleges of higher education) on the other. The steering committee is supported by working groups (on data, funding, quality, and technical options), with a similar representation of the government and the HEIs (and, for technical issues, their software developers). The working groups have an advisory role toward the steering committee.

The primary goals of this new database were, at the outset, to provide data input for the funding mechanism, to determine the eligibility of students for funding, to

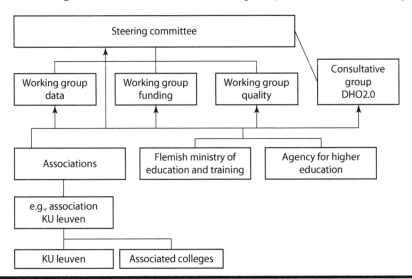

Figure 9.1 Governance of the higher education database.

monitor the parameters, and to provide data to inform policy and to report—to policy makers, to external organizations (EU, OECD), and to the institutions. Also, the data in the database were meant to be the basis for other policies: deciding on applications for study grants, calculating child allowance, giving input for the public database holding all degrees and certificates (*Leer- en ervaringsbewijzendata-bank*, see www.ond.vlaanderen.be/led/).

A new phase of development of the database (version 2.0) started in 2014 and is currently being implemented stepwise. The new phase stems from new governmental policy (*Regeerakkoord 2014–2019*). The government wants to reduce administrative burden, meaning that it commits itself to digitalize data, and to combine databases. The underlying point of view is that a government should not ask information of citizens when that same information is already available at the governmental level.

In the second phase of the database, new goals have been formulated. Because of stricter language regulations for higher education, meaning that only a limited amount of programs and courses may be taught in a language other than Dutch, the higher education database will be used to monitor the compliance of the higher education institutions with these regulations. The European 20-20 goals with regard to mobility (20% of graduates should have a mobility experience by 2020) are also within the scope of the reformed database, which implies that student mobility will have to be registered in more detail by the HE institutions. Another goal is transparency. Both students and institutions should receive information to monitor and assess study pathways and study progression (individual information for students, aggregated information for HE institutions), or more generally, information that can be used to assess the quality of higher education.

In the framework of the commitment by the government to digitalization and reducing the administrative burden for citizens and higher education institutions, and given the set of goals now attached to the database, the second phase of the database aims to connect the higher education database with other governmental databases. Within the higher education sector, the database will be connected with the Higher Education Register (www.hogeronderwijsregister.be), the official register of all programs that may be offered by the higher education institutions. Also, a portal will be built ("MyEducation") where aggregated information will be made public, where more detailed information will be available for HE institutions, and where citizens will find information on their own trajectory in higher education. Broader connections will also be established, outside the HE sector, through the Crossroads Bank for Social Security (https://www.kszbcss.fgov.be/en/international/home/index.html), allowing, for example, the linking of education data with labor market data. Establishing these broader connections has of course brought up privacy issues. For that reason, authorization was sought and acquired from the relevant official bodies: the Crossroads Bank for Social Security (*Kruispuntbank Sociale Zekerheid*), the Flemish Surveillance Commission for electronic administrative data transfer (*Vlaamse Toezichtscommissie*), and the national

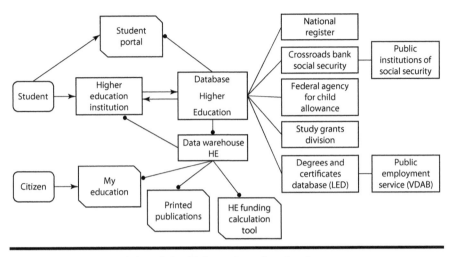

Figure 9.2   Connectivity of the higher education database.

register (*Rijksregister*). Figure 9.2 shows the connections that are established to and from the higher education database.

On the technical level, a secure Internet connection was established between the various governmental database servers and the servers of each institution. Whereas in the past, data was sent from institutions to the government in batches, asynchronously and without updates, the new database allows synchronous event-based registration, in (nearly) real time, through web services. Each higher education institution has a real-time connection with this database in order to register students' programs, courses, and results. The database includes identification data (name, address, etc.), nationality data, entrance requirements, study trajectory, study contract, registration and deregistration data, results, exchange data, and others. When connecting to the database, the institutions also receive information back, such as official student identification data, or data on the students' fundability (the so-called "learning account" indicates how many credit points a student has registered for and for how many of these the student was successful).

With the new database, and particularly the data warehouse that has been built, queries on the data have become possible. The data warehouse thus allows, first, the provision of basic data and aggregated reports to the HEIs, to be used for the validation of the data and for internal management decisions on, for example, student progression and dropout (see the next paragraph). Second, the data warehouse is also the basis for information provision to the broader public. See for instance the website www.onderwijskiezer.be, where data is provided on the study results of students in their first year in higher education, broken down by their previous study in secondary education and their program in higher education. Third, the data warehouse is the tool that allows reporting to the international level (e.g., the registration of mobility in the framework of the Bologna mobility goals, as mentioned in the preceding section).

9.5.2 KU Leuven

The data in the higher education database are also used within the higher education institutions. To provide a concrete illustration of this, we describe how one university incorporates these data in its functioning, namely KU Leuven, which is the largest university in Belgium, has campuses in eleven cities, and is associated with five colleges of higher education (www.kuleuven.be).

As illustrated in Figure 9.2, KU Leuven receives data from the higher education database in two ways. First, basic data are provided to the university directly from the database via web services. These basic data, for instance the number of credits remaining in the learning account of a student, are then captured and stored in the university's own database. The data are then used in operational processes, for example when a student registers at the university the student administration checks whether the student has a sufficient amount of credits in the learning account to be entitled to enroll. Second, via the data warehouse of the HE database, the university receives aggregated data on its own students and benchmark data of students in other institutions (sector-wide data, or data about students in comparable study programs at other institutions). These data are, in the first place, used to validate the data in the higher education database. In addition, the data are utilized as management information, for example to calculate the market share of study programs, and to benchmark study programs against programs at other institutions in the framework of the quality assurance system. More generally, the university is increasingly directed toward data-informed decision making. This has led, for example, to analyses of study progression and the factors determining study failure, leading to the introduction of new university-wide study progression measures (De Wit et al., 2015).

Besides the increased role of the analysis of Big Datasets at KU Leuven, the visualization of data is also becoming more important. For example, an education dashboard was developed, to provide decision makers at all levels with easy-to-interpret figures about enrolment, study progression, dropout, time to degree, student surveys, and alumni surveys. This education dashboard has become part of the new quality assurance system established in the academic year 2015–2016. It provides data and information, not only for internal use on the level of study programs, faculties, or the university, but also as input for the external quality assurance process, involving an institutional accreditation. Figure 9.3 shows some excerpts from an (anonymized) dashboard.

The education dashboard combines "hard" administrative data (registrations, exam results, diplomas awarded, etc.) with "soft" information gathered from questionnaires (student evaluations, alumni surveys, etc.). Within the data warehouse of the university—which forms the basis on which the dashboard is built—these

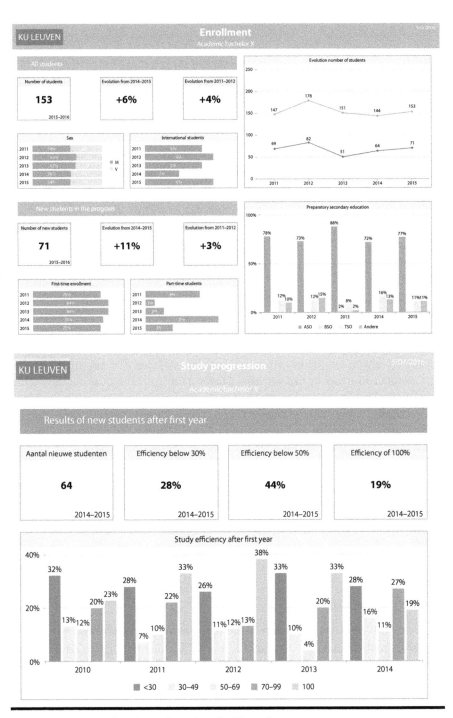

Figure 9.3   Example of an education dashboard.

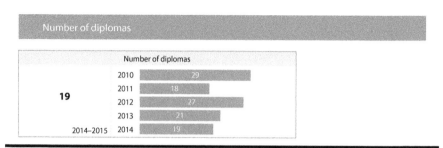

Figure 9.3 (Continued)   Example of an education dashboard.

data are further connected to other types of data, for instance population figures (provided by a federal government agency), and of course also to data received from the higher education database.

Furthermore, research projects are being developed that combine administrative data on study progression and performance with data regarding library access, the use of the online learning platform, feedback to and from students in a student dashboard, mobile app data gauging student opinions, to name but a few.

These developments have been made possible by a leadership that has put increasing value on evidence-informed decision making. The organization was itself adapted to make better use of available data. An IT unit is charged with developing the IT structure necessary for connecting with the higher education database. A business intelligence unit makes sure that data is available in a data warehouse system and in applications such as the education dashboard. And a policy unit is responsible for the content of these applications, as well as for university-wide analyses of the available data. The results of these visualizations, analyses, and research projects feed into the policy-making process, making difficult and controversial decisions possible, because they are underpinned by management information addressing all angles of the situation, made to measure for the issue, and objectifying or falsifying "hunches" (De Wit et al., 2015).

9.6 Conclusion

The concept of Big Data refers to the volume, velocity, and variety of data that are available, but also to a new way of looking at data, because their value, veracity, and visualization lead to analyses and insights that previously could not be achieved. In other words, Big Data have the potential to improve policy-relevant information.

At the moment, however, this potential is far from being achieved, in the public sector in general, and in the higher education sector in particular. A number of technical problems need to be addressed (providing the infrastructure and the tools needed for Big Data analytics), but as important are the non-technical issues that define how the results of Big Data analytics are used in higher education policies. Provisions have to be made regarding the organization and the human resources needed to exploit Big Data, the leadership must be supportive of Big Data analytics, and the policy and culture of organizations and the sector as a whole have to be favorable toward Big Data analytics.

It seems that, in higher education, academic analytics is not yet being embraced, notwithstanding the potential it shows to improve data-informed decision making. The situation in Flanders illustrates that steps are being taken, at the micro, meso, and macro levels, but that further development is needed. We contend that academic analytics can only achieve its full potential if the governance of Big Data is elaborated. This entails, first, IT governance geared toward the appropriate technical solutions, data quality, and security of the data. Technical possibilities should not distract from ethical issues regarding privacy, but also concerning how to deal with the results of academic analytics. For instance, if we "know" from our analysis that a student with specific characteristics (family background, home region, previous education, media use, etc.) will fail in the first year of higher education, do we then not allow this student to enroll, do we take study guidance measures, do we inform the student in advance or not?

Second, internal governance of Big Data means, at the meso level, adapting the organization and organizational processes with a view to improving their efficiency and effectiveness, and similarly at the macro level. In our case of KU Leuven this was, for example, achieved by clearly defining the tasks of both IT and business units at the central level, in order to facilitate the collection of data, their analysis and interpretation, and the dissemination of the information, for example in the education dashboard. Academic analytics can thus improve both operational processes and strategic, data-informed decision making at all levels.

The third layer of Big Data governance is external governance, which involves focusing Big Data analytics on cross-organizational outcomes. This requires timely and accurate data and predictive models in support of strategic decision-making processes, and presumes that those in strategic positions strive for the adoption of Big Data analytics. A point of note is that Big Data analytics can also be misused and a critical perspective should be taken (compare Selwyn, 2015). As with other kinds of data, it is important to be aware that not everyone is necessarily represented or equally represented in the data. For instance, if you examine the activity of students on social media, you might miss those students that are not active users of social media. Another risk is that Big Data analytics, with its stress on efficiency, (cost) effectiveness, and performance, might be used to strengthen the mainly economic discourse that is still ubiquitous in higher education. In our view, exploiting the full potential of Big Data analytics in higher education should involve its application to improve higher education's public value for society at large.

References

Bichsel, J. (2012). *Analytics in Higher Education: Benefits, Barriers, Progress and Recommendations (Research Report).* Louisville, CO: EDUCAUSE Center for Applied Research. http://www.educause.edu/ecar.

Broucker, B. (2016). Big data governance, een analytisch kader. *Bestuurskunde*, 25(1), 24–28.

Broucker, B., and Crompvoets, J. (2014). E-governance and the future of innovative public sector organisations (paper presented at the Public Administration Review Anniversary Conference: *Next Steps for Public Administration in Theory and Practice: Looking Backward and Moving Forward.* 16–18 November 2014, Guanghzou, China).

Broucker, B., De Wit, K., and Verhoeven, J. C. (2016). Higher education for public value: A research agenda (paper presented at the EAIR 38th Annual Forum, Birmingham, United Kingdom, 31 August–3 September 2016).

Campbell, J.P., P.B. DeBlois, and Oblinger, D.G. (2007). Academic analytics. A new tool for a new era. *EDUCAUSE Review*, July/August, www.educause.edu.

Chen, J., Chen, Y., Du, X., Li, C., Zhao, S., and Zhou, X. (2013). Big data challenge: A data management perspective. *Frontiers of Computer Science*, 7(2), 157–164, doi 10.1007/s11704-013-3903-7.

Cook, T.D. (2014). "Big data" in research on social policy. *Journal of Policy Analysis and Management*, 33(2), 544--547.

Cukier, K. (2010). Data, data everywhere. *The Economist*, Feb 25th. Spatial report: Managing information, http://www.economist.com/node/15557443.

Cukier, K., and Mayer-Schoenberger, V. (2013). The rise of big data. How it's changing the way we think about the world. *Foreign Affairs*, 92(3), 28–40.

Daniel, B. (2015). Big data and analytics in higher education: Opportunities and challenges. *British Journal of Educational Technology*, 46(5), 904–920, doi:10.1111/bjet.12230.

Data Revolution Group. (2014). *A World That Counts. Mobilising the Data Revolution for Sustainable Development.* New York: United Nations, http://www.undatarevolution.org.

De Wit, K., Verhesschen, P., Heerman, C., and Beullens, M. (2015). Data-driven decision-making on study progression at KU Leuven. (Paper presented at the EAIR 37th Annual Forum 2015 *From Here to There: Positioning Higher Education Institutions*, Krems, Austria, 30 August–2 September 2015).

Dunleavy, P., Margetts, H., Bastow, S., and Tinkler, J. (2005). New public management is dead—long live digital-era governance. *Journal of Public Administration, Research and Theory*, 16, 467–494.

EDUCAUSE (2013). The rise of big data in higher education. *EDUCAUSE Brief*, December, http://www.educause.edu.

Eynon, R. (2013). The rise of big data: What does it mean for education, technology, and media research? *Learning, Media and Technology*, 38(3), 237–240, doi: 10.1080/17439884.2013.771783.

Fosso Wamba, S., Akter, S., Edwards, A., Chopin, G., and Gnanzou, D. (2015). How "big data" can make big impact: Findings from a systematic review and a longitudinal case study. *International Journal of Production Economics*, 165, 234–246, doi: http://dx.doi.org/10.1016/j.ijpe.2014.12.031.

Greve, C. (2015). Ideas in public management reform for the 2010s. Digitalization, value creation and involvement. *Public Organization Review*, 15, 49–65, doi: 10.1007/s11115-013-0253-8.

Higher Education Commission. (2016). *From Bricks to Clicks. The Potential of Data and Analytics in Higher Education.* http://www.policyconnect.org.uk/hec.

Höchtl, J., Parycek, P., and Schöllhammer, R. (2015). Big data in the policy cycle: Policy decision making in the digital era, *Journal of Organizational Computing and Electronic Commerce*, 26(1–2), 147–169, doi: 10.1080/10919392.2015.1125187.

Irani, Z., Elliman, T., and Jackson, P. (2007). Electronic transformation of government in the U.K.: A research agenda, *European Journal of Information Systems*, 16(4), 327–335.

Janssen, M., van Veenstra A. F., and van der Voort, H. (2013). Management of large transformation projects: Challenges and failure factors. In Y. K. Dwivedi, H. Z. Henriksen, D. Wastell and R. De' (Eds.), *Grand Successes and Failures in IT: Public and Private Sectors*, 121–135, Berlin: Springer.

Kellen, V., Recktenwald A., and Burr, S. (2013). *Applying Big Data in Higher Education: A Case Study.* Arlington, MA: Cutter Consortium.

Kitchin, R. (2014). *The Data Revolution. Big Data, Open Data, Data Infrastructures and Their Consequences.* Thousand Oaks, CA: Sage.

Kitchin, R., and McArdle., G. (2016). What makes big data, big data? Exploring the ontological characteristics of 26 datasets. *Big Data & Society*, 3(1), 1–10, doi: 10.1177/2053951716631130.

Laney, D. (2001). *3D Data Management: Controlling Data Volume, Velocity and Variety.* META Group, http://blogs.gartner.com/doug-laney/files/2012/01/ad949-3D-Data-Management-Controlling-Data-Volume-Velocity-and-Variety.pdf.

Lavertu, S. (2014). Big data and the mismeasure of public administration: Confronting a growing threat to realizing public goals (paper presented at the 75th Public Administration Review Anniversary Conference: *Next Steps for Public Administration in Theory and Practice: Looking Backward and Moving Forward.* 16th–18th November 2014, Guangzhou, China).

Linders, D. (2012). From e-government to we-government. Defining a typology for citizen coproduction in the age of social media. *Government Information Quarterly*, 29(4), 446–454.

Long, P., and Siemens, G. (2011). Penetrating the fog: Analytics in learning and education. *EDUCAUSE Review*, 46(5), September/October 2011, http://www.educause.edu.

McAfee, A., and Brynjolfsson, E. (2012). Big data: The management revolution. *Harvard Business Review*, October 2012, 60–68.

Millard, J., and Wimmer, M. (2012). *Analysis of Current FP7 Projects and Future Research Challenges.* Brussels, Belgium: European Commission, Directorate General for Communications Networks, Content & Technology.

Mullich, J. (2013). *Closing the Big Data Gap in Public Sector. Survey Report.* New York: Bloomberg Businessweek Research Services.

Nedović-Budić, Z., Crompvoets, J., and Georgiadou, Y. (2011). *Spatial Data Infrastructures in Context: North and South.* Boca Raton, FL: CRC Press.

OECD. (2015). *Government at a Glance 2015: A Dashboard of Key Indicators to Help You Analyse International Comparisons of Public Sector Performance.* Paris: OECD Publishing.

Pérez-Mira, B. (2010). *Validity of Delone and McLean's Model of Information Systems Success at the Web Site Level of Analysis.* Baton Rouge, LA: Louisiana State University.

Peters, M. A., Besley, T., and Paraskeva, J. M. (2015). Introduction: Global financial crisis and educational restructuring. In M. A. Peters, J. M. Paraskeva, and T. Besley (Eds.), *The Global Financial Crisis and Educational Restructuring*, 1–10, New York: Peter Lang Publishing.

Picciano, A. G. (2012). The evolution of big data and learning analytics in American higher education. *Journal of Asynchronous Learning Networks*, 16(3), 9–20.

Pollitt, C. (2014). *Future Trends in European Public Administration* and *Management: An Outside-In Perspective. Coordinating for Cohesion in the Public Sector of the Future.* COCOPS Report Work Package 8, http://www.cocops.eu/wp-content/uploads/2014/04/FutureTrendsInEuropeanPublicAdministrationAndManagement.pdf.

Power, D. J. (2014). Using "Big Data" for analytics and decision support. *Journal of Decision Systems*, 23(2), 222–228, doi: 10.1080/12460125.2014.888848.

Reichman, O. J., Jones, M. B., and Schildhauer, M. P. (2011). Challenges and opportunities of open data in ecology. *Science*, 331(6018), 703–705.

Rigg, C., and O' Mahony, N. (2013). Frustrations in collaborative working: Insights from institutional theory. *Public Management Review*, 15(1), 83–108.

Romijn, B. (2014). *Using Big Data in the Public Sector. Uncertainties and Readiness in the Dutch Public Executive Sector.* Delft: Delft University of Technology, Faculty of Technology, Policy & Management.

Sauer, C., and Davis, G. B. (2012). Information systems failure. In M. J. Bates (Ed.), *Understanding Information Retrieval Systems: Management, Types, and Standards*, 285–300, Boca Raton, FL: CRC Press Taylor & Francis.

Savin-Baden, M. (2015). Education and big data. In M. A. Peters (Ed.), *Encyclopedia of Educational Philosophy and Theory*, Singapore: Springer Science+Business Media.

Savin-Baden, M. (2015). Education and big data. In M. A. Peters (Ed.), *Encyclopedia of Educational Philosophy and Theory*, 1–7, Singapore: Springer Science+Business Media.

Selwyn, N. (2015). Data entry: Towards the critical study of digital data and education. *Learning, Media and Technology*, 40(1), 64–82, doi: 10.1080/17439884.2014.921628.

Siemens, G., Dawson, S., and Lynch, G. (2013). *Improving the Quality and Productivity of the Higher Education Sector. Policy and Strategy for Systems-Level Deployment of Learning Analytics.* Society for Learning Analytics Research, www.solaresearch.org.

Silvia, C., and McGuire, M. (2010). Leading public sector networks: An empirical examination of integrative leadership behaviors. *The Leadership Quarterly*, 21(2), 264–277.

Sin, K., and Muthu, L. (2015). Application of big data in education data mining and learning analytics, a literature review. *ICTACT Journal on Soft Computing*, 5(4), 1035–1049.

Snijders, C., Matzat, U., and Reips, U. D. (2012). Big data: Big gaps of knowledge in the field of internet. *International Journal of Internet Science*, 7(1), 1–5.

Streitwieser, B., and Ogden, A. C. (Eds.) (2016) *International Higher Education's Scholar-Practitioners. Bridging Research and Practice.* Oxford: Symposium Books.

Uhl-Bien, M., Marion, R., and McKelvey, B. (2007). Complexity leadership theory: Shifting leadership from the industrial age to the knowledge era. *The Leadership Quarterly*, 18(4), 298–318.

Van Wart, M. (2013). Lessons from leadership theory and the contemporary challenges of leaders. *Public Administration Review*, 73(4), 553–5565.

West, D. M. (2012). *Big Data for Education: Data Mining, Data Analytics, and Web Dashboards.* Washington, DC: The Brookings Institution.

World Economic Forum. (2011). The future of government. Lessons learned from around the world. Cologny/Geneva: World Economic Forum, http://www3.weforum.org/docs/EU11/WEF_EU11_FutureofGovernment_Report.pdf.

Chapter 10

Evidence-Based Education and Its Implications for Research and Data Analytics with an Application to the Overeducation Literature

---

Wim Groot and Henriette Maassen van den Brink

Contents

10.1 Introduction

Our society is rapidly changing, becoming more complex and diverse. This is also true for education. As a result, the demands made of education have increased as well. Many of the most important challenges in life are thought to be best addressed through education. The Dutch essayist Karel van het Reve has pointed out the contradiction in our thinking about education. Many of us believe that educational standards and educational practice used to be better in the past than they are now, yet we cherish the belief in progress or, as van het Reve (2003) puts it, "schools and all the other things are always becoming better and that mankind will be better off five hundred years from now."

The increased complexity and rapid changes call for a further integration and application of scientific knowledge in educational practice. Teaching should become more "evidence-based" and questions of "what works" in education should guide educational policy and practice more than they do now. This calls for a body of knowledge on the cost-effectiveness of educational interventions.

Evidence-based education is the philosophy that education should be based on the best evidence of what works. This means that specific educational interventions, strategies, and policy science should be evaluated before they are recommended or introduced on a wide scale. If that has not yet happened, these interventions should be introduced on an experimental basis, such that the effects of each intervention can be evaluated scientifically. Performance-driven teaching includes some elements of evidence-based education, such as working with measurable targets and systematically evaluating whether these objectives are met. However, the evidence-based approach is more than that. Evidence-based education emphasizes the scientific basis to educational interventions. It is choosing a method or approach based on scientific knowledge about what works, and it is the systematic scientific evaluation of whether the objectives are met.

Evidence-based education emphasizes the investment nature of expenditures on education: education is an investment that yields a positive (and high) return for both individuals themselves and for society as a whole. With an investment approach, the allocation of resources to interventions with a favorable cost-benefit ratio are socially profitable. This applies to any educational investment, but in particular to investments in young people from disadvantaged groups. Or, as Levin et al. (2006) noted, "The investment criterion is a simple one: public investments are worth making if the benefits exceed the costs. Even if education is expensive, poor and inadequate education for substantial numbers of our young may have consequences that are even more costly. Such an analysis goes beyond the more basic question of social justice. If life chances depend heavily on education, it is important that inequalities in education associated with race, gender, immigrant status, language, and handicap be redressed as a basis for equalizing opportunities in a democratic society. But, even beyond the issue of injustice is the question of whether a poor quality education has consequences for the larger society. Social science research shows that poor education imposes social burdens via lower incomes and economic growth, lower tax revenues, and higher costs of such public services as health, criminal justice, and public assistance. In this respect, it is possible to view efforts to improve educational outcomes for at-risk populations as a public investment that may have benefits for the entire society in excess of investment costs."

This chapter focuses in particular on the need for and implications of evidence-based education. The discussion on evidence-based education has largely focused on the attitudes and skills professionals require to work in an evidence-based environment. For education to be evidence-based, teachers need to know how to use and apply knowledge about "what works" in the classroom and policy makers need to apply it in educational policies. Much less attention has been paid to the supply side of this equation: how evidence-based are the empirical findings offered by academic researchers? Evidence-based education has two components: the systematic review of the existing evidence and the production of new evidence through the evaluation of interventions in experimental designs. This chapter focuses on the first component and questions how systematic a review of the evidence is presented in academic research. We do this by presenting a critical review of review studies. We ask ourselves how systematic these review studies are that have been conducted, and how much these review studies have contributed to evidence-based education. We apply this to the literature on the incidence of and returns from overeducation in the labor market. Over the past 40 years there has emerged a vast literature on overeducation. A simple search for "overeducation" in Google Scholar yields nearly 200 studies with "overeducation" in the title. Most of the studies on overeducation have been conducted by economists. This literature has been motivated by concerns about mismatch between skills supplied and skills demanded in the labor market, the concern that the education system produces too many people with a higher education degree, and that these higher-educated workers displace lower-educated workers on the labor market. The outcomes of these studies on overeducation can have important implications for education policy, most notably on policies to increase the number of higher-educated people. As this literature is rather abundant, a number of review studies on the topic have been published over the years. As systematic review studies are an essential element in evidence-based education, this enables us to assess how useful for evidence-based education policy these reviews have been. It furthermore illustrates the potential contribution of the information gathered through data analytics to promote a more evidence-based approach to educational practice and policy.

The remainder of this chapter is divided in three sections. First we will make the case for evidence-based education. Next we will assess whether the review studies on overeducation can contribute to evidence-based educational policy making. Finally, we draw some conclusions.

10.2 The Need for Evidence-Based Education

As a consequence of the previously mentioned changes in society, the demands on education have changed. Education is no longer just about knowledge. Education is expected to contribute to socio-emotional development, is expected to prepare young people for citizenship and for the labor market, to mention just a few of the many things that are regarded as the tasks of education. Simultaneously, the student population has become more diverse: the diversity in (ethnic) origin and the development of students has increased. Thus, the number of students with a disability—such as dyslexia or attention deficit hyperactivity disorder (ADHD)—that require remedial teaching and additional support has greatly increased. Teachers take the nature and development of their pupils more into account, and know that more can be achieved if they take the right approach to pupils. Finally, the importance of education has also increased. Knowledge is our most important production factor. The number of jobs for higher-educated workers has increased, while employment of unskilled workers has declined. Harnessing talent is critical to a well-functioning economy and society. All this (and more) puts greater demands on education.

As a result of this, there is a continuous discussion about education. Expectations about what education can achieve are sometimes unrealistically high. This has led to a call for more transparency and accountability of educational performance. Central testing of students and comparative international tests such as PISA and TIMSS make the performance of schools and countries more transparent and make clear whether schools deliver what is expected of them.

At the same time—as is clear from the quote from Karel van het Reve—there is widespread dissatisfaction about the quality of education. This applies to all levels of education. The demand for greater transparency and accountability of performance has been accompanied by the application of forms of "new public management" in education. This has resulted in management on measurable targets. It has also led to an increase in bureaucracy and management in education. In recent years this has led to a backlash. The idea that managers have overpowered professionals has become common currency. A widely held view is that the quality of education would improve if teachers and lecturers are no longer bothered by rules and meddling managers and directors. Give education back to the teacher. Let the teacher again exercise his or her profession.

The claim that the quality of public services suffers from stifling rules and accountability procedures has also received support from scientists. In the Netherlands, the Scientific Council of Government Policy (WRR)—a government think tank—in its report "Evidence of Good Services" ("Bewijzen van goede dienstverlening") has argued for a revaluation of the professional (see: http://www.wrr.nl/). Accountability and management on measurable targets should—in the view of the think tank—be replaced by a culture of trust. Recognition of the value of the professional should, however, not take the form of uncritical adoration.

Greater freedom and autonomy for professionals go together with a greater sense of responsibility.

Management and accountability are often depicted as organized distrust. Accountability, however, compels self-evaluation and, if well applied, contributes to better performance. Management and accountability are not organized distrust but should be the means to improve professionalism. The rejection of all forms of management and accountability is often nothing more than a call to be left alone and not interfered with. This does not usually contribute to a better quality of education.

A greater reliance on and trust in professionals requires a strengthening of self-reflection among professionals. Do I still function properly as a teacher? Am I not stuck in my work? Human resource management, training, and career counseling are often poorly developed in schools. Professionals often believe that they can take care of their own human resource development, but all too often this is lacking.

A professional attitude also requires that knowledge and skills are maintained and further developed. Continuous training is essential. The willingness of teachers to keep up with developments in their field and to participate in continuous training and development is sometimes lacking. Frequently, there are no strict requirements about the amount of time teachers should spend on their own training and development. More stringent requirements for further training are therefore a prerequisite for the professional development of the teaching profession.

The developments outlined here are not unique to education: demands and expectations have increased in many areas of society, and, with the increase in complexity, the demands for transparency and accountability have also increased. A response to the increased complexity and diversity in many sectors of society has increasingly been a stronger nexus between scientific knowledge and professional practice, and hence between knowledge institutions such as universities and the professional field. Data analytics can in part be seen as a response to this challenge. In the agricultural sector there is a strong link and collaboration between farms and agricultural universities and associated research institutes. In health care, professional practice has become almost completely based on evidence-based guidelines. Evidence-based medicine has become the norm.

Compared to 30 or 40 years ago, our society has also become more pragmatic and rational. The times of great ideologies that guide our daily living appear to be behind us. Indeed, ideologies and those who proclaim them are now found to be suspect. In Western societies ideologies have been replaced by a belief in, and reliance on, scientific knowledge.

There is another development that contributes to the importance of scientific knowledge in educational practice; namely, the diminished authority of professionals. As indicated in the preceding paragraphs, society demands from professionals that they are accountable for their actions and behavior. Education is also expected to be accountable for the results it achieves. For teachers and educational administrators, this means more focus on performance by setting clear objectives and examining systematically whether these objectives are met.

In its Education Report 2011, the Dutch Education Inspectorate qualifies performance-driven teaching (*opbrengst gericht werken*) as the main key to educational improvement. An analysis by Visscher and Ehrenberg (2011) showed that performance-driven teaching mainly involves three practices: teachers should set clear targets to be achieved in a week, a month, or a year by a pupil; describe which approach or method is most suitable to achieve this; and acquire knowledge to make use of the most effective methods and instruments. Performance-driven teaching also requires data and the use of an evaluative cycle: defining goals and standards, collecting information, recording of the data, interpreting the data, and decision making based on the information obtained from this process. Data analytics can make a valuable contribution to making education more evidence-based.

Performance-driven teaching can be seen as a form of evidence-based education. The term *evidence-based education* refers to the idea that educational policy and practice should be based on the best available evidence of "what works." It also refers to an evidence-based *attitude* of policy makers and educational practitioners. Key to evidence-based approach is that only those innovations and modernizations that are proven to be (cost) effective merit wider implementation and dissemination. Where such proof is not available, there should be ample room to experiment with these innovations and modernizations, as long as these experiments are accompanied by a sound scientific evaluation that enables an assessment of the causal impact of the interventions.

Despite its attractions, there is resistance to performance-driven teaching and evidence-based education. This resistance is fueled by the contrast created between rationality and intuition. However, when taking the right decisions, both kinds of knowledge—rational and intuitive—can be valuable. With an evidence-based approach, a rational method is assumed. What is heard in the corridors, in the group, in the staff room as informal subjective information can be useful soft information. By gathering all relevant information and critically assessing the available evidence, better decisions are made. This dichotomy between rationality and intuition also exists between teaching and financial management in education. The allocation of the educational budget and the way we teach our students are closely related and mutually affect each other. Here again is a potential role for learning analytics, to improve the efficiency of the relationship between teaching and its outcomes and financial management of schools. There is a lot to be gained here. Currently, cost-effectiveness analyses are rarely or never performed in education. In contrast to other areas of the public sector—such as the health care sector and infrastructure, where large research programs exist to increase the evidence base on the cost-effectiveness of investments in health care and infrastructure—there is no systematic attention being paid to generating evidence on the cost-effectiveness of interventions in education. The availability of data analytics again could be a stimulus to a research program on cost-effectiveness in education.

Whether we spend the money in education on the right things is a question that is indeed frequently asked, but is rarely studied systematically, let alone used in financial decision making in education. In school organizations, there is a wealth of information about cognitive performance and social and emotional development of students, there are good pupil tracking systems, there are parent, student, and teacher satisfaction surveys. However, there is a lack of systematic analysis of the available data. Also, the link between the goals and objectives in teaching and the financial management of the schools is rarely made. It must immediately be added to this that systematically linking the objectives of the teaching activities with financial management decision is not easy, but requires a systematic approach and sufficient skills and abilities of people involved to work in an evidence-based manner.

In education, the gap between educational practice and educational science is still large. The use of scientific knowledge in educational practice is still uncommon. This is partly because the scientific research on education is not always useful to its practice. Thus, there are shortcomings on both sides: teachers do not know how to find and use scientific knowledge, researchers often study subjects that are not interesting and relevant to practice, or do not bother to hand over their findings in forms accessible to professional practice. Alternatively, they may not bother to present their work in a way that contributes to evidence-based education, as will be illustrated in the next section of this chapter.

The consequence of this gap between science and practice is that unproven practices in teaching can prevail. Or, as the journalist Carly Chynoweth described in *The Times* in 2009: "Few patients would want doctors to make decisions based on their ideologies; when our health is at stake, we want to know that health professionals are drawing on evidence founded in rigorous scientific research. According to Sir Jim Rose, the former director of inspection at Ofsted, the education watchdog, and author of a government review of the primary school curriculum, the same should be true in education. 'Very often [educational practices] take off much more from an ideology about how children learn rather than research,' he says. 'That needs to be held up to the light'" (Chynoweth, 2009).

Knowledge, about what works and what does not, keeps ideologies and unproven assumptions and beliefs outside the door. It makes teaching less vulnerable to what the British sociologist Frank Furedi has called the "fetishization of change," the assertion that we live in an era of unprecedented change and therefore every conceivable education reform is justified. Evidence-based education offers a counterbalance to this "fetishization of change." Evidence-based education not only establishes that teachers should be the primary agent of innovation in education, but also provides the professional knowledge and skills necessary to implement innovations that really improve the quality of education.

Some years ago, *The Economist* published a lengthy article on education reform under the title "The Great Schools Revolution." *The Economist* identifies four factors that contribute to successful reforms: educational decentralization (giving power back to schools), extra attention for students with learning disadvantages, providing a choice of different types of schools, and putting high demands on teachers.

At least three of these factors come together in the development of evidence-based education: evidence-based education gives power over educational innovations and reforms to teachers and their schools. Schools that put evidence-based education into practice can distinguish themselves from other schools, and evidence-based practice improves the quality of teachers. This is also endorsed by the European Commission, which stressed in 2006 that there was a need for a culture of evaluation and more systematic use of evidence as a basis for modernizing education and training systems.

Developing a body of evidence-based interventions in teaching requires high-quality research that is relevant for educational practice. Academic research on what works in education is not sufficient, however. Knowledge about "what works" needs to be disseminated to the teaching practice, that is, to teachers. For this, teachers need to have the skills to interpret research results to make appropriate decisions in their teaching methods. Teachers who want to work from an evidence base must also themselves be able to conduct scientific research in their school, and to implement the results of these scientifically evaluated interventions in their school.

An evidence-based approach also means that specific educational interventions, strategies, and policies should be evaluated before being recommended or introduced on a wider scale. If that has not yet happened, these interventions should be introduced on an experimental basis, such that the effects of the intervention can be evaluated scientifically. Evidence-based education on the one hand refers to the set of interventions that have been positively evaluated, on the other hand to an attitude of teachers and policy makers to work based on evidence-based education. Evidence-based education emphasizes the scientific basis underlying educational interventions. From a normative perspective, it gives preference to educational methods and approaches that are based on scientific knowledge about what works, and it focuses on systematic scientific evaluation of whether the policy or teaching objectives have been met.

An evidence-based approach to educational policy and practice is based on a judicious, explicit, and rigorous use of current best evidence. An evidence-based attitude involves the teacher or the policy maker who is aware at every step of the decision process:

> Is there is evidence to support this decision?
> How strong is this evidence?

An evidence-based attitude requires continuous scientific reflection on professional behavior. It assumes that interventions in educational practice or policy cannot be undertaken without consideration of the scientific evidence on this intervention and has as its goal that the choice of a particular intervention is based on the best available knowledge about the effectiveness of this intervention. The objective is to make use of the results of research that uses the highest possible standards of scientific rigor. This, preferably, makes use of design based upon randomization over treatment and control groups. An evidence-based teacher or policy maker is both a user and a developer of evidence-based knowledge.

10.3 Overeducation and Underemployment: What Is the Evidence Base after 40 Years of Research?

To meet the need and demand for evidence-based education, an accessible supply of systematic reviews on "what works" in education is necessary. However, researchers not always cater to the needs of educational professionals like teachers and policy makers, but frequently have their own agenda. Although in many fields—for example, medicine, psychology, and educational sciences—well-defined standards and guidelines for systematic review studies are available, these standards and guidelines are not always applied. In some disciplines, for example, economics, these standards are also rather unknown, or at least not imposed very stringently. This also becomes evident if—as is the purpose of this section—we review the review studies that have been published on overeducation, the mismatch between skills supplied and demanded, in the economics literature.

Mismatch between supply and demand of skills on the labor market can take different forms. Vertical mismatch occurs if there are jobs for higher-educated workers, whereas there are lower-educated workers searching for jobs, or vice versa. Horizontal mismatch occurs if there are vacancies for some occupations or industries, while workers are (being) educated for other occupations and industries. Finally, there can be curriculum–job requirement mismatches: students are taught skills that are not needed or used in jobs, or the skills and knowledge graduates need in their job are not taught at school or university. In this chapter, we look at a specific form of vertical mismatch: overeducation. Workers are overeducated for their job if their education level is higher than the level required for the job. Overeducation may lead to displacement of lower-educated workers by higher-educated workers, where lower-educated workers find that their chances of finding a suitable job diminish because higher-educated workers enter their jobs.

With the expansion of higher education, the concern that workers may have become overeducated for their job has increased among academics and policy makers. On the other hand, the persistent finding that unemployment rates are higher among lower-educated workers than among higher-educated workers has raised the concern that higher-educated workers are taking jobs intended for lower-educated workers, leading to a displacement of lower- by higher-educated workers. This has focused attention on estimating the incidence of overeducation in the labor market. Overeducation may be inefficient and lower the returns to investments in education. Subsequently, attention has been paid to estimating the rate of return from overeducation in the labor market.

The incidence of, and returns from, overeducation have received attention from both economists and sociologists. Economists have focused more on overeducation, focusing on occupational mismatch—the mismatch between a worker's level of education and the level of education required for the job—and the waste in investments in human capital witnessed by the lower rate of returns from years of overeducation compared with the returns from years of education required for the job. Overeducation views the years of education the worker provides to the job relative to the educational requirements of that job. Sociologists, on the other hand, have focused more on inequities in access to the workplace by emphasizing the displacement of lower by higher-educated workers and the underemployment of lower-educated workers that results. McKee-Ryan and Harvey (2011) distinguish four perspectives on overeducation and underemployment: a focus on individual and organizational outcomes by management scholars, overeducation and its returns by economists, the impact on society and social structures by sociologists, and health outcomes and community effects by community psychologists. Other perspectives can be added to this, such as the effects on (job) satisfaction, as studied by scholars in happiness studies.

Although both the overeducation literature and the underemployment literature focus on the mismatch between demand and supply of skills, there is an important difference in emphasis between the two strands of the literature. Almost by definition, overeducation is more likely to occur among higher-educated workers, as they have more opportunities and are more able to take up jobs with lower educational requirements. The underemployment literature, on the other hand, focuses more on the position of lower-educated workers, as they are more likely to drop out of the labor market altogether, and unemployment rates among lower-educated workers are almost always higher than those among higher-educated workers. Overeducation and underemployment may be related through a process of displacement of lower-educated workers by higher-educated workers. Higher-educated workers displace lower-educated workers to become overeducated in their job. Lower-educated workers become unemployed or—in turn—displace even lower-educated workers than themselves, if they find that all jobs which match their qualifications are already occupied. This process results in workers with the lowest educational attainment—who by definition are unable to displace lower-educated workers than themselves—becoming unemployed.

Underemployment emphasizes that workers cannot always fully employ the skills they have in their job. The sociological literature has taken a somewhat broader perspective, and has also looked at unemployment and at working part-time or fewer hours than desired as indicators of a mismatch between supply and demand for labor (for a more elaborate set of definitions of underemployment, see McKee-Ryan and Harvey, 2011). Feldman (1996) distinguishes between five dimensions of underemployment: being overeducated, being in a job outside one's area of formal training, having skills that are not utilized in one's job, working fewer hours than desired or being involuntarily in a temporary or intermittent job, or earning 20%

less than in one's previous job or as one's peers. From this perspective, overeducation is only one of the perspectives on underemployment.

Studies on overeducation and underemployment have developed as two separate strands in the literature, the one dominated by economists, the other by social scientists. In this chapter, we treat them on an equal footing. Both strands of research—on the incidence of and returns from overeducation, and research on the rate at which lower-educated workers are underemployed and displaced by higher-educated workers—have turned into niches in the social sciences literature. Over the past 40 years, quite a few studies in these areas have appeared. A search of *EconLit* showed that, at the beginning of 2015, there were 191 papers with "overeducation" or "over-education" in the title, and 217 articles with the word "underemployment" in the title. This proliferation of the literature has led to a number of studies that have reviewed the evidence on overeducation and underemployment. We count about a dozen studies that have summarized and reviewed the state of the art in these niche areas of research. The first study on overeducation—"The Over-Educated American," by Richard Freeman—was published 40 years ago, in 1976 (Freeman, 1976). The origins of the underemployment literature are ascribed by McKee-Ryan and Harvey (2011) to the seminal article by Feldman (1996), published 20 years ago. The existence of a number of review studies is evidence of the fact that research on overeducation and underemployment has matured during the past four decades, and that a niche in the literature has grown into an established strand in research.

As is not uncommon in social sciences, research in both areas has developed quite independently of each other, without much cross-referencing or exchange of ideas and findings. Buchel (2001) published one of the few studies to relate overqualification/overeducation to un- and underemployment. According to him, "The analogy between overqualification in general and unemployment lies in the fact that both are due to the aforementioned lack of demand for particular skills—with unemployment reflecting a total absence of demand and overqualification a shortfall in the volume of demand." He also observes that this analogy has received little attention in the academic literature so far.

This chapter aims to bring together these related, but until now quite separate, niches in the social sciences literature. It does so by providing an integrated review of the existing reviews of the research in the two areas. The aim of this review of reviews is to show how much this literature has contributed to evidence-based education. We do so by focusing on the two main topics that provide the motivation for research in this area. First, what can we learn from the literature about how pervasive overeducation and underemployment are in the labor market? Much of the research in this area originates from the concern that overeducation and underemployment are widespread, and that the incidence of overeducation and underemployment is increasing. Directly related to this observation is the concern that overeducation and underemployment negatively impact on the individual and on society. Overeducation and underemployment may carry a wage penalty, meaning the rate of return from a year of overeducation is lower than the return from a year of education required for the job. These negative effects may be especially harmful if overeducation and underemployment are persistent and the negative effects of overeducation and underemployment continue to impact later on in the employment career.

Our review of reviews ignores methodological issues in estimating the incidence of, and the returns from, overeducation. These issues have been satisfactorily addressed by others elsewhere (see, e.g., Leuven and Oosterbeek, 2011). Our focus is on the findings of the review studies rather than on the methodological discussion. We organize the discussion of the reviews around a few themes:

- What is the incidence of overeducation/underemployment, and is it increasing?
- What are the returns from overeducation and how have these returns evolved?
- What are the causes of overeducation/underemployment?
- Does overeducation lead to displacement of lower-educated workers?

For our review of review studies on overeducation and underemployment, we have identified papers in the literature on overeducation and underemployment that use a meta-perspective, that is, studies that synthesize existing empirical studies, e.g., through a meta-analysis, and studies that describe the state of the art in this field. For our review of reviews, we searched *EconLit* and Google Scholar using the following keywords: "review," "overeducation," "over-education," "overschooling," "overqualification," and "underemployment." We scrutinized the reference lists of the review studies in our initial search for any missing and additional studies that met our inclusion and exclusion criteria.

The inclusion criterion was that the paper must represent a review of existing studies in the field and not original research. We excluded from our review of reviews studies that used primary empirical data and had as their primary aim to estimate the incidence of overeducation or underemployment, the rate of return from overeducation or other effects of overeducation or underemployment. Our search yielded 11 review studies published in academic journals and one book that are included in this paper.

Most of the review studies were written by authors from the United States, the United Kingdom, and the Netherlands. This reflects the empirical studies in this field which are also primarily conducted in the United States, the United Kingdom, and the Netherlands (Kucel, 2011). Some summarizing characteristics of the studies included can be found in Table 10.1. The summary of findings in Table 10.1 shows that most of the reviews were not systematic reviews, but rather a selective reading of the literature. Also, a critical appraisal of the literature was very often lacking. As most of the studies were correlational studies using regression analysis to relate the incidence and the returns from overeducation to a number of observable characteristics, questions about the causal nature of the relation, the validity,

Table 10.1   Characteristics of Review Studies Included in the Review

Author	Title— Reference	Objective	Number of Studies and Estimates Included	Summary of Main Findings
Smith (1986)	Overeducation and underemployment: An agnostic review. *Sociology of Education* 59, 85–99	Discussion of overeducation and underemployment	—	The increase in the number of higher educated seems to have had minimal impact on American society
Hartog (2000)	Over-education and earnings: Where are we, where should we go? *Economics of Education Review* 19, 131–147	Review of literature on incidence and returns from overeducation with emphasis on confrontation figures with theoretical models	—	There appears to be an asymmetry in the returns from overeducation and undereducation, as well as in mobility and ability
Groot and Maassen van den Brink (2000)	Overeducation in the labor market: A meta-analysis. *Economics of Education Review 19*, 149–158	A meta-analysis of the estimates on the incidence and the returns from years of overeducation and required education	25 studies yielding 50 estimates on overeducation	Average incidence of overeducation is 23%, average rate of return on a year of overeducation is 3%. No evidence mismatch has increased.
Rubb (2003)	Overeducation in the labor market: A comment and re-analysis of a meta-analysis. *Economics of Education Review 22*, 621–629	Paper comments and expands meta-analysis of Groot and Maassen van den Brink (2000)	85 estimates on overeducation from 23 studies	Average return from year of overeducation is 5.2% and on year of required education is 9.6%

(Continued)

Table 10.1 (Continued)   Characteristics of Review Studies Included in the Review

Author	Title – Reference	Objective	Number of Studies and Estimates Included	Summary of Main Findings
Sloane (2003)	Much ado about nothing? What does the overeducation literature really tell us? In *Overeducation in Europe: Current Issues in Theory and Policy*	Paper reviews the literature on a number of issues in overeducation	–	There is support for the substitutability hypothesis where overeducation is substitute for lack of other human capital. Whether overeducated workers crowd out lower-educated workers is far from clear, but for large groups of workers overeducation is a permanent rather than a temporary feature.
McGuinness (2006)	Overeducation in the labour market. *Review of Economic Surveys 20*, 387–418	A review of the literature on overeducation and assessment of findings with theoretical frameworks	33 studies generating 62 estimates on overeducation	The impact of overeducation is non-trivial and potentially costly to individuals and society
Kucel (2011)	Literature survey of the incidence of over-education: A sociological approach. *Reis 134*, 125–142	Main objective is a review of the incidence of overeducation covering the period 1983–2009	52	Overeducation is not a negligible problem that affects only a minority of workers. The incidence of overeducation has increased considerably over time in various countries

(Continued)

Table 10.1 (Continued)   Characteristics of Review Studies Included in the Review

Author	Title— Reference	Objective	Number of Studies and Estimates Included	Summary of Main Findings
Leuven and Oosterbeek (2011)	Overeducation and mismatch in the labor market, Discussion paper series. *Forschungsinstitut zu Zukunft der Arbeit*, No 5523	Survey of the economics literature on overeducation	42	Estimates of the returns from overeducation may suffer from omitted variable bias and measurement error
McKee-Ryan and Harvey (2011)	"I have a job, but …": A review of underemployment. *Journal of Management* 37, 962–996	Survey of literature on underemployment and their effects	—	Recessions increase underemployment and an increasing number of workers will face underemployment during their career
Scurry and Blenkinsopp (2011)	Under-employment among recent graduates: A review of the literature. *Personnel Review 40*, 643–660	What is underemployment among recent graduates	—	Individual volition and meaning making are important issues that remain under-researched in relation to graduate underemployment

and the generalizability are highly relevant. However, very few of the review studies actually raised these questions. Furthermore, the main findings of the reviews were rather diverse.

10.3.1 Incidence and Evolution of Overeducation and Underemployment

The oldest review of the overeducation and underemployment literature is by Smith (1986). This review is focused on college graduates in the United States and reviews the literature of the 1970s and trends in the supply and demand for college graduates for the period 1947–1982. Smith concludes from his reading of the literature that overeducation/underemployment of college graduates has had no effect on college enrollment, and that despite the concerns about the social waste of overeducation/underemployment it remains unclear whether it really constitutes a social problem. What appears from this review—and what has been corroborated in subsequent reviews—is that the frequently pessimistic predictions that overeducation has increased or will increase in the future, that the rate of return from education will decline, and that overeducation has a scarring effect on workers which they will carry with them for the rest of their careers, is not supported by the evidence and has not materialized. These pessimistic predictions are mainly based upon demographic changes: the idea that the large birth cohorts after the Second World War and the increased enrollment in higher education would lead to an oversupply of college graduates, and, when the increase in the demand for high skilled workers would slow down, result in overeducation/underemployment. But, as stated by Smith, "the grim forecasts of the mid-1970s have not come true." It seems that Smith is a bit confused by the belief that overeducation is increasing and the value of a college degree is declining on the one hand, and the figures which do not quite support these beliefs on the other.

Fourteen years after the review by Smith, two new reviews were published. One was a narrative review of the literature (Hartog, 2000), the other a meta-analysis on the incidence of, and returns from, overeducation (Groot and Maassen van den Brink, 2000). These reviews distinguish between three different ways of measuring overeducation. These are described by Hartog as (1) the systematic job analysis method, where for each job title the required level of education is determined; (2) the self-assessment method, where workers indicate what education is required for the work they do; and (3) the realized matches method, where the required level of education is derived from the mean or mode of the actual education level of workers in a job. Leuven and Oosterbeek (2011) provide a more detailed and richer classification of the measurement of overeducation, although their measures of overeducation can also be grouped in the three described by Hartog. As argued by Hartog, each of the three methods has its attractions and limitations. However, the job analysis method is identified by Hartog as the best and the conceptually superior method, as it produces the least bias in the measurement of overeducation.

Groot and Maassen van den Brink (2000) show that, of these three measures, the first—the job analysis method—generally provides the highest estimate of overeducation, while the realized matches method yields the lowest estimates of overeducation. The incidence of overeducation calculated by the self-assessment method is similar to that of the job analysis method. On average, the job analysis method yields an estimate of the incidence of overeducation which is approximately twice as high as the realized matches method. McGuinness (2006) draws a similar conclusion, although with smaller differences: he finds that that the objective measures of overeducation indicate an incidence of overeducation which is about a quarter less than the subjective measures.

Reviews that address the incidence of overeducation frequently come to the conclusion that the incidence of overeducation is high. Kucel (2011) claims that between a quarter and a third of the workers in advanced economies are overeducated for the work they do. This is similar to what Leuven and Oosterbeek (2011) find: the mean and median incidence in the studies in their review is 30%. Groot and Maassen van den Brink (2000)—although including a smaller number of studies on the incidence of overeducation for a more limited time period—find an average incidence of overeducation of 23%. The common conclusion of these review papers is that the estimates of the incidence of overeducation vary, and that the incidence of overeducation is generally estimated to be high but depends on the way it is measured.

Scurry and Blenkinsopp (2011) use a classification developed by Feldman (1996) which defines a person as underemployed if they

- Possesses more formal education than their job requires
- Are involuntarily employed in a different field from that in which they received their formal education
- Possess higher-level skills than the job requires
- Are involuntarily engaged in part-time, temporary, or intermittent employment
- Are earning 20% less than the average earnings of their graduating cohort in the same major or occupation track

As this definition shows, underemployment is a much broader and more diffuse concept than overeducation. Because of that, exact figures on the incidence and extent of underemployment are scarce. McKee-Ryan and Harvey (2011) state that the incidence of underemployment in the United States ranges from one-sixth to one-third of the workforce, depending on what is included in the definition of underemployment. As with the estimates of overeducation, there is substantial diversity in the estimates of underemployment.

A frequently asked question is whether the incidence of overeducation is increasing. The reviews included in this review provide diverging answers to this. According to Kucel (2011), a review of 52 studies on the incidence of overeducation shows that "over-education is not a negligible problem affecting only a minority of the labor force, and that its incidence has increased considerably across time for various countries." Unfortunately, Kucel (2011) provides no statistical tests for an increasing trend in overeducation. McKee-Ryan and Harvey (2011) also conclude that "the number of underemployed workers continues to rise," but do not provide figures to substantiate this claim.

Hartog (2000) comes to a somewhat similar conclusion. He concludes that for the three countries—the Netherlands, Spain, and Portugal–for which he has comparable data over time, the incidence of overeducation increased during the period 1970–1995. For the United States, he concludes that overeducation followed a U-shaped pattern between 1969 and 1977, but that overeducation decreased between 1977 and 1984. Leuven and Oosterbeek (2011) come to the somewhat similar conclusion that overeducation declined from the 1970s to the 1990s. They also find that overeducation increased in the 2000s.

Slightly different conclusions are drawn by Groot and Maassen van den Brink (2000) and McGuinness (2006). Groot and Maassen van den Brink find, in a regression analysis on 50 estimates of the incidence of overeducation taken from 25 studies, no statistically significant differences in the incidence of overeducation between the 1970s, 1980s, and the 1990s. This conclusion is confirmed by McGuinness, who observes that the incidence of overeducation has been rather stable over time.

Fluctuations in the incidence of overeducation can be explained by business cycle fluctuations and by skill-based technological change. Groot and Maassen van den Brink account for that by including the growth in the labor force and the unemployment rate for the year in which the data were gathered in a meta-regression on the incidence of overeducation. They find no effect of the unemployment rate on the incidence of overeducation, but they do find that a one percentage point higher growth of the labor force increases the incidence of overeducation by about two percentage points. However, McKee-Ryan and Harvey (2011) conclude that economically or personally difficult situations or, as they call it, "facing challenging conditions," increase the likelihood of underemployment.

In general, the reviews conclude that the incidence of overeducation is high, although the estimated incidence of overeducation differs widely between studies. Many of the reviews also argue that the incidence of overeducation is rising. The high incidence of overeducation raises questions: What does the high incidence rate of overeducated workers mean? Does it indicate widely prevalent mismatches on the labor market? The high incidence, in combination with an alleged increase in overeducation, suggests a labor market that is greatly distorted. Alternatively, we may doubt the validity and reliability of the measurement of overeducation. According to Sloane (2003), "It seems clear that a substantial part of what is referred to in the literature as over-education simply reflects the heterogeneity of individual abilities and skills within particular educational qualifications."

10.3.2 *Returns from Overeducation and Underemployment*

Smith (1986) argues that the human capital theory fails to explain why people go to college, despite the increase in overeducation and the decline in the rate of return on the investment in human capital that results from it. The figures presented by Smith seem to suggest that the ratio of mean earnings of college graduates to those of high school graduates in the United States declined in the 1960s. This decline was reversed somewhere around 1974. As Smith reports, the college earnings premium continued to increase through 1983. This finding is corroborated and extended by the meta-analysis of the returns from education in Groot and Maassen van den Brink (2000). They find that the rate of return from a year of required education was 4% points higher in studies using data for the 1990s than in studies with data for the 1970s. The rate of return from a year of overeducation was 2.4% points higher in studies for the 1990s than in the 1970s, although this effect was not statistically significant. McGuinness (2006) concludes in his review of studies on the returns on overeducation that the three approaches used to measure overeducation—the job analysis method, the self-assessment method, and the realized matches method—"generate broadly consistent evidence" on the returns from overeducation. In a re-analysis of the meta-analysis in Groot and Maassen van den Brink, Rubb (2003) finds that the rate of return on a year of required education was 2.59% points higher in studies with data for the 1980s, and 3.98% points higher in studies for the 1990s, than in studies using data for the 1970s. He finds that the rate of return from a year of overeducation was 2.88% points higher in the 1980s, and 1.79% points higher in the 1990s, than in the 1970s. Both meta-analyses clearly show the rising trend in the return from education since the 1970s.

The third and most recent meta-analysis on the returns on (over)education—aside from Groot and Maassen van den Brink (2000) and Rubb (2003)—is Leuven and Oosterbeek (2011). They find in their meta-analyses of returns somewhat larger differences between the rate of return from a year of required education and a year of overeducation. They find that, on average, the return from a year of required education is around 9%, and the return from a year of overeducation is about half of that. They do not observe a systematic pattern in the rates of return from education over time, only during the 1990s returns from a year of overeducation appear to be somewhat lower (–1.5%) than in studies that use data for the 2000s. Somewhat contrarily, the rate of return from a year of required education is 1.8% higher during that same period in the studies in their sample. They further find that in the 1980s the rate of return from a year of required education is 1.4% lower than in studies using data for the 2000s. The latter also suggests an increase in the return on years of required education.

If we compare the returns from overeducation in the review of Leuven and Oosterbeek (2011) with those in Groot and Maassen van den Brink (2000) and Rubb (2003), those in the former review appear to be larger than those in the latter two reviews. Leuven and Oosterbeek (2011) also find a higher rate of return from a year of required education than Groot and Maassen van den Brink and Rubb. This is consistent with an increasing trend in the returns on education since the 1970s due to the demand for higher-educated workers outpacing demand.

It is interesting to note that both the meta-analysis of Groot and Maassen van den Brink and that of Leuven and Oosterbeek find that the way that overeducation is defined and measured has a great impact on its reported incidence (with the measure with the highest incidence identifying about twice as many workers as overeducated as the measure with the lowest incidence), but that there are no statistically significant differences in the rates of return from a year of overeducation and a year of required education between the different methods to measure skill mismatches.

Hartog (2000) observes that the estimates on the rates of return show that undereducation is less severely punished than overeducation is rewarded. From this, he concludes that the more able workers are found among the undereducated, while the abilities and skills of the overeducated do not differ from those of workers who are correctly allocated. Taking this conclusion a step further, it seems that workers who are undereducated attain position on the labor market based on their abilities and despite their (lower) education level, while overeducation seems to be more the result of chance or lack of luck in finding the right job or not.

Underemployment also has negative wage effects. McKee-Ryan and Harvey (2011) report wage losses after a spell of unemployment of 14%–35% per year. They also specify a range of other areas such as job satisfaction, organizational commitment, and well-being on which underemployment has a negative impact. Other reviews come to more qualitative conclusions on the returns on overeducation. According to Sloane (2003), "over-education has long-run as well as short-run effects on wages. There appear to be scarring effects for those workers who do not obtain a good match early on in their careers."

10.3.3 What Are the Causes of Overeducation and the Lower Returns to Overeducation?

Overeducation can be seen as an indicator of mismatch between skills supplied and demanded on the labor market. The lower rate of return from a year of over-education relative to a year of required education is therefore informative about the efficiency losses of this mismatch. However, other interpretations of overeducation are also possible. Overeducation may indicate lower abilities or a lack of other aspects of human capital. One of the arguments in Groot and Maassen van den Brink (2000) is that overeducation can—at least partly—be explained as a substitute for the lack of other elements of human capital such as on-the-job experience and training. They support this argument by noting that workers with lower other forms of human capital (like tenure, experience, and on-the-job training) and workers with career interruptions (like unemployment spells and spells out of the labor market or working part-time) are more likely to be overeducated. Sloane

(2003) also concludes that formal education is one aspect of human capital, and education deficits can be remedied by other aspects of human capital, such as on-the-job training. Alternatively, overeducated workers may be more attractive for employers as they need less on-the-job training.

McGuinness (2006) relates this theory of overeducation as a compensation for a lack of work-related human capital to the permanent or temporary nature of overeducation. If the compensation theory is correct, overeducation may decrease as workers accumulate more tenure and experience over time. McGuinness notes, however, that it is unclear to what extent the trade-off between education and experience is the result of human capital substitution or cohort effects. As noted by Kucel (2011), overeducation is only consistent with human capital theory if it is temporary and compensates for lack of other skills, such as experience or (on-the-job) training.

The alternative line of reasoning views overeducation as the result of labor market inflexibility and "bad luck." In this argument—first put forward by Thurow (1975)—there are only a limited number of jobs for higher-educated workers. With an excess supply of higher-educated workers, some fail to find a job that matches their skills and have to take a lower skilled job for which they are over-educated, thereby displacing lower-educated workers who may fall out altogether and face unemployment. Education is seen as a way to get ahead in the queue for the best available jobs. Overeducation, in this view, is the result of an excess supply of higher-educated workers. Some support for this claim is found in Groot and Maassen van den Brink (2000).

10.3.4 Does Overeducation Lead to Displacement of Lower-Educated Workers?

Overeducated workers may displace the lower educated. However, overeducation does not necessarily affect the labor market position of lower-educated workers. If there is an oversupply of higher-educated workers, but a shortage of workers for lower-educated jobs, overeducation may be a way to balance supply and demand for lower- and higher-skilled workers and jobs. According to Scurry and Blenkinsopp (2011), there are three explanations for underemployment. The first is similar to the compensation argument for overeducation, and says that underemployment can be a temporary period used to acquire additional skills and experience, a stepping stone to a better fitting job or to cover a period before career decisions are made. The other explanation is that underemployment is a way to avoid unemployment. The third explanation they offer is that underemployment is part of a lifestyle choice. While these explanations focus on why individuals may end up in a job for which they are overeducated or underemployed, others have looked at the implications of overeducation. An issue that has attracted attention both in the academic and the popular literature is whether overeducated workers displace or crowd out lower-educated workers. Especially if overeducation is a long-term state of affairs, overeducated workers may crowd out lower-educated workers. Sloane

(2003) provides a review of the academic literature on this issue and concludes that "the evidence for crowding out is rather thin, being limited to outflows rather than inflows of workers with relatively low levels of education."

Whether overeducation leads to a crowding out of lower-educated workers depends—among other factors—on the incidence and persistence of overeducation. The higher the incidence and the greater the persistence, the more overeducation will crowd out lower-educated workers. As we have already addressed the incidence of overeducation, we shall now focus on the evidence for its persistence. Are many workers temporarily overeducated for the work they perform some time during their career, or are some workers permanently in a job for which they are overeducated? The studies reviewed by Sloane do not seem to provide an unequivocal answer to this question. Sloane therefore comes to the somewhat unsatisfactory conclusion that more research is needed using panel data with direct questions on overeducation. Leuven and Oosterbeek (2011) come to more specific conclusions and claim that "various studies corroborate that for many workers overschooling persists." Unfortunately, they do not provide figures to support this claim.

10.4 Conclusion

In many areas, there already exists a strong nexus between scientific knowledge and professional practice, and thus between knowledge institutions such as universities and the professional field. In the agricultural sector, a close link exists between farms and agricultural research. In health care, evidence-based medicine has become the standard. It may be worthwhile to note that much of the field of evidence-based medicine has only recently been developed. The term itself has only become commonplace since the early 1990s. In many areas in medicine, there is still very little or no scientific evidence, but in the areas where this is not the case, evidence-based medicine is widely accepted and has become the standard of practice. Much of the evidence is also put into guidelines to which physicians are expected to adhere. Meanwhile, in nursing, social work, psychotherapy, occupational therapy, physiotherapy, and speech therapy the evidence-based approach is widely embraced and accepted.

A doctor who does not adhere to evidence-based treatment guidelines is likely to face disciplinary charges and risks losing his or her license to operate. Rightly so. A doctor who does not work according to the best available knowledge can do much harm to patients. But the same can be said for a teacher. A teacher who does not use effective teaching methods can do much harm to children as well. A poor education can have lifelong negative effects. A bad teacher can be worse than a bad doctor, as a bad teacher may be harmful from a young age onwards until the end of one's life. As education has an effect on many areas in life—ranging from one's income to one's health—the damage done by a bad education can be far more extensive. Research by Peter Tymms et al. (2009) shows that having a bad teacher at the beginning of one's educational career can have lasting effects. The negative effects of a bad teacher in the first grade of primary school are still discernable in the eighth grade.

Education is still very much based on ideology rather than science. Teachers, like doctors, should work on the basis of the best available knowledge about "what works."

To enable teachers or policy makers to work in an evidence-based manner, academic researchers should supply them with systematic information and knowledge about "what works" in education. Especially in the economic science, but also in the social sciences at large, there is a lack of systematic evidence on what works. We have illustrated this in this chapter, by critically reviewing the review studies on overeducation and underemployment. Overeducation and underemployment are topics that have received considerable attention from academic researchers over the past 40 years. This attention mostly originates from a policy perspective: the notion that overeducation and underemployment imply a waste of talent and resources. Over the past 60 years, the educational attainment of the labor force has increased dramatically. In many countries, enrollment in higher education has increased tenfold during this period. This has raised concerns about overeducation of the workforce. As described, many studies on the incidence of overeducation and underemployment have supported the idea that overeducation is a result of the increased educational attainment of the labor force. This suggests that the increase in educational attainment has come at the cost of the overeducated worker. As noted by Tinbergen (1975), the rate of return on education is determined by the race between demand and supply of skills. If we look at the literature on the rate of return to education, we can conclude that during the past four decades this race has been won by the supply side. The literature on the rate of return on education shows that in virtually all Western countries the rate of return from a year of education has increased (cf. Groot and Maassen van den Brink, 2000 and Leuven and Oosterbeek, 2011), suggesting that because of technological changes the demand curve has shifted outward, leading to a higher rate of return, even as the supply of higher-educated workers has increased. There seems to be a discrepancy between the overeducation literature, which raises concern about the consequences of the increase in educational attainment, and the literature on the rate of return to education, which suggests that because of the more rapid increase in the demand for educated workers, income inequality between lower and higher-educated workers has increased. As the policy relevance of the topic is high, it is important to know whether the academic research provide any useful tools for evidence-based policy making.

We find that, compared with studies that have looked at horizontal mismatch (between the type of education demanded and supplied within a specific education level) or intercurricular mismatch (between the specific skills learned in a specific educational program and those demanded from graduates by employers), the attention paid to vertical mismatch, or overeducation, has been quite substantial.

Reading through reviews on overeducation and underemployment, one can concur with the point made by Scurry and Blenkinsopp (2011) that "preoccupation with measurement of underemployment has stymied the development of research that might help in understanding the dynamics of the unfolding experience of graduate underemployment." Sloane (2003) states that the main contribution of the overeducation literature has been to highlight that it matters where a worker is employed.

In this chapter, we have analyzed to what extent the literature on overeducation and underemployment contributes to evidence-based education. A necessary condition for a contribution to evidence-based education is that reviews on this topic should be systematic reviews. This implies that the reviews contain an explanation and description of the search strategy and the inclusion and exclusion criteria used to select papers for review. We found that very few of the review studies on overeducation and underemployment are systematic reviews. In the large majority of the review studies the search strategy is not described at all, it remains unclear on what criteria studies have been selected for inclusion in the review, and basic information about the studies included are not presented. Also, a critical appraisal of the studies and their findings is often lacking. Most reviews take the claims made in the studies reviewed at face value. Very few reviews raise issues like the causality in the relationship between overeducation and its returns and about the validity and generalizability of the findings. From this, we conclude that the usefulness and relevance of these review studies for evidence-based education is limited to say the least. Even after 40 years of research, the evidence base on overeducation and underemployment in the labor market remains slim.

The overeducation literature can be criticized for its rather static nature. Any worker with more education than required for the job is considered overeducated. This ignores the fact that overeducation may be conditioned by experience, tenure on the job, and on-the-job training. A middle-aged worker with a university degree who works for ten years in management support may be overeducated, whereas a recent college graduate whose first job is in management support may not be really classified as overeducated.

How useful is the overeducation and underemployment literature for evidence-based education? The answer to this question must be that its usefulness is limited. The first caveat is that the returns on overeducation—which may indicate the welfare losses of mismatch—may be biased and do not reflect causal effects. Second, there is evidence to assume that for many workers overeducation and underemployment are temporary phenomena and not a permanent state. Many overeducated or unemployed workers find more fitting jobs over time. Third, there is evidence to assume that overeducation—at least partly—compensates for a lack of other productive skills. Some of these other skills are accumulated over time—e.g., experience—thereby reducing overeducation. All of these arguments limit the need and potential for policy interventions. Finally, and from an evidence-based perspective rather importantly, very few of the reviews on this topic are systematic reviews. Most of the reviews seem to be based on a rather selective reading of the literature.

The authors of the reviews almost never make clear how the search for the literature has been conducted. At some points, one gets the impression that authors have searched for the literature that supports their ideas about the incidence and effects of overeducation and underemployment, rather than letting the findings speak for themselves.

References

Buchel, F. (2001). Overqualification: Reasons, measurement issues and typological affinity to unemployment. In P. Descy and M. Tessaring (Eds.), *Training in Europe*, Second report on vocational training research in Europe 2000, Cedefop Reference Series.

Chynoweth, C. (2009). Campaigning for evidence-based education. *The Times*, December 10, 2009.

Feldman, D. (1996). The nature, antecedents and consequences of underemployment. *Journal of Management*, 22, 385–407.

Freeman, R. (1976). *The Over-Educated American*, Cambridge, MA: Academic Press.

Groot, H. and Maassen van den Brink, H. (2000). Overeducation in the labor market: A meta-analysis. *Economics of Education Review*, 19, 149–158.

Hartog, J. (2000). Over-education and earnings: Where are we, where should we go? *Economics of Education Review*, 19, 131–147.

Kucel, A. (2011). Literature survey of the incidence of over-education: A sociological approach. *Reis*, 134, 125–142.

Leuven, E., and Oosterbeek, H. (2011). Overeducation and mismatch in the labor market, Discussion paper series, *Handbook of the Economics of Education*, 4, 283-326.

Levin, H., Belfield, C., Muennig, P., and Rouse, C. (2006). The costs and benefits of an excellent education for all of america's children, http://www.literacycooperative.org/documents/Thecostsandbenefitsofanexcellentedforamerchildren.pdf.

McGuinness, S. (2006). Overeducation in the labour market. *Journal of Economic Surveys*, 20, 387–418.

McKee-Ryan, F., and Harvey, J. (2011). "I have a job, but …": A review of underemployment. *Journal of Management*, 37, 962–996.

Rubb, S. (2003). Overeducation in the labor market: A comment and re-analysis of a meta-analysis. *Economics of Education Review*, 22, 621–629.

Scurry, T., and Blenkinsopp, J. (2011). Under-employment among recent graduates: A review of the literature. *Personnel Review*, 40, 643–660.

Sloane, P. (2003). Much ado about nothing? What does the over-education literature really tell us? In F. Büchel, A. de Grip, and A. Mertens (Eds.), *Overeducation in Europe: Current Issues in Theory and Policy*, Edward Elgar Publishers, 11–45.

Smith, H. (1986). Overeducation and underemployment: An agnostic review. *Sociology of Education*, 59, 85–99.

Thurow, L. (1975). *Generating Inequality*, New York: Macmillan.

Tinbergen, J. (1975). *Income Distribution*, Amsterdam: North Holland Publishers.

Tymms, P., Jones, P., Albone, S., and Henderson B. (2009). The first seven years at school, *Educational Assessment Evaluation and Accountability*, 21, 67. doi:10.1007/s11092-008-9066-7.

van het Reve, K. (2003). Ik heb nooit iets gelezen en andere fragmenten, van Oorschot, Amsterdam, the Netherlands, p. 344.

Visscher, A., and Ehrenberg, M. (2011). The simplicity and complexity of revenue focused werken. Analysis commissioned by the Knowledge Chamber of the Ministry of Education, Culture and Science. Vakgroep Educational Organisation and Management, University of Twente, July 2011.

Index